Praise for *Enough*

"*Enough* is a memoir reflective of the arduous, often non-𝗅𝗂𝗇𝖾𝖺𝗋 journey of growth through mental illness and the after-effects of trauma. Zachry's honest, genuine, and direct descriptors of her symptoms and experiences will help countless others who are facing their own struggles navigating mental illness."

—Dr. Kari Jones, licensed psychologist

"There is little BILPOC representation when it comes to memoirs about trauma and mental illness. In *Enough*, Zachry takes on these hard subjects with writing that is beautiful, powerful, and compelling. You won't soon forget this brave, important book."

—Claudia Love Mair, author and coordinator of the
Kentucky Black Writers Collaborative

"In this compelling debut, Zachry takes the reader on an unflinchingly honest, heart-wrenching journey."

—Anastasia Zadeik, author of *Blurred Fates*

"*Enough* is the story of one woman's journey to find her place in the world, despite a nagging sense of abandonment, racial insecurity, a history of trauma, and the unfortunate stigma associated with mental illness. Zachry captures it all with grace and illuminates the art of healing."

—Rica Keenum, author of *Petals of Rain* and
Which One of Us is Broken

ENOUGH

A Memoir of Mistakes, Mania, and Motherhood

Amelia Zachry

SHE WRITES PRESS

Published 2022
Printed in the United States of America
Print ISBN: 978-1-64742-291-2
E-ISBN: 978-1-64742-292-9
Library of Congress Control Number: 2022907070

For information, address:
She Writes Press
1569 Solano Ave #546
Berkeley, CA 94707

She Writes Press is a division of SparkPoint Studio, LLC.

For my daughters,
the lights of my life, the seeds of my strength.
There are no wrong cards.

PROLOGUE

Majestic red rocks towered over me, baronial in their exhibition. This was my first time to Sedona, Arizona, and I felt the strength of the mountains, the power of being enveloped in their magnificence. This marvelous scene was a humbling reminder of how far I'd come over these past seventeen years, a journey that had too often been a downward spiral. Only recently had I discovered my own internal net—how to catch myself, to speak again, to bear the weight of my being on my own two feet. These mountains seemed a symbol of this newfound strength. I had just turned thirty-six, and this trip was part of a delayed celebration.

People travel to Sedona from all over the world for spiritual revival, restoration, or reenergizing. In the desert, I felt ablaze with energy, love, and life—things that had often felt elusive in the past nearly two decades. That rusty red against a beautiful, blue, clear spring sky tugged at my heart. I felt as if I was always meant to touch this red dirt, to bathe in this energy vortex, allowing my energies to open up and soar freely. I was home.

Daniel, my husband, agreed that I needed a break from the daily demands of being a stay-at-home mom, every ounce of my essence spent on mothering. My two beautiful daughters were my entire reason for breathing, but they were draining—especially Mandy, my profoundly

1

gifted firstborn who was only five but required education plans galore. Then there was Allison, my sweet baby, two years old and demanding of my attention. Both tested my strength and resilience as a mother, even as I reveled in their blossoming into incredible individuals. Motherhood humbled me. The mind-boggling intellectual debates with my oldest and the needs of my youngest had me in a state of enchantment and constant disarray. When my friends suggested this trip, Daniel supported it immediately. I knew he worried that I was in a prolonged depressive episode, and we both hoped this would be the remedy.

My two best friends and I had initially planned to go to Portland, Oregon. Jenny is the outrageous one, a bold optimist, and Sara is my calm, quiet rock. I wasn't keen on going anywhere, but I was happy to be with my best friends for a few days. This trip came about as a result of one of my episodes. This recent one had lasted almost a year.

I had been depressed and detached from everyone around me— except Jenny and Sara, whom I relied on for comfort. Jenny supported me from hundreds of miles away in Los Angeles. Sara lived in Georgetown, about an hour from where I lived in Lexington, Kentucky. We met less often these days, with the demands of the daily grind, and our phone calls became my lifeline. There was no telling where this episode came from. Perhaps it was the stress of raising children or the strain I put on my marriage, pushing Daniel away as he tried to convince me of my worth. Perhaps it was simply biological. It was Jenny who assured me, "A trip is just what you need. Just get away from everything for a bit and recharge."

Though Jenny and Sara didn't know each other well, the time all of us had spent planning brought them closer together. When we settled on Sedona, everything fell into place. We were all drawn to the mystical vortex, the sound healing, and all the quirky things Sedona is known for.

~

I was nervous. This was the kind of situation in my life where anxiety took over. This time it was about not having Daniel by my side to take care of things. Arriving at the Phoenix Airport in Arizona made me realize how much I had leaned on him through the struggles with my mental state, and also how much I depended on him, which allowed my mind to go on autopilot.

For this trip, my two friends were more than happy to take charge. I know autopilot to be my defense mechanism, taking over my body as if I've been evacuated to survive the experience. They understood this, and therefore were the best travel companions.

I made it from the arrival hall to the rental car counter to the car with no recollection of our progress. The racing in my brain intensified as the discomfort of being without Daniel grew. Once inside our car, however, my friends made it their mission to make me laugh, and they were successful. I was laughing so hard that my face hurt. I'd always wanted to get a trucker to pull the horn. We passed by a few, and I pulled at the invisible cable above my head. They were not amused. One stared at me with a worn face, and he may as well have flipped me the bird. But nothing could dispel my upbeat spirit, and I had a wide grin the whole way to our Airbnb.

Once we got off the highway, I saw a serene blue. Against the desert and the red sand, the sky was an incredible shade of the deepest aqua. I took a deep breath to bring the thoroughbreds in my brain to a slow trot. I looked out at the beautiful cacti and bushes that seemed to have grown in perfect alternation. This was a far cry from the rich green rain forests of Malaysia, my home country. A lot of field trips in my childhood were filled with hiking the oldest rain forests in the world. The smell of the mud, and the beautiful, lush green brush under the massive canopy was fresh in my mind. I missed home more than I ever thought I would. I'd been gone for nine years, and though I knew I'd never live in Malaysia again, I felt like it was awaiting my return. I'd left because I'd wanted to. In many ways, I had to. Daniel provided me an opportunity for escape, to get far away from mistakes I'd made almost twenty years earlier that still haunted me.

The beauty of this desert was of my heart. This drive to Sedona had me overcome. Neatly dispersed cacti lived on dry dirt, which looked barren to the naked eye but was so rich in nourishment, keeping all the life on the desert alive. I felt similarly forlorn, alone in my being with hardly anything flourishing. With this trip, I was determined to change that—to find some water to quench these longings and pains I had carried for so many years. The road was not too busy. I watched the lines pass on the side as the dust floated into the air, dancing in the desert sun. It was magical. It seemed that this land spoke.

~

We stopped at an ancient cave dwelling by a river and walked to the end of a trail with beautiful rapids. Oh, the rush of that foaming river on the rocks, and the birds! I focused my gaze to find the river bottom. *How strong is that current? How quickly would the water fill my lungs? How long would it take for me to lose consciousness if I hit one of those rocks in the rapids?* A familiar sensation flowed from my mind to my body. I wished for the thoughts to end every time they came, but the emotions were overwhelming and no contest against my rational mind.

"Let's take a picture here, guys!" Jenny, ever enthusiastic, knew I would want photos to remind me of this trip later. They would serve as evidence that I was capable of enjoying life.

I thought about the ancient cave dwellers as I smiled for a selfie. How wonderful and beautiful it would be to farm, forage, and fish as my only goals. No fitting in, no demanding child, no gifted-learning plans, no complex marriage struggles, no *what the fuck am I doing with my life*, no goals I will never achieve. Being alive would be the only goal.

This retreat was to last four days. It was an intimate coven, just the three of us. I read somewhere that witches were often put to the stake for their predictions and premonitions. These might have simply been superior intelligence, mistaken by community members who were unwilling to comprehend given the highly chauvinistic, misogynistic ways of the times. In our coven, I knew the three of us were remarkable women. Jenny and Sara were self-assured, with no inhibitions or shame about who they were. They followed their true calling, never swayed by the wayward touch of circumstances. They were enlightened and fierce in their convictions. I longed to find a self I had no recriminations for, one in which I felt fulfilled. During my healing and growth process over the years, I'd found little space for relationships. Jenny and Sara provided me the kind of friendship I needed and a sense of belonging.

I had once belonged to a family I adored, but I'd lost them all to my own distancing, secrets, or unwillingness to let them in. My father had recently suffered brain damage in a medical incident and lost significant cognitive abilities, including the ability to recognize me. I'd left him, chosen America over Malaysia. Even though I'd been here six years, I had yet to find my footing. Inside this trinity with Jenny and Sara, however, I felt connection. Daniel was my safe place and sanctuary, but this vortex of feminine power made me feel more empowered, whole, and awakened. Beneath the soles of my feet, I felt the dirt that assured me I was standing, holding my own.

That afternoon, we took a hike up Cathedral Rock. I was immediately in love with the red rocks and the beautiful formations. I had seen them at the Garden of the Gods in Colorado, but this was different. There was an operatic power about Sedona. The air felt calm, and the red dirt seemed a part of me. I moved toward it with an ancient familiarity. I touched the earth. I needed to feel it, and it needed me to feel it.

We climbed that natural sandstone butte, walking most of the way single file, chatting until we all fell silent. Jenny had gone inward. Her breathing got heavy. She was struggling, almost in tears, and I realized she was afraid. I knew she was afraid of heights, but the climb had been gradual, and she'd never been one to back down from a challenge. But suddenly she grabbed my arm, struggling to say that she was freaking out. I was freaking out too. But Jenny needed me, and this was something I could give her. I thought about how many times she'd rescued me—come to watch the baby so I could sleep, come to sit with me because I couldn't be alone. She'd pick up the phone in the middle of the night when I couldn't stop crying. I found words from a deep reservoir of courage I didn't even know was there. "You don't want to stop now, Jenny," I said calmly. "You'll be so disappointed if we don't push to the top. I'm here. Let's do this."

Sara is a natural leader and sensed what was going on. She jumped in front of us. "I'll go first, okay? You guys just follow this way." She gave me a reassuring smile. How did she always know what to do? I trusted Sara as much as I trusted myself to make the rest of the climb.

As we got closer to the summit, there was a presence in the air, like a crescendo. You could almost hear strings, like those of a viola, heavy with the boldness we presented, yet light with the glee of our skipping hearts. As I stepped up to the flat top, my heart was full. We hugged each other and talked to others who'd summited. We took a moment to connect with the beautiful butte we'd just scaled. I looked out at the sun setting behind another gorgeous red mountain. A shudder ran through me. "I made it to the top," I whispered.

Sara heard me and stepped closer, put her arm around me, and squeezed my arm. "You did it." She understood what this meant. She understood my struggles in life, my inability to do the most benign things due to the merciless fog in my mind. It came to visit in cycles that I had grown so familiar with and even come to manage gently. There was a celebration in this. I reached the summit fueled by my newfound courage. I saw myself for what was within me, what had been seeded and growing for so many years.

My heart swelled. For the first time in a long time, I was grateful to be alive. I found a new meaning. I didn't know what it was or what to name it, and there were no words assigned to this understanding. I was there, and I was grateful I was there. It felt like a lifetime ago that I'd suffered the violation that sent me into an emotional cyclone, which hadn't quelled after all this time. In these moments with my friends, something within my soul was opening up. I was capable of something I had not thought possible without the security Daniel provided me with his mere presence. Something was shifting within me, though I couldn't grasp its origin. I didn't understand how or why it would have been part of my journey, but here I was. I looked to my side, and there stood these two gorgeous women, glowing and seemingly magical. Their power and auras radiated.

An old friend once told me that in his Buddhist faith, they believe that no one meets anyone with no purpose. We are in timeless reincarnation. Someone you merely brush shoulders with today may have come from a deep karmic relationship. What a beautiful take on relationships—that we are here today deepening relationships from a past life. It occurred to me in that moment that I'd chanced upon my sisters. Sara had been surrogate aunt to my children. She understood my displacement and how I made bargains in my head about the family I left behind. She understood how I longed to belong and for my children to have extended family, and how I sometimes berated myself for the distance I'd put between them and my family of origin.

Jenny, too, had been there for my girls. Even from California, she participated. She helped with the planning of Mandy's birthdays or the environmental campaigns in Kentucky for my little activist, making my children feel special. She did this because she loved them as her own, just as I loved her son as my own. Sometimes I forgot that I was not alone, and my friends were the best reminder of that truth. I was looking for grounding, and already Sedona had delivered. In the past, life was bleak. I endured it and moved through it, but now it seemed like a reckoning with my past was opening up a new world.

~

Later that evening, Sara and I sat out on the patio of our Airbnb, looking at the butte we had just hiked. It stood amid the vastness of the desert—I could almost touch it. I was soaking in the desert sounds: the trill of crickets, the buzzing and flitting of insects, the cacophony of a sweet symphony for my fatigued spirit. The beautiful calls of the coyotes in the dark were like a call to my soul—a message that there was no pain, no harm that could wound me. I closed my eyes, and I felt the desert breeze brush against my cheeks, my hair in my face. My physical being was open to something here. Sedona was calling. She knew my name, and she welcomed her child home.

Jenny and I shared a room that night. She reminded me to take my medications and checked if I was all right. "I'm here for you, always," she said as she drifted off to sleep. I'd missed her so when she'd moved to Los Angeles. I grappled with how to navigate life without the familiarity of my best friend, whom I had depended on all those years, though of late I was doing better. I'd been learning to be steadier on my own, less reliant on those around me for comfort and security.

Waking up the next morning and realizing we were still in this fantasy, I felt a rush of excitement. My soul hadn't been this awake in twenty years. I noticed that my autopilot had been rather quiet. I seemed to have discovered peace in my body and allowed myself to experience all this trip had to offer. Though I had come to rely on autopilot, I felt relieved by its absence. I was eager to feel every breeze Sedona breathed into me.

We went on another hike, and the first feeling I identified was freedom. We climbed up and sat on the beautiful Devil's Bridge, which was fifty-four feet over the desert forest. We sat holding hands, eyes closed. I let go and planted my hands on the flat rock we sat on. Jenny held on tight to the boulder. She tried to force her body to ground and connect with the nature around us, though I found her mostly to be holding on for dear life. I tried not to laugh and lauded her efforts in committing to grounding despite dying to get out of there, away from the danger of falling to our deaths. Looking out on the vast red rocks and sprinkle of vegetation, feeling the gritty sand on the rock beneath me, I felt a connection to the universe. I was a speck in this vastness, a part of something larger than myself. I believed I was connected and had a purpose. Sara stayed silent; she likes her silence. I breathed in the power of the mountains, and the cool breeze reminded me I was in my own skin, and I felt gratitude for this. I noted how far I'd come to be able to feel this way.

I watched Sara's soft face as she stared into the open. I knew her to be truly grounded in her thoughts, with little that could sway her. I thought back to another trip, almost ten years ago, when I sat on the top of Mount Fuji with Sara. It was a different time. I was unsure about myself and so afraid. I'd just moved from Malaysia to Japan to be with Daniel. Had I known what was ahead of me, I would have been filled with joy. Daniel and I had been through so much, and it was only now that I was finally healing, settling into my own power.

Sitting on Devil's Bridge was exhilarating and calming all at once. I closed my eyes again and pictured all the things I was grateful for. My youngest daughter, almost three, was beginning to find her voice in this loud world. My oldest daughter, my poppy, had a precociousness that ensured a life through intriguing lenses. Barely five years old, she'd been obsessively reading a book about rocks and minerals and had made a specific request for me: "Mommy, buy me an azurite, please. It is blue and green, with a little bit of light brown like this. I love it because it looks like earth." She had Googled on her iPad that azurites could be found naturally occurring in Sedona. I was proud of the little girl she was growing into, leaving the baby coos behind. My heart filled with gratitude.

～

The next day, on another adventurous hike, we ended up lost with no cell service and no other human in sight. We came to a river we needed to cross to get back to where our car was parked, and I was faced with a dilemma.

"We'll use these branches as walking sticks to dig into the ground to hold balance," Sara instructed as we made our way into the almost waist-high water. All my fears surfaced—of water serpents, of creepy crawlies, of drowning. I tripped at that thought and held on to the branch with all my might. As I found my footing and made my way to the riverbank, I had an epiphany. I wished not to die. Having previously longed to die, wanting *not* to die was a release so visceral that it took over my body. My body was to remain mine, as I belonged to it, and it belonged to me.

There was something special that I couldn't name in Sedona, but I knew it had to do with my friends. Destiny, karma, or the energy from the vortexes Sedona is so famed for seemed to find us at every corner. We had to explore the world of psychics and mystics we found there. As we stood outside one of the many crystal shops that line the main streets, we were approached by a woman. She was warm and kind.

"May I interrupt you ladies for a second?" she asked. "My guides are telling me I need to talk to you."

"Sure," I replied, because I knew we were all curious. She told us about each of our characters. While skeptical, we were open. She told us that we were three very strong energies, which together made a beautiful color. We were a vortex. Our energies were strong and pure and complementary. I'd longed to be a part of something for so long that it nearly bowled me over to realize what she was saying—that among these women I admired, I now stood toe-to-toe with them. No longer was I the timid, insecure, lost girl of the past.

I had arrived at the perfect time. I was wrapped in the love of my friends, of nature, and of strangers and their kindness. In that love, I saw myself for the first time. I was part of something bigger than myself or my inhibitions. It had taken me almost twenty years to accept what had happened to me as a violation. With that acceptance, I knew my life was in my hands. The state of mind that was abrupt and unpredictable was within my control. I was finally open to learning. All that had happened in the past was by design—stepping-stones that led me to my present. I had stepped into my magnificence. I was worthy.

The past was the past. There was no changing it, but at least now I had the power to change the lens through which I understood what had happened to me and finally know it was not my fault.

CHAPTER 1

At seventeen, I was on top of the world. I had been living with my grandmother for the past four years. I was among the best in my high school graduating class, a track champion, and a debate speaker to beat. I had lots of friends and was on the precipice of adulthood. I had been built by my grandmother's love and my aunt's and uncle's guidance. Their spiritual guidance and my own introspection brought me closer to discovering myself.

I had been prepared. When I was fourteen, my younger brother and I were handed over to our grandmother, Amachee. We went to live with her in Alor Star, five hours away from my friends and everything I knew. My paternal aunt, Devi Atthey, and her husband, Uncle Bala, lived two doors down. All of them stepped in as surrogate parents for the four years my parents were in Ghana. My parents entrusted my grandmother, aunt, and uncle with the daunting task of raising us, which my surrogate parents threw themselves into wholeheartedly.

While we wailed at the Kuala Lumpur International Airport as our parents left, I saw the sadness in my uncle's face, not knowing how to comfort a pain he didn't understand. I saw Uncle Bala whisper to my father what I imagined to be words of comfort. There was a new broadcasting station that needed setting up in Ghana. It seemed there was no one else other than Mommy, a TV producer and director, and Daddy, the only engineering director, available to do the job. They chose advancements in their careers over their children. There wasn't even a discussion. My brother and I were left out of the equation that would shape my life.

My heart was broken, and every ounce of this burned like acid. Alor Star was a world away from Kuala Lumpur. I did not want to leave everything I knew, everything that was mine, in Kuala Lumpur to go live in that small town in the North. I couldn't believe they were leaving. *Who does that? Why would they leave us?*

We got McDonald's at the airport as my parents waited to go through the gates. I couldn't stop myself from questioning their decision. My father insisted the schools were better up North. I'd protested, "But I don't want to go. I want to be with you." I was angry they were leaving me, and my whole body froze with the weight of the world. Immobile from fright, I felt captive in this horror reel.

"It is not safe for you in Ghana. It's better for you here," my mother added, as if that would be helpful.

The excuses piled up, and I believed none of them. Nothing in my brain would tell me that there was a reason for my parents to leave us. I didn't understand how they could do this to me, but especially to my brother, who was still at such a tender age. I'd always thought he was their favorite.

"We will see you soon. You can come visit us," my father said, trying to reassure us as we sobbed.

It was no reassurance. I was still a child who felt lost and abandoned. I felt so insignificant. My parents didn't love me enough to need me close. I could never make sense of their choice. I was in my formative years—stepping into my sense of self and taking space in the world. I didn't know who I was, never mind who I'd be in a new town. This was to be my life, a life without Mommy and Daddy, with maybe a promised trip to Africa at some point in the future.

Kuala Lumpur was a metropolis—think New York City—with theater, concerts, enormous shopping malls, sidewalk cafés, and cuisines from all over the world. Alor Star was a small town, with one large shopping mall, a handful of schools, and no highways. A fish vendor parked his truck in front of Amachee's house, and all the housewives congregated to share gossip. It may as well have been Timbuktu. I was not a small-town girl. I didn't want that life.

I stared at the floor, my milkshake untouched. We walked to the security checkpoint for our last goodbye.

"Be good, yeah? Stay sharp in school," Daddy said. "You can write to me. I will call you. Everything will be okay. Daddy loves you." The tears streaming down his face didn't unlock my own tears. I was in shock, in pain, and angry. This was a mistake—surely I would never find forgiveness for this show of cruelty.

"Amy, take care of Adik, yeah? Don't give Amachee problems." Adik, my little brother, held on to Daddy's hand luggage as he sobbed, knowing his big sister did not want that responsibility. He then controlled his sobbing to be strong for my parents, to give them comfort even though they were hurting us. Adik, like me, must have been dying inside from the pain.

"You will be okay. We will see you soon, okay?" Mommy was always the more emotionally disguised one. I could never tell what she was feeling.

She hugged me, and I found myself frozen. My hands gripped her red wool sweater, and I couldn't let go. My uncle coaxed me to let go, and what felt like an enormous two-hundred-foot wave came crashing down on me. I was hysterical. I wanted them to miss their flight. I wanted them to stay. I wasn't ready. I screamed and cried, causing a scene at the airport. I didn't want to be without them. The hysteria hit my brother, and he cried profusely. My parents tried to calm us down, but there was nothing they could say. I watched the fucking handkerchief pass over Daddy's eyes over and over. My mother sniffled as they walked away, waving as if they were going on a quick vacation.

My parents walked through those gates. I wouldn't see them again for a year and a half, at the one reunion I had been promised. They were gone for four years. The next day, we made our way to our new home with my grandmother. On the drive to her house, I found myself afraid and resistant. I stared out the window, feeling resentful, crying the whole way.

"It's going to be okay." My uncle reassured us on the drive through the highways lined with limestone and paddy fields. My eyes kept a steady gaze on the nature outside, watching the striations on the mountainsides.

"You'll find new friends, and you'll find your way. It will be different from Kuala Lumpur, but you'll find your way. Just focus on your studies." I knew he was trying to make me feel better.

"Why didn't they take us with them? Tell me the truth." I stared at him from the passenger seat, and I watched his face drop. He looked straight ahead.

"I don't know, but I know you're better off with Amachee. You'll see."

The tears were like a leaky faucet I couldn't turn off. My brother sobbed quietly in the back seat.

⁓

Because my father was Amachee's favorite son, we had historically kept up with weekly phone calls to her. We were very close, so arriving at her house meant a sense of continuity.

Adik was eleven. Our oldest brother, Aziz, was twenty-four and at university in Switzerland. We had a sister, Maryam, who was twenty. She had already been living with my grandmother for the past three years due to my parents' inability to keep up with her challenging shenanigans. This was telling of my parents—shifting the responsibility of their children to others when they couldn't handle it. *Was I out of hand?* I did everything right. I had promised not to talk back if they took me with them. I was willing to be a good girl. They didn't tell me what I had done wrong. This felt like punishment for a crime I had unknowingly committed. The three of us lived in a tiny 1,600-square-foot home with my two other cousins. They were already living with my grandmother so they could attend the better schools in the area.

The small town was conservative and predominantly Muslim. Adik and I tried to fit in. He did better than me because of the lighter, olive skin he had inherited from my mother. It matched the skin of the Muslim Malays, the favored race in town. My mother was Malay by ethnicity and Muslim. All Malays in Malaysia must be Muslim, as mandated by our constitution. My father, who was Indian and Hindu, converted when he married her, as was the law in Malaysia. Neither of my parents were particularly religious, so we learned the Islamic faith at school, where it was mandatory. We were not pious people, and this would create a world of humiliation and pain for me in Alor Star.

I was born with a skin shade belonging to neither parent. I was not dark enough to be Indian like my father, nor nearly as light as my mother. This posed problems in our new town, because the fairer skin was evidence of your faith as well as your ethnicity. Biracial people were seen as oddballs. I looked almost Indian with my lighter-brown skin. Indians were generally Hindus or Christians, but I was Muslim on paper. My grandmother, aunt, uncle, and all my cousins I lived with were Hindu. The forced connection to my legal faith left me in a forever seesaw of belonging, but not belonging, to either parent's culture. None of this mattered in cosmopolitan Kuala Lumpur, where everyone I knew was a mix of something. We all spoke English and the subjects of race and religion were rarely in the forefront.

I soon found out that I didn't speak the Malay language with the correct accent in Alor Star. I was constantly made fun of for my curly hair and dark skin by the Malay girls in my neighborhood. I endured name-calling and exclusion. Among the darker Indians, I was not accepted, as I didn't speak Tamil. I wasn't dark enough to be one of them. I learned all this the hard way on my first day of school.

Dress codes were a focal point in my new life. There was the dress code policed by my grandmother: no midriffs or short skirts allowed. Short skirts included anything that showed the knees. No baggy jeans were allowed. "You look like a hoodlum" was the judgment cast by all the adults, including my grandmother. There were to be no sleeveless tops, no spaghetti straps, and no ripped jeans. The list went on. I was furious but wore the same acceptable things over and over again.

On the first day in form 2, the equivalent of eighth grade in America, I walked into a trap of fear and humiliation. My new school, St. Nicholas Convent, inherited its name from our colonial past. Malaysia used to be a British colony, so the education system is based on the British education system. Prior to independence from British rule in 1957, schools were run by nuns and priests. My new school was girls only and used to be run by nuns. In modern times, all public schools are run by the federal and state governments, but names were kept in remembrance of history. It was a hundred-year-old school, an historical landmark, intact as it was a hundred years ago. I liked that history, and my aunts, cousins, and sister had attended this school.

But when they went to school, the leadership had been more liberal. Under new local leadership, the rules had changed. My grandmother and aunt hadn't realized what an issue the uniforms had become since the time my sister and cousin had attended.

The uniforms were a point of contention. There were two versions of the public-school uniforms. One was a white button-down shirt under a powder-blue, knee-length pinafore. The other was the Malay traditional version, worn by both Muslims and non-Muslims alike. It was the *Baju Kurung*, a long white tunic that reached the knee with a powder-blue, ankle-length skirt underneath. White socks and white shoes were to be kept clean. Muslim girls wore the *Baju Kurung* and chose to wear a hijab, a head covering revealing only the face, which was practically mandatory in conservative Alor Star.

I arrived looking spiffy on my first day, in my crisp, pressed Ministry of Education–sanctioned pinafore. My grandmother had agreed I looked smart and coiffed. When I got to the classroom, however, I felt like I was naked. The other students looked at me and whispered. I counted the students—thirty-five. It was clear as soon as I walked in that the students had self-segregated. The Chinese girls in their pinafores lined the front of the class, and behind them were rows of Malay girls in long tunics and hijabs. In the far corner were the dark Indian girls, also in pinafores. My feet froze to the ground as I tried to be calm. I felt displaced and disoriented, not knowing which group I belonged to. I wore a pinafore, but I was clearly meant to be in the tunic and hijab by the stares I was getting. Here, religion trumped race. The heat started to get to me. There weren't windows in this classroom, just four large doors. The ninety-degree heat smothered me. As I found a place to sit, the girl next to me looked at my notebook and saw my full name.

"Why are you dressed like that?" she asked me in Malay. I took note of her hijab. It was a large white scarf that draped over her head, long enough to cover her chest. I felt the heat rise in the room, making it difficult to breathe.

"Like what?" I asked, feigning ignorance and now self-conscious of my Kuala Lumpur accent, which differed drastically from hers.

"Like a non-Muslim," she said loudly enough that the person in front of us and the teacher heard.

"She ran out of cloth, it seems," the hijab-wearing teacher said, insulting me. I came from a family where religion was something that was close to the heart and personal, not exhibitory in nature, and definitely not something to be endured. A woman covers her hair in modesty and submission to the Lord's decree of the sacred nature of a woman. A woman, in her relationship to God, chooses to wear the hijab or not. It should have been my choice, but here it was not. I wish I had known this. My grandmother would have been appalled and mortified had she known this beforehand.

~

"Worst day of school" would be an understatement. I'd never been publicly humiliated like that before. Devi Atthey, my aunt, consoled me later that afternoon when she got home from work. She assured me things would be okay.

"It's okay, ma, just wear the *Baju Kurung* from now on. People here are a little bit narrow-minded, so just deal with it best we can, okay? Your mommy and daddy are not here. Don't make trouble. It's just a small thing." She'd always been very pragmatic in her consolation. The humiliation surprised her too. She explained that the shifting political climate was changing the norms. An über-conservative political party had been close to winning the elections two years before, so the incumbent's campaigns had turned up the dial on religious campaigning. They won and so did their hyperbolized religious values. She said it was hard to predict how these emboldened actions were going to pop up. Now we knew, and we would deal with it by submitting to society's expectations to avoid further confrontation. I knew she was right, but I didn't want to submit to such pressures. I was angry that I had to deal with any of this, that what I wore each day would be another thing for me to endure.

Two months into the school year, we got a new principal who made an arbitrary rule that all Muslim students were required to wear a hijab. I was the only Muslim girl not wearing a hijab, so I was singled out and forced into submission.

I cried over this new rule. I felt violated that anyone would make me do something I didn't want to and snatch away my freedom to choose. Nevertheless, I wore a hijab every day. In an act of rebellion, at the end of the school day, I would take it off at the entrance while I waited for the bus to arrive.

My insolence and reluctance to wear the hijab puzzled my teachers. The religious teacher, the rude one who'd humiliated me about the head coverings, decided it was time to question me. I was nervous when I was called to the principal's office. I was met by the religious teacher and another teacher. The two women began their police-style interrogation. All that was missing was the bright lamp in my face. The questions were relentless. Why wasn't I living with my parents? Why was my grandmother's name Hindu? What did I eat at her house? Did she have a dog? (Muslims were not permitted to have dogs.) They informed me of their intent to remove me from my grandmother's Hindu home to be placed in a boarding school for Muslim girls. I wasn't sure if they had the legal right to do so, but I was terrified. Given the political climate, anything was possible.

As they seemed close to a verdict, the principal walked in and sat across from me at the teak desk. The long stretch of the table mirrored the distance that was growing between them and me.

"Where are your parents?" she asked with both scorn and deep concern.

"Ghana," I said.

"Who are you living with here?" I knew she had the answers to these questions. I'd been through this line of questioning already, multiple times.

"With my grandmother, who is my legal guardian." I offered that they should speak to my parents or to our family lawyer. "I'll be happy to arrange a phone call," I spat out, nervous about standing up for myself. My whole body was hot and sweat came through the back of my white tunic.

"Can you pray in your grandmother's house?" she pressed. *What a preposterous question.*

"Don't people pray on dirt?" I asked. I was referring to the mass prayers in which Muslim people prayed outside full mosques with their prayer mats on the dirt. She'd posed a ridiculous question. I did not care for the scrutiny. "I want to call my parents now. You have no right to ask me these questions." My body was shaking. I was certain they were going to remove me, and there was no one to challenge it. My parents were the only ones whose opinions mattered, and they were thousands of miles away. I held back tears, to be brave and to show them they couldn't mess with me.

"You brat!" she exclaimed in frustration. She sent me out of the room.

∽

I didn't breathe a word of this to my grandmother, for fear of worrying her. I wasn't sure what kind of trouble I might have been in or what the principal might do. It was clear they were trying to remove me from my grandmother's home, the only place I had. My grandmother never heard from them, so I figured I had called their bluff, though I never understood the point of the interrogation in the first place. Perhaps they were just trying to put me in my place, to put an end to my insubordination. Whatever the reason, I was glad their nosy questioning ended at the principal's office that day. I'd stood up for myself and put on a brave face. I'm sure I seemed full of myself, but in fact I had pretended to be courageous, as I'd done so many times in the past.

This was just one more stressor I'd endured since arriving in this terrible place. I missed my parents. I didn't fit in at school. There was the hijab fiasco, then the threatened removal from my grandmother's care. It all wore me down. I didn't belong.

My friends in Kuala Lumpur all spoke English, which we called "Manglish" because it was English with a sprinkling of Malay words. Most everyone in Alor Star spoke Malay, even the Chinese and Indian girls. I tried to gain favor with the Malay girls so I wouldn't be so lost during religious classes and didn't get into more trouble with the religious teacher. But the only way to do that was to pretend I was more religious than I was. If I could pretend to be a pious Muslim in class, there would be no need for further interrogations, so I strategized. I hid behind my Malay friends and copied everything they did. They didn't exactly befriend me, but at least they were kind.

The non-Muslim crowd seemed to get along great among themselves, but there was an exclusivity to their circle. They spoke English with each other. I spoke English, but I was an outcast because they couldn't figure me out. I was not one of them, I was biracial, and I came from Kuala Lumpur. It intimidated and confused them.

For weeks, I endured the stress of not belonging. Finally, one afternoon at school, a few minutes before the end-of-day bell rang, my social standing was determined. Our teacher walked in with the final scores for the midsemester examinations.

"Number two, Amelia," she said.

Everyone gasped, and all eyes were on me. I ranked second in all of the thirty-six students in the classroom, in all eight subjects tested, even the religious class. Whispers in the room made my hair stand up under my tunic. My sense of pride mixed with embarrassment.

"How did you do that? Where do you go for tutoring?" They were talking to me. I was the center of attention. That afternoon at track practice, a friend from the front of the classroom, a Chinese girl, sat to chat with me. For the first time, she asked about where I was from. She lived in the same neighborhood as I did, and we trained for track together after that. Academics got me into the circle I so wanted to be in. School became a little more tolerable after that. I had to keep my real self on the down low under the head scarf I wore, masking my resentment. But I kept my scores up and made new friends. There were no more rehoming suggestions by those "well-meaning" teachers after the first-semester grades came out.

~

Within six months of being without my parents and with external factors under control, I felt better. I grew closer to my aunt and uncle. Devi Atthey, my father's younger sister, became my closest ally. She taught me to stand on my own and be considerate of others, no matter what I wanted. She loved us all. She was a banker and worked a routine nine-to-five job. We'd all wait for that little red hatchback to pull into the driveway in the evenings. This cute lady, just shy of five feet, would strut down the driveway as we all rushed to greet her. We were bathed and clean, with hurried reports of our chores done so she would take us to get frozen yogurt. She would oblige with a tired smile on her face. My brother, my two cousins, and Devi Atthey's three children raced to the car to claim seats. We piled on each other in the tiny hatchback—seat belts and car seats were not legal requirements at the time.

She tirelessly cared for us and wore her affection on her sleeve. There was one thing she did not teach me, however, and that was self-care. Instead, she modeled absolute sacrifice. She put on a brave face and a strong front to endure all that she had to handle. She was raising all of us and her children, holding a professional job, and caring for her husband and her mother. She had to be exhausted dealing with us, but she wore a smile at all times, a mask just like mine. She was one of the most giving people I knew. She carried herself with dignity and honesty, and she strived for success professionally and in her home life. This would be something I'd try to emulate for the rest of my life.

Her husband, Uncle Bala, was a mentor for me. Sometimes I would tell him my problems at school, and he would ask me to sit quietly with him. I tried to meditate as I watched him. In the evenings, he sat at the Hindu altar in the prayer room at his house, two doors down from Amachee's house. He lit the incense, and we were to be in complete silence. I admired all the little statues and pictures of Hindu deities adorned with marigold garlands and flowers we helped picked in the evenings for his prayers. He would sing Sanskrit prayers, then sit cross-legged on the floor, eyes shut as the smoke from the incense filled the room with the scent of sandalwood. He would sit in silence for what seemed like hours to me, who found it hard to pass a minute in silence. Still, I sat with him quietly, wanting the blessings from the incense to take away the restlessness, the void in my heart from missing my parents, and the trauma of being uprooted.

He delved into his deepest thoughts, and he instructed me to do the same. I breathed in the incense and watched the lit camphor on the table. After these meditations, we usually discussed anything that was bothering me—troubles with friends at school, missing my parents, or hardships with studies and my grandmother. It seemed that through his meditation, he gained clarity about any issue I was having. He always gave me sage advice. It was not a farce with him; everything was clear and simple. "The right thing to do is usually the hardest thing to do. But we must carry on, find a way." He gave me comfort when I didn't fit in at school. He had all the practical and spiritual guidance on any predicament I put forward. He was truth in my eyes and someone I trusted. His advice never failed me.

In my parents' absence, I focused on school. I was constantly under scrutiny. There was nowhere to hide. One blistering hot afternoon, I came home smiling, trophy in hand. I had just won the state elocution competition. Amachee was waiting at the front door with a tray of lit camphor. She stopped me at the gate, circled me three times with the tray, and kissed me. She had me go straight into the house as she discarded the contents of the tray without me seeing. This was done in order to rid all evil eyes on me, so my energy would be cleansed of envious thoughts and malice from others. The savory smell that filled the house told me there was a feast waiting. My favorite dish, mutton *varuval* with a delicious spicy rub, and three other dishes were on the dining table.

She came into the house, washed her hands, hugged me tight, and congratulated me. "Eat! I cooked your favorite," she said. "Muthu from the school told me the news this morning. You beat all of them, ah! Good job!" I was filled with the pride and love I no longer longed for. She did seemingly mundane, normal things, but I realized how invaluable those gestures were.

Approaching the anniversary of our first year of living together, I fell into a groove. School was going well, and my grandmother's dress code didn't bother me. I looked forward to coming home to a house full of people and spending time with my cousins and siblings. I was preparing for the second-semester, year-end exams. I studied late at night when everyone was asleep. I sat in the dining room, and Amachee sat in the rocking chair facing the TV. I could see her back through the doorway. She had the television on to prove she wasn't staying up for me, so I wouldn't feel bad. She watched her show and then the nighttime newscast. My gaze shifted from my chemistry textbook to her head flopping and bouncing back. The television broadcast had ended, and she was fast asleep. I chuckled and told her to go to bed. She insisted she was still watching TV, but she was actually keeping me company so I wouldn't feel alone. No one had ever shown me such care. I was used to being independent and doing what I needed on my own. Back in Kuala Lumpur, I never even did homework. In her company, I studied and had special lunches awaiting me every day. We shared stories over popsicles on the porch. She was invested in me as no one else had ever been. I found myself less lost, and there was a settling of my shattered pieces. The rage at my parents had simmered down. I no longer resented my life with my grandmother. I knew in my heart that she persisted in keeping me company during my pursuit for success because she cared.

After the realization that I was indeed home, I dug in my heels and attempted to be part of this new world. I was no longer a stranger in my own life. I got involved in extracurricular activities at school. I was good at track, and I entered public speaking competitions, poetry readings, debate, and anything else that allowed me to use my gift of gab. I won many of the competitions, and I finally understood what it meant to be in love. I was on top of the world. I never wanted to leave the stage when my name was called, because my ears rang with the sound of my Amachee standing up in the crowd. She would cheer and tell everyone around her, "This girl, this is *my* granddaughter! She's a very good girl!" It wasn't about her words, but about the pride I felt. It flew off her, straight to me. She was mine, and I was hers.

Her love filled the void left by my parents. Amachee showed me what it meant to love, despite all her meddling and nosiness. She loved me in a way no one else ever had, not even my parents. She was invested in my life and wanted to protect me from harm or any deterrents to success. The torment of fitting in, like trying to shove huge feet into tiny stilettos, didn't go away. But she made me believe I could endure and even thrive.

~

The first time my parents arranged for my brother and I to come visit them in Ghana, I was fifteen and already in my second year at the new school. We were escorted by my mother's colleague, Nora, to board a flight to Ghana, with a layover in Heathrow. We got a scare at Heathrow when Nora was interrogated by British immigration officers on suspicion of traveling with minors not related to her. The officer seemed ten feet tall to me.

"Where are you going?" he asked, staring straight at me.

"I told you I'm taking them to meet their parents in Ghana. You have the documentation," Nora said sharply. She stroked my hair gently to calm me, knowing we were afraid.

"I wasn't talking to you. You will remain silent or be removed." The officer raised his voice as another officer motioned for her to step away from us. Then he turned to me. My little brother clutched my hand. We were both nervous.

"I'm visiting my parents. This is my little brother. My parents work for TV3 Ghana. We're going to visit them. This is my mother's colleague. She's taking us there." I shivered as I spoke, holding back tears.

They pulled Nora aside and engaged her in a heated discussion. I was afraid of what was going to happen. I was worried they were going to take us away from her, and we wouldn't get to see our parents. I put on a mask, one I knew how to wear well. I acted brave and happy. I chatted with a female officer next to me.

"Is there snow outside? I would really love to see snow," I said cheerfully.

"No, love, not in London. It has been raining a lot," she said, smiling kindly at me. I knew my act was going well.

I asked Nora for my water bottle. She handed it to me, and I hugged her, to show that this was not child trafficking. I was fast on my feet and had my wits about me. The stern, large man asked me again about meeting our parents. He looked through our passports and documents and finally let us go. Putting on a show was easy for me, and so was getting out of sticky situations. Years of practice paid off that day. We enjoyed our layover with a picnic outside the airport, watching the airplanes take off and land.

We landed in Ghana. This airport was quite different from the ones we had in Malaysia and a far cry from the one in London. The sign read: KOTOKA INTERNATIONAL AIRPORT. It was small and not very brightly lit. There were lots of people everywhere, but they weren't all travelers. This was definitely different than what I had seen before. The only people of African descent I had ever seen had been on TV. There were men in colorful shirts, all offering to carry my luggage, which was very curtly denied by our chaperone.

We spent three weeks in Ghana. Everything was peculiar, funny, and made me feel so alive. My parents' house was similar to houses in

Malaysia. It was a stand-alone house, with marble flooring and tiled kitchens and bathrooms. There was a large living room with a television and surround sound, a formal dining room off the living room, and a hallway leading to the master bedroom and two other rooms. The yard surrounding the house was rather bare but for the potted plants my mother nursed along the porch. Water was rationed. There was no water except for what came from the water truck, which visited the neighborhood to fill our containers once a week. My parents also had containers outside to catch rain. Showering was scheduled. Bathwater was collected to use for flushing, which was restricted to number two only. Rear-end cleansing was prioritized; a bucket of water sat next to the toilet. This was the life they left *our life* behind for? Great stories would be shared when we got home to Amachee. I couldn't wait to tell her.

At my parents' house, they had a live-in housekeeper, Ajwa. There was also a driver, Kweku, and a guard, Fred. The guard and housekeeper entertained me while my parents were at work, which was quite an experience. Even during our visit, my parents would work many of the days, leaving us with the three strangers I quickly befriended. I was invited to spend days at the new TV station, but after a couple of tours, I tired of it. My mother asked me to accompany her to work to watch her edit her latest documentary. I declined sitting in the editing suite for eight hours. *Thanks, but no thanks.* My father was overseeing the equipment rigging of a new studio, and my brother happily joined him. I preferred to stay home with my new friends and the option to kick back and watch TV.

Ajwa braided my hair and taught me songs in Twi. Her kind eyes grew wide with surprise when I failed a Ghana trivia test. She'd grab my hair in a quick second and turn me to face her, nose to nose, to get indisputable confirmation that I did not know Kofi Annan was from

Ghana. "Little girl, you know great men come from Ghana, okay?" she said with a stern look. She was proud of where she came from. I took serious note of Kofi Annan's origins, which were in the little town of Kumasi, about four hours from where we were in Accra.

I was fascinated by Ajwa and her animated way of talking about her hair salon visits. "It takes seven or eight hours to look this good." Her eyes would light up and bulge at me to make a point. Her lips were full and smooth. I loved watching her speak with so much expression as much as I liked listening to her stories about Anansi. I took comfort in her warmth. Sometimes she would sing, and I would beg for her to teach me. One of the songs told the tale of a woman, Abena, who didn't know she had lost her family to bombs because she had left her home village. She was very much like Ajwa, who had to live away from her family to make a living. My heart ached for Ajwa as much as it ached for Abena. I now knew and would always have a heart for this conundrum. My parents had done the same, though I never understood their reasoning.

My father took us to the outskirts of Accra the second weekend we were there. We drove away from the city. The farther we went, the more we saw little children, younger than me, walking while balancing buckets of water on their heads. They rushed down the dusty street with those heavy buckets. I couldn't make out if it was water streaming from the buckets or tears from the pain and struggle of transporting water for their family. They made many trips, I was told. A few miles down the same road, we came to a village of makeshift houses. These houses had walls and a tarp roof, or zinc walls that finished mismatched brick walls, topped off with zinc. There was no flooring, just the laterite dirt for the children to rest their bones on after bringing home water. The air in the car grew thick. I couldn't breathe from the guilt and pain I felt for those families.

"Be grateful for what you have," my father told me. "When you think that you don't have enough, there are people who have it worse."

My heart was heavy. My father felt the sadness too—I could tell from his tone. But he did not want to miss out on a parenting moment, one in which I was learning to be grateful for what I had. I could not be the privileged, spoiled brat who would surface periodically. I felt survival guilt. *They were born into this. I was not. Why do I get to live and visit their homes as if on a safari of life lessons, while they toil in their daily survival?* Since then, I've never taken for granted the concept of having nothing. I couldn't quiet the whispering in my mind.

Was he showing me how much more difficult my life could be? Was I to compromise my pain of abandonment with the fact my life isn't as bad as these children's?

I don't know if my father's lessons stemmed from the guilt of having left us behind, but I willed myself to believe it was gratitude I was supposed to learn. I had to make it okay in order to carry on the next two and a half years without them.

After three weeks of waiting while my parents were busy at work, only having them in the evenings and weekends, we went on a trip to London. I rode the double-decker busses down busy London streets. I saw all of London and the Thames and even walked across the London Bridge. At the end of the week, we traveled to Montreux to meet up with my older brother. I played in snow, in the mountain town of Gstaad in Switzerland, for the first time in my life. I was the happiest fifteen-year-old there was. I was living in a fantasy adventure with my parents while we traveled the world. Sometimes I felt connected to my parents. The four of us in a hotel room together for those two weeks made me feel close to them again. I had missed them so much, and our time together in these foreign lands eased the longing I'd had. I yearned for the warmth and familiarity that I used to know. We said goodbye to my older brother in Switzerland.

My parents returned to Alor Star with us, and once we got to Malaysia, my emotions caught up with me. Listening to their tales of life in Ghana made my blood boil. Oh, what a grand old time they were having without us—all the funny stories about *their life*. It seemed to me they didn't care at all about my struggles. My old friend resentment whispered in my ear. I distanced myself to show my discontent with them. I was so full of resentment that I hardly remember the visit. Our vacation in Africa and Europe had been a special time, but once back in Malaysia, the distance between us grew. They returned to *their* home in Ghana. This time there would be no tears when they left. I was convinced that I no longer belonged to my parents.

Once they left, I was more open to my new home. I had already learned to accept and live with the abandonment. I'd already accepted it as my reality.

That trip was meant to close the gap between my parents and me but did nothing of the sort. Instead I woke up. I had figured a few things out. I belonged to my grandmother, Devi Atthey, and Uncle Bala. They were my home. I would never understand my parents' willingness to part from me and my brother. I would never under-stand their indifference to our pain. Perhaps they figured the love I would find with my grandmother, aunt, and uncle would serve as stand-in love and suffice. It did not.

To survive the pain, I had to replace them. I pretended they only existed in phone calls and letters we exchanged. I abandoned all expectations and understanding of their willingness to part with me. In my mind, I found new parents in Devi Atthey, Uncle Bala, and

Amachee. My real parents were just a fact of my biology. I dropped my anchor with surety in the soil I called home.

~

In my grandmother's house, there was a lot of praying, fasting, fire and incense, and cleaning and cleansing. She prayed for everything and all of us. The end of high school was coming and with that a series of examinations that I needed to pass in order to graduate. I'd worked so hard all these years, and these exams would determine my future. I had it all mapped out—I'd get great results to qualify for the Australian Year 12. From there, I'd go on to the university of my dreams in the land down under. I was so excited about my future.

The day before exams, I followed Amachee to the temple as she was praying for me. Offerings to the gods would ensure my success, she said. That afternoon, I went for a walk with my cousin to pluck flowers that grew in the neighborhood park. A beautiful bunch of white jasmine were to be part of the offerings.

We ate an early dinner, then headed to the temple. I arrived feeling such urgency. I needed everything to go well to ensure the future I had planned. We removed our shoes and washed our feet at the entrance. My heart pounded. I took a moment, struck by the beautiful marble structure. Gorgeous white pillars held up the tiered roof, which was adorned with carvings and statues of the temple guardians in all the colors of a palette. The statues depicted animals and fierce men.

At the main altar, a shirtless priest stood with three white stripes of sacred ashes drawn across his forehead. My grandmother handed him the offerings in a small coconut shell: bananas, betel leaves, betel nuts, and the jasmine I had picked. The priest rang his bell as he sang in Sanskrit, and I heard my name in the song. Words strung together quickly in my mind: "Please help me. Please help me. Show me the right answers. Let me remember everything I studied." Then he brought the lit camphor. Amachee put her hand to the fire and quickly pulled it away. I bowed my head, and he blessed me, assuring me all would be well. "Top marks," he said. He pointed firmly to the sky, as if to insinuate he had spoken to the gods about my outcome. He smiled at me. My grandmother also smiled, satisfied that her part had been done. The deities had heard her call for my success in exams. I felt confident in the efforts.

I aced those exams and attributed it to my hard work but also to my grandmother's extensive devotion to my success.

It surprised me that I'd grown so comfortable those past four years and that I'd so easily let go of my former self. I grew into a new person, one who was thriving. I was a little more submissive, to please my grandmother, the teachers, and the gossipmongers. I put on masks to get along with my friends at school. I pretended to be pious to protect my living arrangement, and I acted strong and resilient so my family would not worry. Through all this pretense, somehow, I also found peace and a place for me.

My parents leaving would be my first major heartbreak, but it would also lead to my first true-love story. I learned what it meant to love, what devotion and kindness looked like. I had found a version of me that I understood. I learned to navigate my life with a new sense of being, a confidence that seemed indestructible. I was strong because my grandmother's blood ran through me.

CHAPTER 2

My parents returned from Ghana in time for my high school graduation. They made all kinds of promises, surely from the guilt of being away for four years. They said I could enroll in any university I wanted. This had been my understanding for as long as they'd been in Ghana—that part of losing them meant I'd get to go anywhere for college. Of course, I had my heart set on one of the best, an Australian undergraduate program for business in Melbourne. Once they got back, we moved to the big city. With my excellent grades, I was readily admitted to an Australian Year 12 program, a prerequisite for college in Australia. Once I completed the Year 12 entrance exams, I wanted to get my Bachelor of Commerce with majors in accounting and business law.

The Year 12 program went as planned. I excelled in school. I would get into the university of my choice, and I would complete my four-year undergraduate degree in three years, working harder and taking more classes per semester. I was excited and ready for my Australian adventure. I wanted to spend the summers traveling the continent. I couldn't wait to see the koalas and wallabies. I wanted to dive in the Great Barrier Reef but most of all live a life independent of my family. I just needed to keep up my tenacity. When I came home with my Year 12 exam results, Daddy looked at my transcripts with tears in his eyes. He asked me to sit beside him, wrapped his arms around my shoulders, and pulled me in for a kiss on my forehead.

"Well done," he said softly. I knew this woeful tone of voice. The flame of my excitement turned to embers as I understood that I was about to receive bad news. I still held on to an inkling of hope and tried to stay positive.

"I'm going to apply to these three universities in Australia. I qualify for all of them. Do you want to see the brochures?"

He sighed deeply and pinched the bridge of his nose to catch the tears.

"I don't think we can afford Australia, baby." I couldn't believe it. My heart filled with pain, like a thick stew boiling. I had trusted him when he'd said the *reason* I had to be without him and Mommy those long four years was to afford my ambitions. Apparently, trust was a luxury I could no longer afford. My dreams were out of reach, and there was nothing I could do. I was devastated. I had worked hard. I had done all I was supposed to, and I couldn't believe I was being betrayed. He picked up the remote to the stereo and turned down the Celtic music.

My heart was crushed. I tried to slump back into the seat and be engulfed in the music as I'd done when I was a child. We would sit on our red couch, turn on Celtic music, and listen together. Daddy would lie his head on the back of the couch, his eyes closed. Some days I'd lay on his chest, breathing in the comforting goodness of my father.

But now Daddy was explaining how he had saved as much as he could in the four years in Ghana, but it would not be enough for me to study overseas given the atrocious exchange rates. We also had to think about Adik, who wasn't far behind me in school. "I had to be away from you all that time to try to secure what you wanted," Daddy said. "But please, with the exchange rates, it's not enough. Can you try to understand?"

I sunk into his chest, my dreams crushed. I had always wanted to study abroad. In many ways, I had been groomed for this overseas adventure my whole life. And here was my father, who knew how much it meant, crushing me and trying to make it okay. They'd gone to Ghana and left me to struggle for four years, in a void that I had tried to fill with the love of others. I had been patient and steadfast in my end of the bargain. What about their promise? The anger stewed and simmered, coming closer to the boiling point with every passing second.

"We can look into Australian satellite campuses here, and you'll earn the same undergraduate degree," he said, trying to soften the blow.

I broke away from his embrace in full meltdown. I thought about the promise of Australia and everything I'd miss out on now. There would be no outback, no koalas or kangaroos. There would be no life on my own in which I'd be my own person, not bound by the social constraints I had endured for the past four years.

"You left me for four years, on the pretense that I could go wherever I wanted, and now you tell me this?"

"I tried my best, baby. It wasn't easy, and I have to think about your Adik too."

I walked away, leaving him on the couch. Once in my room, I heard the volume turn up on the Celtic music. It pained me to know that my father was disappointed, in a shrunken state on that couch, but the fury of betrayal ate at me. My anger deflated eventually, my vexation no longer like cymbals crashing. Guilt abated my frustrations. I knew that it didn't matter how hard I tried. There was no remedy to this financial predicament. Every time they'd said we were closer to my dreams in those letters—which I waited on with bated breath and blind faith—it was a lie. It was only closer to a *version* of my dream, not my actual dream. They had returned to crush me further than I had already been ground down. The guilt of feeling angry was not enough to placate the ache in my heart for dreams foregone, promises broken.

For my entire life, I had been groomed for a life outside of our country. Daddy always felt strongly about the art of table manners, social graces, and self-presentation—all social norms of Westerners. He was particular about us knowing the basics, at least: which hand held the fork and which held the spoon. In Malaysia, we ate almost everything with our hands, except soups and noodles. He taught me not to clank my cutlery on the plate and not to blow on my soup. "Always spoon your soup outward in case it spills, so it won't be on you. No blowing of tea, just a light stirring. Don't act like a ninny—you're going to need this when you grow up and live overseas," he'd say. I'd always had this expectation, and I'd always think about how I'd get to present my impeccable table manners at an Australian dinner table.

He had filled my head with wonder and yearning for a faraway life ever since I was a little child. My father traveled a lot for work conferences and training. He traveled to America, England, Germany, Italy, Australia, Qatar, and the UAE. I listened to all his stories upon his return from foreign lands as he handed out the gifts he brought home. I heard stories of the gambling escapades in Vegas, dampened by the exchange rate. I heard about immigration officials at the London airport scrutinizing him, despite his credentials and the fact that he was attending a training hosted by the British Broadcast Corporation. He talked about the long highways lined by cacti and tumbleweeds in America, the deserts and riding camels in Oman. It felt impossible to contain all those feelings of wonder and amazement.

I longed for a life abroad, for the foreignness of everything different and new. But now financial burdens and consideration for my brother squashed all those dreams. I was always going to live overseas and experience that life of adventure. But now I was here, sobbing in my bedroom, ruminating on the fact that this would never be. I would not experience the travel escapades promised to me in stories, and dreams would remain dreams.

~

I spent a week sulking and trying to accept my fate. My father and I toured satellite campuses of the Australian universities in Kuala Lumpur. At least this way I would still get an Australian undergraduate degree that was prestigious and more valuable in the job market than one from the local public universities. Walking into the large foyer of my chosen university, I was filled with confidence, knowing I would get in. The tall white pillars, which were so grand, and the mosaic tiles gave me a sense of pride and grandiosity. I was about to be part of this sophisticated institution.

I watched the college students reading by the garden. Some were in groups, deep in studious discussion. Students were rushing to classes. Everyone was in plain clothes, and some had nose rings and torn jeans, midriffs showing, and tattoos. Others were more conservative as I was in my tank top, jeans, Chucks, and a backpack. I already felt I fit in here. I just needed to get in and find my squad. We walked over to the tables, the banners advertising various program options. I walked straight to the Bachelor of Commerce banner, my dream. A lady locked eyes with me as soon as I approached. She had a warm smile and grabbed a packet. But when I reached for it, my father stopped me. He pointed toward the Bachelor of Engineering table, to which I simply said, "No." I turned back to the lady whose arm was still outstretched. The packet held an enrollment form that I couldn't wait to fill out.

We walked back to the car as Daddy held onto my hand, but he was deep in thought. The car ride was heavy with the air of my father's discontent. "I'm worried you will not have a good future with a business degree. Something like engineering or the sciences is the way of the future. I don't want you to make the wrong choice and ruin your future." I stayed silent. *First he's saying that I can't go to Australia, and now he's saying what I get to study?* I had to bite my tongue as my mind raced in a fury. I was not the one who was fickle with my words or choices. I had done my part. With the betrayal of not being able to go to Australia fresh in my mind, I was not letting this part of my dream go. I refused to pay mind to the horrifyingly wicked idea that I was going to spend the next few years doing yet another thing I didn't want to. I'd had to make horrendous choices from the time I was a little girl. I wouldn't have a future but for sheer luck. I'd actually had to make life-or-death decisions at a much younger age. I didn't see why choosing an undergraduate program was of dire contemplation.

If anything, I was independent and responsible. I was charged with my own safety and security by the time I was eight. My younger brother, then five, was always with a babysitter after kindergarten. My older sister was fourteen, living with my grandmother. I was alone at home every day after school but for the rare occasion my oldest brother would be home straight from high school. My memories of coming home and policing myself filled me with pride and terror.

As would be expected of any eight-year-old, there were days I forgot the keys. On those days, I rested my feet and sat at the gate until someone could let me in. There was a concrete bench with no shade at the gate, and the sun was rarely forgiving in Malaysia. I'd wait out there on the hot bench. It was usually about three hours before either Mommy or Daddy came home. On some of those days, I fell asleep. Once, someone that I didn't know saw me there, woke me up, and invited me to his house to wait for my parents. I was perplexed by the idea of riding in a stranger's car. But the sweltering heat made it feel as though my forehead was melting onto my nose. My dry throat and the ferocious rumbling in my belly made me weigh the odds differently. He mentioned my father's best friend's name and said he was his brother. I studied his heavy jowls and stern eyes as well as his primped suit, signs of a respectable person. I jumped into his Mercedes. I had gauged the risk and decided he looked legit. I was willing to be rescued from the heat. I got lucky, because once we got to his house, his wife fed me the amazing and exotic Laughing Cow cheese wedges—what a luxury! But later I couldn't help but think about the other possible outcomes had the man not been who he said he was—had he not been kind, with a wife at home. They let me watch TV until my parents got home.

It was a quiet and reflective drive home from the university. Neither me nor Daddy uttered a word. Once we got in the house, my father's disappointment with my choice of studies bothered me. He locked himself in his bedroom upstairs to avoid further confrontation with me. I walked into the kitchen to find my mother gathering the coffee sets.

"Mommy, I want to live on campus, please," I begged. She stopped midstride, hands on her hips, annoyed.

"Why? We live but fifteen minutes from the campus, and Daddy can send you and pick you up on the way to and from work." She turned away from me and got back to the coffee sets. I was intent on getting the independence that would have been part of living overseas.

"When you said I could go to Australia, I was going to live on my own anyway."

Her eyes grew wide as if she were surprised. She explained that it was not a financially feasible idea, seeing as we lived so close to campus. Then she added more salt to the wound with the idea that I wouldn't be able to care for myself well enough. "It's how you'll get into trouble. You'll see. You'll be distracted from studies. It's not safe for a girl to be out and about at night for dinner and all that you will have to do on your own," she insisted.

I was starting to see a pattern here. I wasn't going to get my way. My parents had thought of every possible excuse as to how my independence would steer me the wrong way. All of a sudden, I somehow needed their supervision and guidance that had been absent for all these years. I didn't have any more fight in me. I chucked the enrollment packet onto the dining table and locked myself in my room to read away my frustrations. I refused dinner that night and went to sleep without saying good night.

~

The next afternoon, the doorbell rang, and there were Uncle Bala and Devi Atthey. My mood lifted immediately. I was excited to show them my university and the program brochures. I also couldn't wait to tell them about the drama my father was orchestrating in protest of my choices. Uncle Bala knew me well and supported me, and I was so grateful to see their faces—until I looked past them and saw three other cars parked along the road. It was *all* my uncles and aunts, my father's siblings. That suddenly explained the coffee sets my mother had been preparing the night before. Now my father walked down the stairs with a choleric look on his face. I saw serious looks on everyone's faces, as I'd seen when they all gathered to discuss Amachee's ailing health.

Daddy invited everyone to sit in the living room. This had to be some serious family discussion if Devi Atthey and Uncle Bala had driven five hours to be here. They were spending the night, and that made me happy. I started up the stairs, excusing myself, thinking this was a grown-up discussion. Then I heard my father's voice boom, "Baby, come sit here." *Oh fuck, what now?*

My mother served everyone coffee. All eyes locked on me as I took a seat next to Uncle Bala, my ally. This was an ambush. My father had called in the cavalry to talk to me. I had walked into an intervention. As it dawned on me that this family meeting was about my choices for my future, the betrayal I'd felt from my parents deepened.

"Sit down," said my father sternly.

"What's happening?" I asked, though I knew. I froze, eyes locked on the marble floor. I swung my toes to graze the floor, keeping focus on the rhythm of the swinging. My heart was pounding. I felt like a child in trouble for stealing candy.

"Why are you throwing away potential on business school? You have the grades to qualify for engineering or medicine or anything else. There are a million business graduates. It's such a competitive field," said my father's brother.

"Well then, I'll be one in a million!" I said, thinking it was a clever retort.

The conversation got heated. Uncle Bala defended me, and everyone else tried to influence me. It was a conversation about me, excluding me. Coffee cups clanked on the table as hands flew everywhere in animated outrage. I essentially had five sets of parents, and they all wanted a say. My aunt shifted uncomfortably on the beige couch. We were close-knit and always in everybody's business. But this was something new, because outside of emergencies, we usually gathered in merriment. I longed for their blessings as they had given me just the previous month at Deepavali.

Had it only been one month ago that I'd seen them all at Deepavali, the Hindu festival of lights? We'd gathered as we always did, at Amachee's house. It was the most anticipated event of the year, as all twenty-plus of us congregated to celebrate. On Deepavali day, once everyone was bathed and dressed, we received blessings from our elders. I got in a line along with all my cousins, starting in front of my grandmother and moving down the hierarchy of my oldest to youngest aunts and uncles. We kneeled on the floor, then touched my grandmother's feet, bringing our hands to our forehead. This was then repeated at all our elders' feet. Our elders touched our shoulders in a gesture to bring us up. My aunt whispered her blessings to me: "All will be well, ma." Then they wrapped us in hugs and kisses, which I always loved.

My gaze lifted from the marble floor to my aunt staring straight at me, the same aunt who had told me at Deepavali that all will be well. She had a look of disappointment in her eyes as she whispered, "Why, ma?" I shrugged my shoulders and looked away.

"Now she wants to live on campus," my mother said, adding fuel to the fire. I had approached her about this in confidence the night before. I could not believe she was bringing this up, pushing me into a corner, drawing everyone's attention to me as if I had proposed something utterly ludicrous.

"Why? That's ridiculous. The school is fifteen minutes from here," said my uncle.

"Because I want to live away from this house. I want to be independent, like everyone my age." I grabbed the cushion I was sitting on, to hold back the anger.

"What do you know about being on your own, Amy?" my aunt chided.

I could not believe these people conveniently forgot that I traveled alone for much of my childhood, since I was six years old.

A few months after my sixth birthday, I had embarked on my first adventure. I was a cast member of a children's TV show that shot on location and required travel. That morning I was up very early. I walked into the big hall at the airport, lined with counters. The lights were so bright, and everything was so white. I had my backpack and my duffel bag filled with everything my mother had packed for me. My mind took in all the sights, but I was nervous.

My parents weren't coming with me, and I was getting on a plane for the first time. We hugged and kissed. My whole body was flushed as the dread of not having my father with me became more real.

Daddy looked straight at me, his eyes knowing, his brows strong, the lines falling into the bridge of his nose. With a stern but endearing look on his face, he nodded. I nodded back. This was what we did at so many of the big moments we shared. My mother waved, chatting with her friends who were working on this production. I knew all of them, and one of the women would be sharing a room with me. The smell of Daddy's cologne lingering on my shirt gave me comfort on the flight. My first time flying was magical. As we flew into the clouds, questions flooded my mind. I tried to make note of them in my head to ask my father later.

While on production, I figured things out on my own. Lessons from others were not always pleasant. Sometimes they were embarrassing, and sometimes they were scary. I also had the additional burden of my parents' reputation to protect. I made sure to memorize my script prior to recording so as not to trouble anyone with mistakes. I learned to curb my enthusiasm and keep focused on the task at hand, even when I was excited. I stayed at hotels during production and kept my own schedule, bathing and dressing myself and showing up at call time. I had learned how to arrange courtesy wake-up calls at the hotels. I learned all of this without my parents' guidance or prompting.

I did this from age six to eleven, traveling six to eight weeks out of the year. I would say I knew a thing or two about being on my own.

Now my mother was staring straight at me, as was everyone in the room, looking for some kind of response. I was annoyed beyond comprehension. My blood boiled with frustration, mixed with the guilt of letting them down and the general faux pas of defying my elders. Uncle Bala, who had taught me to listen to my inner voice, was the only one defending me. He recalled my independence and success in all my endeavors at school. He was the only one in my corner and was met with great disagreement from all around. They noted, for some reason, that "this was different."

"It's not safe, Amy, a girl like you living alone," my mother said, sitting on the chair next to my aunt.

"I won't be living alone. I'll have roommates."

"You still have to go out for meals and all at night, and it's just not safe. Bad things happen." It was clear to me that her raised voice and strained throat were a result of her terrible discontent. I could feel my temples pulsing with frustration. I tried to hold it together.

As if a jolt of energy shot her up, my mother's back straightened as she sat tall, declaring some newly discovered fact she had to share. Her voice raised to drown out the others in the room. "I know why you want to do this. You want to party and go out at night and get into trouble. People go missing like that, you know, and other things happen to girls at night like that. Just listen, please. Stay home." This was her ending the conversation about living on campus. I watched the vein in her neck ease.

"Bad things don't only happen at night," I said.

How could it be that I was trusted when I was six on public

transit, solo? To be alone for weeks at a time, to travel with strangers? No one shifted their gaze from me, and their stares made me feel nothing but guilt and contempt.

"You have your daddy's brains. Use them. You know he could be a doctor if your grandfather could afford the fees and bribes for him to continue in medical school? That was a shame he only got one year in. Top of his class." My aunt's added tidbit was apparently supposed to change my mind.

"I don't want to be a doctor. I want a career in the corporate world," I said.

"Amy, this is a mistake. I'm telling you. There are so many jobless business graduates now," she continued.

"This is what I want. Why is this such an issue?" I said, knowing my tone was disrespectful.

Huffing and puffing and withering glares came my way to burn me for disrespecting my elders. My path in life had groomed me for independence and adventure, yet there was confusion over my ability to make the right choices.

I backpedaled now, knowing I'd stepped out of line. Out of respect, I smiled and nodded and agreed to take their words into con sideration. But as soon as I left the room, I cried. I felt like a failure, a disappointment because I didn't meet their standards. Whatever success I was about to have in my choice of study was trumped by their expectations of me based on some bullshit pedestal. In my bedroom, I sobbed and listened through the door to them consoling my parents. *What the fuck? Why do they need consolation? It's my future everyone is spitting on, because I will not submit.* I heard everyone leave, and my parents continued hushed conversations with Uncle Bala and Devi Atthey. I couldn't make out what they were saying, but I figured it was a continuation of the consolation my parents so direly needed. I had defied them that day, risking their blessings that were crucial to success, but I did what I was compelled to.

The next day, Uncle Bala patted my back in an endearing gesture of defeat. "It'll all be okay. Don't worry, Amy."

It didn't feel like it was going to be okay. I continued my strike in my room, and I didn't talk to anyone for days. Finally, after three or so nights, Celtic music was blasting so loud that I couldn't hear myself think. I walked downstairs to find my father smiling on the couch. He gestured for me to join him. I sat next to him. He held me and gave me a strong kiss on the forehead. He pointed at the table. The Bachelor of Commerce enrollment forms had been filled out, and a neatly signed check sat on top. He turned down the music and took my face in his hands. "It's your life, baby. Daddy just wants what's best for you. If you insist this is what you want, then do your best, and make me proud." His words breathed life into me. I grabbed him in a big hug and lots of kisses. I'd won this battle, at least. He assured me that I had his blessings for the program choice, but we agreed that living on campus would be a huge dent in our resources and could be money better spent elsewhere. Though I was disappointed, I was elated that I was at least going to pursue studies that excited me.

My father had come around, knowing that I had always been resourceful and resilient. I had made good choices in the past without his guidance, and my independence was what made me successful. Emotions ran high in my family, but more than that, my father could not bear my disappointment. Perhaps Uncle Bala had gotten through to him. Whatever the case, it was going to be okay, just as Uncle Bala had said.

CHAPTER 3

D addy dropped me off at college for my first day. I walked into the beautiful foyer. White-and-gray tiles decorated the floor, and marble pillars were on either end. I was about to embark on an exciting journey that I had dreamt of since elementary school. I was familiar with this building, as it was the same place where I had attended Year 12.

The first day of business school was momentous but bittersweet. I had an anxiety ridden start. Ruth, Sophia, and I had been inseparable since we were fourteen. We'd planned for years to move to the big city to attend university after high school in Alor Star, and we'd stayed close in Year 12. Now Ruth was in the biotechnology program, and Sophia was at a different college. I was nervous because even though Ruth was enrolled in my school, she was in a different program. Most of our friends from Year 12 had gone to Australia as we'd all planned. This was starting over. I was on my own.

The previous year, I'd had a glorious social life with friends aplenty. Within the first month of Year 12, I had my first boyfriend. He was studious and well-mannered. He had won my father over during tea and detailed conversation. I had met my match in studies, conversation, and philosophical discourse. He was a Taoist and taught me about his beliefs, which included vegetarianism and a commitment of kindness to all beings. I was fascinated by his views on respect and gratitude for all life forms. He wouldn't even eat certain candies because they were made with protein from bees. He lived a life seeking detachment from material needs and was exploring the applications of his beliefs. I was intrigued by this worldview, having always been drawn to things that were different.

Despite our differences, we did agree that we would not sleep together. For him, this decision was based in religion. Mine was based in my feminist belief that sex should be a choice I made at the right time, with the right person. I am a romantic and believed that my first experience was going to be magical, with someone I loved deeply, and I wasn't convinced we were deeply in love.

About ten months into our relationship, I met his parents. I discovered his mother's discontent immediately. "What is your race?" she asked me.

"My father is Indian, and my mother—" I started, but she interrupted me.

"Some kind of mix, I know. My son is Teochew and Hakka. We are Chinese, okay, and he cannot be with you. It will not work out." That conversation hurt, reminding me again how the color of my skin and my origins were a point of contention. I withheld tears, humiliated. The cut was made deeper by my boyfriend standing by with no defense, respect, or care for me. He later convinced me that it would have been a futile attempt. His mother had nothing but contempt for our relationship, and there wasn't anything that could change her mind. His obedience and filial piety confirmed his mother's demands that we break up. I wasn't heartbroken over it but offended by the overt racism that seemed to negate all the openhearted discussions we'd had in the prior months about his religion and way of life, which was supposedly rooted in kindness and love. After our breakup, I lost the friends who were his friends first. I learned firsthand how fragile friendships could be.

Thoughts of that past year dispersed into the air with the reality of my first day of school and the coming year. I walked straight to the cafeteria, where Ruth was with her boyfriend, Damien, and his friends. Sophia's boyfriend, Craig, was also there. I knew all of them from the previous year. The large part of the building at the back of campus was used by a local private college where Damien, Craig, and all their friends attended. Everyone congregated at the cafeteria any-time we were not in class. There was always someone there. I watched them gather their backpacks, which I doubted held anything course related. They were loud and rude and picked fights with people who looked at them the wrong way. Something about the way they spoke, their crudeness, really got under my skin.

My father had never approved of Craig. He'd been over with his friends a lot in Year 12, as there was a time when Sophia was practi-cally living at my parents' house. "They are the kind of friends that will get you into trouble," my father told me more than once. Their disrespectful behavior whenever they visited our home was infuriat-ing. They barely acknowledged my father. He asserted that this was a sign that the boys had not been raised right. They didn't show respect to elders. I stayed silent, as I still kept their company to remain close to my best friends.

My father's words clearly rung in my ears now, as I listened to a trio of them already planning to skip class to smoke a joint off campus. What they saw as a bit of fun, I saw as tempting fate. I wanted no part of it, because capital punishment was in full effect in Malaysia, and drug-related offenses could land you on death row. I couldn't understand how they didn't see how monumental the con-sequences could be.

I looked at the boys and realized I had no idea what they even planned to study, probably because they didn't study. They were always in a dalliance with nothingness—no direction, no ambition, no real purpose. Smoking, drugs, partying, and skipping classes were the focal points in this group. I was an oddball in this circuit, and most of them didn't like me as a result. I knew they could tell I judged them. I often told them how stupidly dangerous the things they did were. One of them stared straight at me then, looking for a reaction to their plan to go smoke marijuana. But I just rolled my eyes and said nothing.

Arrogance was how I handled them. I didn't realize at the time how grating that was. But as much as I behaved like I was better than them, I was also trying hard to fit in, always proving my worth with my wit and smarts. They liked Ruth and Sophia, and I was the odd friend that came with the package. I had to have thick skin to repel the insults and condescension thrown my way. "Stuck up," "snob," "snoot," and "bitch" were words they commonly used to respond to my comments. When I heard those words, I was embarrassed, and I responded as a smart-mouth in self-defense. The feelings were mutual, and because I was outnumbered, I tried to hold back my thoughts and opinions.

The boys were still there, lingering. I listened in on a conversation about the girl at the next table possibly not wearing panties under her skirt.

"Can you see, Amelia? Is she or is she not wearing panties?" Craig asked.

"I have better things to do than concern myself with what's under someone's skirt. Fucking pathetic," I said, separating myself and making my values clear.

"You think you're fucking better than us. You're full of shit," he responded, highly animated. Ruth grabbed my arm and rubbed my back softly as a sign for me to calm down, to silence me in order to avoid further confrontation. Perhaps it was arrogance, snobbery, or just plain awareness of the better choices I was raised to make. I was not liked for asserting my values. I tried my best not to correct them, but it was nearly impossible. I tried to stay silent during their idiocy, but my budding feminism made their misogynistic remarks hard to ignore. Ruth and Sophia were so enamored and entranced by their show of masculinity, however toxic it might have been. I wanted them to be out of those relationships but did not dare risk my friendships.

I got up to get lunch. I had thirty minutes before my next class started. When I returned to the table, the topic had changed to an upcoming talent show. I was invited to sing with their hip-hop band. These talent shows were meant to be icebreakers for starting the year, and at least one performer had to be a student at the university. Because they all attended the private college next door, I was their ticket into the show. We'd done two of these performances in the past year. I agreed, mostly because I had enjoyed our performances, and partly because this was my friend group, love them or hate them.

After the first day, I resolved to be less assertive around the boys. I befriended a few of Damien's and Craig's friends who were kind to me. I'd actually had a few smoking sessions with those boys in my last semester in Year 12, and I'd learned to appreciate their company. I started meeting up with them at the smoking corner every afternoon after class. It was there that I met new friends from my program toward the end of that first week. I was starting to find my place and felt more comfortable, the anxiety of being alone dissipating with the new connections I was making.

～

Two months after our first conversation about the talent show and many rehearsals later, it was time for the big day. I was on a high on that stage, my voice blaring through the speakers. I felt confident and self-assured. The applause that followed affirmed this. I looked over to the boys onstage with me. Damien walked over to hug me, and the rest of them cheered. I saw a glimmer of sincerity in Damien's eyes. Perhaps there was true friendship to be had here. Perhaps I could let down my guard and befriend them.

I did a couple more performances with them over the course of that semester, and they were kind enough to include me. There were more than a few slights and backhanded compliments, but they always said they were joking, and I had made my commitment not to talk back so much. Plus, I was enchanted by the idea of belonging to this group, and I began to enjoy their company. I was intoxicated by the stage performances, chasing a high. The more time we spent together, the more tolerable they became—to the point that I even looked forward to spending time with them.

I was getting comfortable at the end of my first semester, four months completed and goals accomplished while my social life was settling. I managed mostly A and B grades. I no longer feared being on my own. I was on track to fulfilling my dreams. My university experience was nearly as perfect as I had imagined it.

∼

I was running for women's officer on the student council during the second semester of my first year. I strongly promoted feminist ideas through my campaigning. I wanted to win. What I lacked in other abilities, I made up for with my gift of gab. There had been reports of mugging and assault in the wooded area near campus, and I was running on a platform of safety for female students.

"Safety of our women should be of utmost priority. Students cannot be at risk getting to and from campus. The surrounding areas should be safe for our girls. We will look into measures of security to take care of our students." I was adamant that women should experience campus life the same way as our male counterparts, without threat to our safety. We were not to restrict ourselves to certain hours when we felt we could be safe on campus. Though my message was well received, my campaign ended in defeat.

In the second semester, smoking and socializing became more of my focal point. I skipped classes to play snooker with my new friends from my program and sometimes with Damien's friends.

I was vocal in class, and professors took notice. Even though there were more than one hundred students, professors called me by name due to my incessant questions and studious application in class. I was confident because I did my work, and then some, to stay ahead in class. Calling attention to myself also meant that I was noticed when I wasn't in class.

Every Thursday afternoon before class had become a scheduled time with my friends, as we had all decided to match our second-semester schedules. I was attending class upon returning from the pool hall, reeking of cigarettes. It was one of my business-law classes, with a professor I already had the semester before. She had noted that if I kept up with my hard work, I was going to qualify for the honors program. This added to my confidence. During the lecture, the professor called on me for an answer. I was fumbling through the pages, flustered. "I'm sorry, Prof. I don't know that case," I managed.

She stared straight at me with her hand on her hip. All that was missing was a wagging finger. She said, "If you spent less time smoking with those thugs out there and more time with your nose in your books, you would know."

I smiled coyly and replied, "I sure would." I was embarrassed but laughed it off. No one was going to affect my studies and my dreams. I was flying high.

The second semester came to an end. I did well, getting mostly As and Bs again. I had found my place in college. I had friends to study with and friends to party with. Paul, a friend I had known from Year 12, rose to the top of my friend group, and he knew Damien's friends too.

~

We went clubbing on a Friday night at the beginning of our second year. It was Paul's birthday. He got a bottle of whiskey at the club, and it was just the four of us—Paul, Sophia, Paul's friend Sean, and me. I looked forward to our weekends together, because I didn't get to see Sophia during the week, as she was at a different college. There were lots of shots, and soon we were joined by people we didn't know. They gathered around to drink with us. There were also people I recognized but did not personally know. Among them were Damien's friends, who I knew didn't like me. I could see Sophia out on the dance floor. Paul and Sean were across the room, laughing with some new friends. I was by the bar, taking in the vibes. A guy I knew to be a ruffian, known for his violent escapades, came to talk to me and handed me a shot. I accepted it even though I was already completely inebriated.

~

The next thing I knew, I woke to cramps, as if my guts were trying to come through my esophagus to escape my mouth. My body was convulsing. I had dry heaves when I opened my eyes and saw the disgusting black grime on the grout in the red tiles, just inches from my face. I was in a filthy bathroom that I did not recognize. There was a loud ringing in my ears, and I had a splitting headache. I was naked on a grimy floor. I pushed myself to stand and hobbled to the sink to wash my face. It was covered in a thick layer of moldy film. At the sight of all this, I vomited again. I was at a loss as to my where-abouts or how I ended up there. My body shivered at the fact that I was on display. I had not been naked in front of anyone for as long as I could remember. A hot flash of urgency raced through me as someone approached the bathroom door.

"Get dressed. Your friends are downstairs waiting for you." It was a man's voice I didn't recognize. I looked up to see a bare room beyond him. The bed was a mess, and there was a bedside table with a large digital-radio alarm clock.

The stench then hit me like a brick wall. I didn't know what to make of all this. Confusion took over. *This is bad. Something bad has happened.* The thought rolled around my head like a tumbleweed in a tornado. There was a musty, moldy, soiled carpet. I saw stains—black, gray, and crusty—all over it. I tiptoed out of the bathroom, scanning the room for my panties and clothes. I found my panties in a bunch, next to two white sleeves that I supposed were used condoms. I'd never used one before. Had I now? I must have, or how else would I be in this condition? I still didn't know where I was. The last thing I remembered was being at the club with my friends. Why was I here with the guy who had given me the shot at the bar? How did I get here? What had we done?

The guy just stood there, a calm and satisfied look on his face. He licked his lips, like a dog after a treat. He glanced casually back and forth from his phone to me as he waited for me to react. Whatever it was that happened was now done. I was in pain, but my face was solemn, my voice buried along with my dignity. I knew in that moment that my dream of one day giving my whole self to a man I was madly in love with had been stolen from me—and it was entirely my doing. All I could think about was the viscosity between my legs and my sore vagina, which was burning like a motherfucker. I could not find my pretty black dress with the beautiful neckline that showed just enough of my breasts, the one that fit so perfectly that Sophia and I had agreed it was worthy of an epic night out.

I was nineteen and not womanly per se, though I had some curves on my petite frame. I had felt so good in that dress. There was a power in feeling alluring. I had never thought of myself as attractive in the typical sense. Charm and wit had always been my go-to. I would have to turn that on in order to make it through this moment. *My friends were downstairs?* I still couldn't piece together what was happening. I looked over at this guy I'd only seen in passing on campus. He was zipping up his pants and buckling his belt. He flipped the brown-and-green, pilled covers back to reveal my dress, which lay there crumpled. I was desperate for it to cover my naked body. I grabbed it quickly. The embarrassment physically hurt. The sheets were stained, and I was filled with disgust, which added to the bad feeling in my head. The spinning escalated with every second I stood there in confused stupor. Had I had sex for the first time? Was I not a virgin anymore? I wanted to die right there. *Let me die.*

As I put on my dress, I saw fresh blood on my panties. Tears streamed down my face. I smelled his sweat, his saliva—the venom of a vicious monster.

I couldn't look him in the eye as we walked down the filthy motel corridor. I squeezed my brain to wring out an explanation, a memory of having traveled here from the club.

In the lobby, the monster paid at the front desk. I heard an exchange about time and rates. I realized that we were at a pay-per-hour motel, the kind I'd only ever heard about. These existed for immoral activities, filthy activities of the sort I must have just been a part of. My body had apparently capitulated to whatever had unfolded, as my mind had abandoned my body, left it to be defiled in that room by a stranger.

As he finished paying, I walked out the front door, disoriented. *Where the fuck was I? How did I get here? How would I get home? Where were my friends? He said they were down here.*

"Amy! What the fuck!" I heard Paul's voice. I ran and reached out to hug him. I was so afraid. How glad I was to see my friend's face, only to be met with a rude push. I didn't understand. Everything started moving very fast. Suddenly there were four other friends. I saw them around me, all yelling. I couldn't make out the words, but I was shrinking by the minute. They were angry at me. My world was spinning. It was impossible for me to move.

The monster came up and said something to me. I heard "fuel ... money." I looked at one of my friends, and he handed me my purse from the car. I opened my wallet, and he grabbed all the cash I had left in there, $60. Was this actually happening? First, I woke up in a bathroom with no clothes, and now he was robbing me.

The tears had stopped. I stood there, immobile, while everyone yelled at me, accusing me of leaving the club with him. I found the strength to walk to the car. They drove me back to the club to find Sophia. They said she was upset and waiting for me. It all happened so fast. I couldn't believe what I'd done. I'd accepted the drink. I'd had too much. I'd blacked out. I was smarter than this, wasn't I? I never thought something like this could happen to me. How could I have made a mistake like this? This was not just a mistake—this was a colossal fuck up. What happened, I didn't remember—perhaps nothing. "Nothing happened," I said aloud, begging for mercy.

No one believed me. The car ride was filled with their shouting and my shame, guilt, and fear. What would happen now? What would happen once everyone found out? The tears refused to descend. I heard "whore," "slut," "irresponsible," "selfish"—all directed at me.

"How could you do this? I thought you were better than this," Paul said, his face fixed on the road as he drove. *How could I have done this? How did I?* The weight of my own disappointment flooded over me, matching the fury in the car. We headed downtown to get Sophia, who was sitting on the curb staring at her phone, crying out of worry. She jumped into the back seat and hugged me tightly. It was the first warmth I had felt all night. It made me realize how cold I had been moments before. She assured me everything was going to be okay and we needn't speak about it until morning. Knowing I needed her, she spent the night with me.

When we got home, I stood in the shower for more than an hour, methodically scrubbing myself. I had to get that saliva, sweat, and cheap cologne off. I scrubbed and scrubbed, but I couldn't get it off. The stench of that foul motel room clung to me, prompting another bout of vomiting.

My body felt grimy. His sweat was still on me. I had a flash of his smooth brown chest pressed to the side of my face, but it was blurry. I had a two-second snippet, followed by that cheap cologne smell. I grabbed the loofah and scrubbed incessantly. My face burned from the scrubbing, as did my chest and my stomach. When I came close to my vagina, I couldn't scrub. I tried, but I winced at the pain. I felt I deserved the pain. I felt light-headed from trying to remember. If only I could remember how this had happened, maybe I could fix it. *I can fix this. I can fix this. I am so sorry. I didn't mean to. Please help me fix this.* I sobbed for salvation from the universe, my parents, my friends, and everyone I had hurt by doing this. I had brought shame and humiliation on my family if they should ever find out. I had to keep this to myself and begged Sophia to do the same, as I couldn't bear my parents' disappointment in me. What felt like the weight of a vault caused me to collapse on the bathroom floor. Sophia banged on the door, begging for me to get out.

~

On Monday morning, I steeled myself and went to school. Daddy dropped me off at the gate. I got out and saw one of Damien's friends. I walked toward the entrance. He smirked and said, "Heard it was a great weekend." News spread like mold to damp. My ears were hot, and I had never felt so small. I turned around. *I can't go in there. I cannot face everyone. Oh fuck, what will I do?* My heart raced like never before. My head was spinning, and it felt like my skull was compressed in a clamp—tighter, tighter, and tighter. I couldn't breathe. I couldn't see. I was so scared, I vomited on the concrete, standing in the spot where I'd smoked every day in the past months with my friends.

I couldn't face anyone, so I walked to the coffee shop. I sat and sipped my coffee, the warmth reminding me I was here. I lit a cigarette, and as I put my lighter down, it went flying to the floor. *What the fuck?* I was being yanked by the back of my collar. My ears were still buzzing, and I was queasy from the vomiting. I heard a lot of yelling, but I had no idea who or what it was until I was slammed into the wall. A louder ringing in my ear followed the hot tingling on my cheeks from the slap I had just received.

"You can fuck around and sit on any dick you want, but don't go after my boyfriend," said the girl. She was taller than me, definitely meatier, and stronger.

"Well, obviously you're not sitting on it enough, or maybe his

dick couldn't handle all of you—that's a lot, babe. Go figure." The
words slipped out because I was vacant of any sense of self. At that
moment, I didn't care about being beaten. I was on my own, and she
had at least sixty pounds on me. I didn't care about my body; it was
now tainted and nasty by whatever I had done with the monster.

She raised her hand again, and someone pulled her away. It was
lovely to have met the mate of the monster. She was escorted out of
the café by her friends.

I sat down and sipped coffee. This humiliation I could handle,
but the shame I had brought upon my family and myself, I couldn't
bear. I didn't understand how any of it had happened. I didn't even
know exactly *what* had happened. I just knew I couldn't stay seated
for too long. The pain grew between my legs.

I texted a few friends, hoping one of them could walk me into
class—I was too afraid. No one answered. They were all Damien's
friends, and they'd been there that night. The story, starring me as
the slut who'd brought this outcome upon herself, was already out
there. I couldn't undo it. The answers to my texts followed in quick
succession:

"Stop texting me."

"Don't text me. Can't believe u did dat."

"About time you got put in your place."

"Free fuck."

"You thought you were better than us. Your cheap pussy had it
coming."

I couldn't believe that my friends were ostracizing me. The fact
that I had made a mistake of epic proportions hit me again and
again as I scrolled through my phone. I didn't have anywhere to go. I
belonged nowhere now. Without Sophia, I was desperate for someone
to talk to.

I called Paul, begging him to meet me. He was my friend, my last chance at regaining my place in college.

"You have to tell me what happened, Amy," he said coldly.

"I don't know. Please believe me! I don't know."

"I can't believe this happened. How could you?" I heard the sound of resignation and the end of our friendship with the click of the phone. It was the last time we ever spoke.

I couldn't attend any of my classes. I was too afraid of the monster. I was afraid of everyone. I couldn't face *anyone*. Sophia was the only one who tried to console me, to comfort me by saying it was all going to be okay. I insisted nothing had happened, lying to comfort her. Ruth sent a message through a friend: "Ruth doesn't want to be associated with anyone who could do what you did." I did not have a reaction. We'd been best friends since we were fourteen, inseparable. I would never hear from Ruth again. Our friendship was done in the blink of an eye, over a moment I couldn't even remember.

~

A week later, I was in pain from the discharge, which by then had changed color and stunk like rotten cheese. I cried and prayed to die with the pain every time I urinated. As an inexperienced young adult, I tolerated the pain because I was afraid. I didn't know what doctor to go to or how to go about finding one—my parents made all my doctor appointments. Because I couldn't disappoint my parents, Sophia helped me find a doctor. No one had ever seen my privates, not since I was a little girl. Now they would be closely inspected.

I thought I had caught a sexually transmitted disease. I thought I might be pregnant. This would do my father in if he found out—his baby girl, defiled. I was terrified that the doctor's office would call my parents if I had an STD or if I was pregnant. What would I do if I was pregnant? I was so afraid and so alone. Other than Sophia, no one was talking to me.

I sat there in a gown, watching the doctor put on gloves for the examination. Sophia held my hand silently, her firm grip assuring me I wasn't alone. "It's going to be okay," she said with a warm but less-than-assuring smile. I stared at the stainless-steel tray next to me. It was filled with tools I assumed would be used to examine me. My thoughts raced about how I had ended up in this chair. My father trusted me. I had always told the truth, and I had convinced my parents that I was fully capable of taking care of myself. Now all I had for all that self-assertion was this life of humiliation, guilt, and regret.

I thought about how the one thing they had feared happening had happened. I had insisted that I was capable of protecting myself, that I was vigilant and streetwise. My stupidity floored me. I'd been so naive and so arrogant. I'd invited this. I was not as smart as I thought I was. I deserved this for being so stupid. The monster took advantage of a situation that I allowed to take place. I had been championing women's rights for security and to be able to walk around campus regardless of the time. I said that we should have the same privileges as men, without threat to our safety. But I had received a rude awakening that this was not possible. We lived in a world where taking a drink from a stranger could end with me naked and defiled. I made a mistake, one I could not undo.

The doctor was pulling off her gloves and pulling the sheet over my putrid nether regions. This was the result of that man's aggression, which had injured me so badly, I couldn't wear jeans for the pain. I felt as if I couldn't breathe, for his actions had left a stench that suffocated me. It was an infection, the doctor said as she wrote a prescription. "Always wash before and after sex to avoid this." As

Sophia and I left the doctor's office, the words played on a loop in my head: *before and after sex . . . before and after sex.*

I returned to school, but my dreams were crushed, my confidence absent, and my will to fight the fear diminished. I had turned from star student to pariah overnight. I could see them all looking at me. I could feel their stares on the back of my neck. I could hear the murmur of voices in the hot air in the café.

I took refuge in the little wooded area off campus. I found a space to sit on the ground, plugged in earphones, and listened to Celtic music. I tried to recreate the times I listened to music with my father, hoping it would bring the same calm. It did nothing but send shame throughout my body, like a swarm of ants under my skin. All that my parents had worried about when granting me independence had come to haunt me for the rest of my life. Their words rung true. I couldn't stop tormenting myself for my error. I lay my cardigan down and sat in silence. My cigarettes kept me going.

CHAPTER 4

Every day for the next four months, I sat in silence as my father drove me to college in the morning. I could tell he was worried about me.

"Baby, is everything going well at college?"

"Yes," I replied, holding back tears. The truth was too painful, even for my father, the strongest man I knew.

"Are you okay?" He knew something was off with me, but he didn't know what to say or do. I assumed he knew I had done something wrong, as he had always known when I was a child.

"Yes. I'm just tired—slept late." I managed, quickly wiping a tear. I stared out the window at the road lines dashing away from me. My mind scrambled to find an excuse to pacify my father.

"Okay. Mommy and I are worried. You don't look well. College can be stressful, but you pace yourself, okay? You'll be okay. You're a smart girl." We pulled up to the entrance of the school.

"Bye." I rushed out of the car with no kiss. My father watched me walk in as he did every day, making sure I got in safely. There was no way he could know that this place was not safe—this was where the monster roamed. I felt my father's eyes on me as I passed the entrance, followed by the soft hum signaling he had driven off. *One . . . two . . . three . . . four . . . five*, I counted in my head, to make sure he had driven far enough away so I could walk back out without him catching me. I turned on my heel and headed out the front gate, lighting my first cigarette of the day.

The months since the incident at the motel had been a hell of humiliation and isolation. I had never bothered to get my driver's license because I had someone to drive me around. The morning drives were my time with Daddy. Some days we chatted, but lately the rides had been silent. I didn't have the words to express what had happened. I didn't feel comfortable being in the same room as my father or mother anymore. I felt disgust for what I had done. The disappointment in myself grew, as did the distance between my family and me. I also had not spoken to Amachee, Devi Atthey, or Uncle Bala during this time. I ignored their calls and sent them texts saying I was busy. I was no longer their little girl. I stayed silent. My anguish over my mistake ripped me away from all the love that I used to know.

I used to kiss my father every day when he dropped me off at school. Now I just couldn't. I couldn't let my lips touch him. My self-loathing knew no end.

The start of my second year of college had coincided with the incident. I started the new school year with a shock to my system, the situation haunting me every day. Now it was June, and I hadn't been to a single class in four months. I knew the monster roamed the halls on campus, and this gave me chills. I was surprised I hadn't received a notice of expulsion. I wanted to at least submit my final assignment so that I could possibly avoid failing. I went to find my professor and ask for an extension. This was the same professor who'd tongue-lashed me about hanging with "thugs." She was almost certain to reject an extension, but what choice did I have? I could not disappoint my father further. I did not want him to find out I was a failure at school. I had to try with the professor. I was afraid, but I mustered what little strength I had left to ask for the extension.

"Something bad happened. Something really bad. Help me, please." I found myself trying to explain. This was the first time I'd opened up to an adult about what had happened. "I went out with them and woke up in a dodgy motel. Then I was sick from an infection I got from what happened that night. I don't know how I got there. I didn't even know the guy. I don't know anything. It is really, really terrible. I don't know what to do."

The words came flying out, against my reservations. I felt nothing but shame in the words that had just escaped my mouth. I didn't know why I wasn't talking about the damn paper. I needed to pass the class. I was lost and desperate. Maybe I was hoping for mercy, guidance on what I should do, or just some comfort. I wanted so desperately to hear that it was going to be fine, it wasn't as bad as I had imagined, and that I wasn't at fault. But all I felt was mortified by my admission.

"No can do. You'll have to make better choices next semester when you retake this paper," she said without an ounce of concern or mercy. "What did you think was going to happen hanging out with thugs?" Her apathetic response left me cold. I was in shock. She carried on, shuffling papers as if I wasn't there. I felt the way she wanted me to feel—invisible, worthless, insignificant. "I have another appointment. Leave the door open on your way out." With no pity, she shooed me out of her office.

Her response only reiterated what I knew—I did deserve what had happened. Even she—an adult, an experienced woman of the world—agreed it had been a choice. I made a choice, and now I had to live with the consequences. I dashed out of her office and off campus. I sat on the boulder at the smoking area and lit a cigarette. I couldn't think. There was a death metal band playing in my brain—the intensity, vibrations, and pressure of it all threatened to blow my skull open. I couldn't breathe. My nails gripped and scraped the boulder I was sitting on. I tried to find my breath. My eyes focused on the gritty concrete beyond the tip of my shoes.

Splat. Something wet and cold hit my shin. *Fuck. Spit.* I looked up in panic and saw an ex-friend with a few girls I recognized.

"Slut," he scoffed. He walked away, followed by the giggles and smirks of the girls. I didn't understand how I was being treated this way. There was hardly any of me left. There was barely enough to make it through the theatrics that kept my father dropping me off each day. I needed him to still see me as the perfect daughter thriving in college, working toward a dream we both had for my future. It would be devastating if he found out I was failing every one of my classes. I grabbed a large leaf from a plant to wipe the spit from my shin. I retreated to my clearing in the wooded area.

I mostly kept to myself. Some days Sophia would meet me at the mall for window shopping, pretending everything was fine. I maintained the lie that nothing had happened, to comfort Sophia and as a defense against all who were chastising me. The nice clothes I tried on at the mall didn't feel like they were meant for my disgusting self. I couldn't look in the mirror and hadn't in months. We'd pass time by eating and hanging out. I had less time to ponder my existence. My time with Sophia was coming to an end, however; in July, she'd be moving to America to complete her studies.

~

Most days at college, I wouldn't eat so I could avoid running into the monster. He was at the coffee shop, the cafeteria, the restaurant, and the boulder where smokers sat, so it was a full-time effort to avoid him.

Six months after the incident, nothing had gotten better. I was retaking all my courses from the previous semester, as I had failed them all. One Thursday afternoon, after I'd eaten nothing all day, I got so hungry that I risked any abuse I might endure at the coffee shop. While I was getting food, an ex-friend, Arvind, invited me to join him. He seemed genuine, and I was desperately lonely, so I sat at his table. He told me the rumors he'd heard from Craig's and Damien's friends.

"There was talk among the boys that *he* wanted you. He wanted to prove that you weren't as hard to get as you made yourself out to be." He didn't have to tell me who *he* was. I knew he was talking about the monster.

My heart sank. It was my own arrogance that had invited this attention. The buzzing in my ears began as I tried to listen to the rest of his story.

"He thought you were cocky, and he boasted how he was going to get your pussy," he continued. "The boys were happy you were going to be put in your place."

I couldn't believe what I was hearing. Did the punishment fit my crime of acting superior?

Arvind said he wished I hadn't agitated them so much. "If only you'd kept your head down and not made them hate you so much." Once again, there was blame. Everyone I spoke to about what had happened suggested I had it coming. I could not digest any of it.

I stayed silent as my mind tried to make sense out of his words. He continued. "The boys saw you being carried out of the club, and they distracted Sophia so she'd look for you elsewhere. They knew exactly where you were—the motel you had been taken to. Everyone knows he takes girls there."

I felt as if I were going to be sick. I could not believe this was real life. They'd paved the way for this to happen and given the monster time to scourge my pussy. And then he emerged with pride, and I handed over $60 for the badge of "slut" and the ostracization that would come after—his prize for fucking me into submission, for putting me in my place.

"Was this some grand plan?" I finally managed. "Everyone wanted me to learn a lesson like this?" I was horrified that my value was reduced to that of my stolen virginity. I was aghast that my confidence had earned me this lesson, and no one felt sorry for me—only victorious while I was reduced to dust.

"I don't believe it was a plan, but I think when they realized what was happening, they let it happen," he concluded, looking me straight in the eye. His own eyes teared up, and he wiped them and took my hand. "It's okay, ma," he said, and with that term of endearment, I thought of my family. I was ashamed. Most of all, I felt devastated that collectively the boys had agreed I deserved what happened. It was all a game to them. I was nothing but an irritation that they'd dealt with in the harshest possible way. Arvind pulled me close, and I let my head rest on his chest. He told me to forget about it and move on, that I shouldn't let them bother me so much. He laid his hand firmly on my head and pushed my hair back as he stood up to leave. He would never speak to me again after that. I knew he felt sorry for me, but not sorry enough to be seen with me.

~

I found peace in the woods. I became practiced in meditation. Not one person cared for me, and it seemed as if the whole world was fine knowing I was at school but not attending classes. No one showed any concern. If this rumor was circulating that I'd been targeted, surely someone would have reached out? But no one did.

I'd sit sobbing for hours on end. The world I used to know had a force field I could not penetrate. I pondered Arvind's words for weeks: *Put me in my place? Where was that? Six feet under?* That seemed a better place to be.

I was in a nightmare as the monster continued to parade his conquest. My body no longer belonged to me. It belonged to strangers who spread nastiness without a care. I knew they were talking about me from the slut-shaming that I endured when I ran into old friends and acquaintances. I imagined what they'd say about me—that I got put in my place, that I wasn't as great as I thought I was.

It finally dawned on me that I had nothing left, no reason to be here. The world carried on without me, no one wanted me here, and my family would only be humiliated by the revelation of this atrocity. It would be better to end this while maintaining the facade of me as a college student, studious and thriving toward my successful future. My parents wouldn't see my treacherous deed. Everyone would be better off with me gone. I wanted to disappear—an escape in death.

My eyes fixated on the tree in front of me. It was tall enough that I could climb onto the first branch to fasten the noose I would fashion out of my pashmina. I thought this through while meditating to Celtic music. My heart softly whispered goodbye to my father and the world. The racing thoughts, pain, and devastation had left, leaving me with nothing. I was numb. I was ready to die. There would be no more sadness, disappointment, confusion, humiliation, and fear— just pure nothingness. My nails gripped the tree as I climbed up the rough trunk. I climbed past the first branch that had touched my head earlier. I knew I needed to go higher to be sure I would definitely die. Once on the largest branch, about eight feet off the ground, I looked down at the dry dirt, burnt by the heat of the afternoon.

I eyeballed the height. It was high enough for my feet to be off the ground. I tied the noose to the branch while crying. Apologies ran through my mind. I saw my father in tears, my mother's stoic reaction as she buried her deep sadness, and my siblings in fury and confusion. As for me, I'd be dead. I finished tying the first end of my scarf.

"What are you doing?" I heard a voice from below.

"What are *you* doing?" I replied. I felt rudely interrupted. Trying to kill myself did not come naturally.

"Come down here," he said with a smile. I didn't know him, and he looked at me kindly. "You want a hit?" He gestured to the joint between his fingers. A friend of his walked over, and both of them stared up at me in the tree, making me feel like an idiot.

"Okay," I said, properly embarrassed. He spotted me as I jumped down.

We introduced ourselves to each other, and that day I learned to puff and pass. This was the first time I ever smoked pot. It was something I had refrained from to keep my immaculate reputation for my family and my future, especially to avoid being on death row. None of that mattered anymore, though, did it? We got acquainted, and a realization came over me. There was a world beyond the monster and this place.

I spent the afternoon chatting with the two boys and confiding in them some of what had happened. My new friends didn't even know the monster existed. They were sympathetic and kind and invited me to a different part of campus where they'd shield me from the monster and his crew. As they walked me out of that wooded area, I had an epiphany. I didn't have to be here. There was a life outside this quadrant of pain dominated by the monster and his posse of abusers.

I tried hard to understand why I had stayed locked in that pattern for all those months. I had subjected myself to anxiety, risk of abuse, fear, and constant humiliation, then hid in the woods like a feral dog. Perhaps it was some sort of self-flagellation, some act of martyrdom—a penance for my sin.

I found a glimmer of hope with my new friends, though they did not remain my friends for long. Still, they would forever remain genial and gracious, and I owed them a debt of gratitude for their unknowing intervention that day.

I found new friends. I found my courage and understanding that not everyone in the entire school had heard what happened. I put distance between myself and the perpetrators of the club plan. I even got my driver's license.

Sometimes I enjoyed studying and was motivated to do well. My grades went back up, but it didn't last long. Just the previous year I'd been a strong, confident student, driven to succeed. Now success was elusive, reminding me that I carried a pain that wouldn't leave me alone or allow me to focus.

By December, I was wrapping up my second year. I finally received the dreaded mail that I had been expecting. I had intercepted it before my parents could read it. "Due to your failure to meet required coursework and grades, we regret to inform you of expulsion from the Bachelor of Commerce program, effective immediately."

~

I didn't have the chance to redeem myself academically. I could not believe how all these bad things kept happening. I was cursed—*I must be*. I did something horrible, and nothing but bad karma had followed.

I lied to my parents about wanting to transfer to another university, concealing the expulsion from them. I convinced them to allow me to transfer my credits into another program at a different Australian university satellite campus in Kuala Lumpur. I made up some excuse, but it didn't matter. They were furious. Finally, they confronted me about my distanced and unpleasant behavior.

My father stewed about the transfer, but the next night, after dinner, he poured me a cup of coffee and asked me to stay. I watched the steam rise from my cup, as did the fear inside me. My father stirred sugar into his coffee gently. I knew this was going to be difficult for the both of us. This was confirmed when my mother sat next to me. She touched my head gently, adjusting my ponytail as she looked at my father.

"Baby, is everything okay with you? Tell me the truth." My father spoke so softly, and there was sadness in his voice.

"Yes, I'm okay. I just need to be in a different program that I think is better," I said with a chirpy tone to mask the fear.

My mother rubbed my back and leaned in to hold me. "We're worried, Amy. You're behaving like there's something wrong. You stay in your room. You go out without telling us. I don't know where you are. I know you're smoking now. What's going on?"

"I'm fine. I'm just doing whatever. I'm fine." I was trying to keep the secrets of the past months, but my body resisted being in on the lie. I was crying and shaking. I wanted to scream my confession. What had happened was so much worse than smoking. What would they say? It was too great a risk.

"I knew it," my father boomed. "Something has happened! What is it? Tell Daddy, please." My father was desperate, but I was more desperate to keep my secret. He pushed the coffee cup away and faced me. He leaned in, but I turned away.

"Nothing happened, but you're making it seem like I did something wrong. You don't trust me, and you're always waiting for me to screw up! What do you want from me?" I screamed hysterically through the tears.

"Amy, calm down. No need to scream and shout. We just want to know you're okay," my mother said softly.

"I'm fine. I was fine until you set up this interrogation." I wiped my tears, gathering myself.

My father pulled me in for a hug and kissed the top of my head, squeezing me in an effort to ease the tension and pain. I got better at lying to them after that day. Of course, they knew something was amiss. Of course, they wanted a reason. They wanted to understand. In truth, I was losing what I wanted and grasping at my dream, which had diminished so much.

~

Over the next three years at my new university, I struggled to keep up. The hopes and dreams I had when I entered my previous university were gone. I just needed to accomplish this one goal, to bury my secret further and keep up appearances. I was distracted and unable to focus. I managed passing grades, but gone were the days of A's on my transcript. I spent most days by myself, though I managed to make a few friendships with classmates to get through group assignments. I had a hard time trusting new people. I figured it had been friends who got me into this mess, so it would be wiser to keep to myself. Any time I made a new friend, I waited for the other shoe to drop, to find out they had betrayed me, that they didn't like me from the beginning. I decided that I was a bad judge of character, and it would be best for me to keep to myself and avoid another epic fuckup. There was one friend I made who seemed to accept my awkwardness and cold personality. Her name was Alia, and she became my partner in classes and the smoking corner. She wasn't pushy or intrusive and was satisfied even when we sat in silence. We chatted over coffee and cigarettes, and she made life at the new university bearable. I only trusted her.

Most days, I watched myself live a life that was supposed to be mine. I lived to accomplish something for my poor parents, whom I had humiliated with my mistake. I was making them fools with my lies, but I had been shamed into silence. I wanted a reset, but I didn't know how to get one. I lived to accomplish a bachelor's degree from an Australian university as my father and I had always planned. At the end of the term, I completed my degree. Six long years had passed since that traumatic night, and I couldn't imagine my life ever returning to how things had been.

After my graduation, nothing much changed. I was still hollow on the inside, living one day at a time. The pain was so great that to call it sadness or grief would be trivializing. Each day, I prayed for the end, for the torment to stop. As much as I prayed to be dead, I also immersed myself in the torture, feeling that I deserved it.

I secured my first job, at a public relations and marketing firm. I was excited for the first time in a while. There was a shift, a glimmer of hope in a new world away from the abusers and the monster. This new venture was exhilarating because I had actually gotten a job in the field I'd majored in. I was keen on getting real experience. The company had several high-profile clients. The rush of deadlines and the high-pressure environment made me feel alive. I had little time to indulge in thoughts of sadness and death.

The biggest skill I learned during this time was how to mask my feelings. I forced myself to make friends and entered into a few dysfunctional romantic relationships. I wanted to be in a relationship with someone who loved me despite my vile mistake. The first two people I dated after the dreadful event were kind and loving, but I didn't feel the sense of security I longed for to shield me from the monsters of the world. I thought my partners were immature and overly romantic in their take on relationships. I broke off the relationships in search of something more secure. I did not know what that looked like, but I believed I would know it when I found it—honest, raw, true love.

~

About a year into my post college life, I ran into an old friend at a party. I knew him from Year 12. We were both born in the same month. That night, we talked about astrology and our shared sign. He was confident and strong, kind and funny, and loved by everyone at the party. I was attracted to his intelligence and felt safe around him. We started dating a few days later, and I was on cloud nine. I thought I had met my soul mate, and I fell in love.

He was the kind of person who knew it all but in an endearing manner. He was tactful with his words and sometimes brutally honest. I admired that. He told me he was attracted to me, because of all the girls he had met, I was *real*. His compliments were genuine: "I love the way your eyes smile with you" and "You're so smart. I love the way you handled that conversation." The compliments of my intellect were the ones that drew me closer to him. He was confident with his physical advances, too. He'd place his hand on the small of my back when we were in public and hold me all night when we were out with friends. He made me feel like I was *his*, and I enjoyed that sense of belonging. I felt like I was being rebuilt, that the reset I'd been longing for might happen through this relationship.

After a while, things started to change. He was frequently irate with me. I believed his patience for me had run out because I was always making mistakes. We saw each other every night after work for dinner, which made the frequency of mistakes more apparent.

ometimes I ordered the wrong drink. Sometimes I ordered the drink too soon before he arrived, and it wasn't hot enough when he got there. Sometimes I chose the wrong booth to sit in. Sometimes the food I ordered for myself was gross to him. There was no way to predict his criticism and discontent. I was living at home, but I hadn't had dinner with my parents in a year. He wasn't interested in spending time with my parents, citing that only once we were serious enough, by his gauge, should we meet each other's parents. He had many rules like that. Initially, I found it attractive that he was so principled.

On the night of my twenty-fifth birthday, we went out to dinner. I watched his eyes as he sized me up. I was in a dress I had bought for my birthday and was feeling rather sophisticated. "Do you have to wear dresses so tight for work? It makes you look cheap."

I was stunned and embarrassed, as it was never my intention to flaunt my body on the job. I agreed and made sure to wear more modest clothing to work. I didn't want my boyfriend seeing me as cheap. I certainly didn't want my clients to see me that way.

The honeymoon period was clearly over, and we entered into a *real* phase of our relationship. He had me convinced that we had to work on things in order for us to secure a future together. All my faults became more apparent, and he didn't spare my feelings when informing me of the ways I needed to improve. I stopped wearing makeup to assure him that I was confident in my natural self and that I was definitely not *whoring* myself out to my clients. When I visited the beauty counter, the clerk, a woman I'd come to know well, expressed concern for me. "Amelia, I don't know if you know, but your boyfriend was here last week. He told us not to sell you any more makeup. Are you okay?"

"I'm fine," I said, brushing it off. "I wonder why he did that. He's so silly. He must be joking." I was mortified.

"He said you're having financial trouble and spending all your money on makeup and that we should help you."

I left without a word and never went back.

The criticisms and the verbal abuse kept coming, and I felt more flawed and inept than ever. Once, when we were out with friends, I mentioned that bourbon can be made outside of Kentucky, although it is a product exclusive to the United States.

"Bourbon is whiskey made in Kentucky. That's just what it is. You don't know this stuff. Don't worry about it, baby," he said, correcting me politely. It hurt, though. I could see the looks of discomfort on our friends' faces, but no one said a word.

A friend attempted to help by taking my side. "Are you sure, man? I think she may be right."

My boyfriend responded, "If you want to sound stupid, sure, man. Bourbon is from Kentucky. That's why Jack Daniels is not bourbon, and Jim Beam is." Then he laughed heartily, and we all fell into silence. I had known this fact because I had read an article about bourbon, but now I distrusted myself. He made it clear to me that I was lucky to have him in my life, and I believed this to be true.

He was a banker who worked a standard nine-to-five job at a local bank, whereas I worked outside conventional business hours. In the second year of our relationship, his berating and abuse escalated. He did not approve of me getting any kind of work done outside the office. That was his time. His disapproval for my job and the company I worked for was a point of continual contention. One night, we were having dinner at our usual spot. I had to respond to some work emails on my Blackberry, and he chided me, "Do you need to do that right now?" I could hear the irritation in his voice, but I needed to reply to a client's email.

"I'm sorry, darling, just a quick e-mail. The event is tomorrow."

I spoke softly, hoping to bring calm to the table. As I hit send on my phone, he slammed his utensils down and gripped the table. I watched in horror as he stood up, tossed the table, and threw money for the bill in my face. He left in a tantrum because I was working at dinner. I picked up the table and the money scattered on the ground. The waiters rushed to my aid but said nothing as they cleaned the mess. They had seen this humiliating display toward me before. I smiled sheepishly at the waitresses as I picked up the money, got the bill, and went after him.

I loved him, and I hated when I made him angry. I wanted him to be happy with me, as I craved his affection and love. His criticism and anger increased in ways I had not experienced before, and it always struck when I least expected. One night we were having a good date, laughing and enjoying our time together, unwinding after a long day at work. I made a joke he found offensive, and we sparred verbally until he elbowed me in the stomach. I was winded, I cried, and he left. I wished I hadn't made that joke. I wished I had not said stupid things. I was desperate for forgiveness, and I didn't want to lose him. He was too good for me, and I knew it.

The abuse varied in its damage and reach. It messed with my mind and sense of self-worth. I believed I was already broken and damaged, not worthy of love. I couldn't look at myself in the mirror without disgust. He was with me despite my mistakes. He forgave me for them and assured me that he believed I wouldn't make the same mistakes again. I found comfort in his words. I felt he would keep me safe from the monsters.

I hated being alone. I did not want to be around my parents mainly because of the guilt from the secret I was concealing. My boyfriend agreed that my parents would not understand, and it would be best to bury my misdeed forever. After all, he'd remind me, it was in the past. I was addicted to him and needed to be with him at all times. I felt safe when I was with him. He insisted that I belonged to him, and I lived in that space of belonging.

About three years into our relationship, I had an important dinner meeting with a client, but my boyfriend wanted to see me before the meeting—just for a drink, he said. We agreed to meet at our regular restaurant, and as I pulled into the parking spot, he was there waiting for me. He came over to give me a kiss, and in a split second, his grip on my arms tightened. When I tried to pull away, he ripped my shirt, popping the buttons off. He started yelling hysterically about my nighttime meeting and provocative shirt. His grip loosened as I begged for forgiveness. "Please don't be mad. I didn't realize that. I'm so sorry."

"You've been going around all day like this! Everyone has already seen! Let them see all of it then, if you must!" He shouted at me, and I shrunk smaller and smaller.

"I won't do this again. I'm so sorry. I'm so, so sorry." I was appalled that I had been showing my breasts and didn't even realize it. I wanted so badly for him not to be angry.

He had lashed out at me for the gap between the buttons over my breasts. I was showing cleavage, he railed. He did not want anyone seeing "his" breasts, so his tantrum ended with my shirt ripping. He was not happy that I was having a meeting with a male client at night and accused me of acting like a prostitute. Thankfully no one was in the parking lot to witness the humiliation.

"Slut! Whore!" he yelled. *That's right; that's me.* I had confided in him about the pain of those labels, which had cut deep for me, and I was mortified that he would use them against me now. I was reduced to the shell I had been in the days following my mistake. I felt as insignificant as I had during the days I was excluded and spat on. It was a feeling I struggled to reconcile, as I supposedly had a boyfriend who loved me unconditionally. He was possessive, but I was convinced that this was because of his care and concern for me.

I fixed a safety pin to my shirt for my meeting that night. My boyfriend's actions did nothing to make me doubt him or his behavior. It only reiterated to me that I was fucked up. I kept messing up when we were together, and I needed to do better. His treatment was classic abuse in all its horrid forms—chokes, slaps, and public humiliation. It was followed by making up and "I love you" and "I promise I will be better." But I didn't recognize it for what it was. If someone had told me I was in an abusive relationship, I wouldn't have agreed. He took advantage of my utterly eroded sense of self and my disconnection from family, which he encouraged.

He frequently reminded me that I was very ugly. He said that we were together only because we had been friends and he thought our relationship would be good, but I was shit. *I was so ugly that I would never be able to be with anyone.* I held on to the relationship with every ounce of strength. Whenever I had panic attacks, which were increasing in frequency, he would leave me in my breathlessness. He would walk out so that I could deal alone with what he called "drama." As I calmed down, a release always came over me. The fear I had of him was overwhelming. The fear of being alone, though, had a far worse effect. I went home to nurse my wounded ego while hiding yet another secret from my parents. First, it was the colossal fuckup with my body. Now, it was this relationship I knew they wouldn't approve of but that I couldn't do without. I lived with even more lies, avoiding my parents altogether by staying out as much as I could.

On and on it went, for another year. At the end of our third year together, I intercepted a text on his phone from a girl whose name I didn't recognize. I had believed he was committed to me and we'd someday marry, so when I saw the text, my stomach dropped.

"I'm missing you, baby. Will you b over tonite?"

I decided to play sherlock and followed his car that night. I watched as he got out to greet her with a kiss. I said nothing to him or anyone else, for fear he would leave me. I was willing to have him no matter what.

It wasn't long after that when our relationship came to an end, but it was not initiated by me. He was driving me to an event that my company was organizing, and I was texting about work with a colleague. My boyfriend grabbed my phone and screamed at me, certain that I was cheating on him.

"Let me see what you're saying here!" he yelled, furious. I stayed silent, not wanting it to escalate to a physical altercation.

The text read, "Kevin: Meet you there at 8:00 p.m. I'll bring the press releases from the office. Cheers, love."

"'Love'? Who the fuck is this?" He demanded an explanation.

"It's Kevin from work. It's not romantic, just something people say. Please don't read into it." I desperately needed him not to be angry with me.

"I can't do this anymore," he said, resigned. "You're a fucking slut and always will be. I don't want this anymore. Just get out!"

"Please, please, darling, don't do this," I begged, but he abruptly pulled over to the shoulder of the road and slammed on the brakes. His hand came an inch from my face. I froze, thinking he was going to hit me, but he just reached over to open the door.

"Just get out!" He pushed me out of the car, yelling as if shooing a dog. I stumbled out of the car. I clutched my purse and stood on the roadside, confused. Familiar feelings of the wooded canopy at college came back. I was abandoned and unloved yet again.

Thirty minutes later Kevin arrived to pick me up. Humiliated and in tears, I tried to keep a brave face. I made up an excuse as to why I was stranded. My boyfriend never answered my calls again. I knew he didn't want to be with me anymore, but the abrupt ending left me feeling lost. I didn't know how to carry on, but the zombie in me knew how.

In the fallout of our breakup, I lost another round of friends. They chose him over me and blamed me for what happened. I deserved what I got, because he was such a nice guy and I had screwed up by being my difficult self. *I am cursed. I am not worthy of any love, not even from this piece of shit that beat me and cursed me.* I never breathed a word of his abuse, a skill I had mastered from masking all the pain I already bore. I was a terrible girlfriend, and that was why he sought comfort and love in another girl. Three years ended with nothing but a crushed heart. I was alone again. The pain was back, but it was not the fierce stabbing I'd had four years earlier, when I found myself in grief and isolation. Now it was a dull ache, a pain I knew and was accustomed to nursing. Deep inside, I understood that I would carry this pain forever.

~

While mourning the end of that relationship, I was forced to mourn another end. I'd avoided my parents over these three years, but I'd also avoided the opportunity to care for my grandmother, who had raised me. In my shame and guilt, I had not spoken to Amachee very often. Our phone calls and visits became more infrequent. When she called, I made up excuses about being busy when in reality I was ashamed. I stayed away to stay honest. I didn't have the heart to lie to her, and my whole existence was predicated on keeping my secret. When I did visit her toward the end, I sat in silence and counted on her dementia to get me through.

She passed peacefully on an afternoon when she said she was ready. I traveled to Alor Star to the home I'd grown up in. I arrived to a house full of cousins and their children, aunts, and uncles, who tried their best to hold everything together. The moment I saw her lying in a coffin, my heart shattered. She wore the green sari she had requested she be cremated in, and she was surrounded by incense and flowers. The reality of her departure from this world hit me like a hundred-mile-an-hour car crash. I was not ready for her to go. She was my one safe place, which I'd been too ashamed to claim in recent years. This was the place I was loved no matter what, the place where popsicles and jokes washed away pain. How had I allowed myself to stay away so long? I was decimated looking into that coffin. I fell to the ground, only to be caught in an embrace by my aunt and cousin. We cried in our shared loss.

I felt guilty about how I had avoided time with my grandmother out of shame. In the last five years of my grandmother's life, she was quite ill and needed tending. All of my cousins, aunts, and uncles— all twenty-two of them—had coordinated schedules. In those final weeks, I had traveled to see her three or four days a month. I sat with her, bathed her, and mostly spoke to her vacant eyes. I imagined there might come a time when I'd spill my guts, but I couldn't muster the courage.

Her funeral, like her life, was celebratory, loud, and joyous. I mourned with my family. We sat around the coffin and spoke to Amachee, warning her of the frenemies who had come to visit. We laughed about the ladies who grieved by screaming and wailing at the top of their lungs. They weren't close friends, but it was the customary loud grieving that was performed at a funeral. We reminisced and talked about the time Amachee jumped out of the bushes to scare me on my way home from night classes. We laughed about her prank calls and all the mischievous things she did. We cackled as we shared these memories with her one more time.

We sang prayers and the Gayatri Mantra. Our voices together created a symphony, so beautiful and clear. After that, a silence fell over the house, a familiar peace and calm. All the noise and chatter stopped. She had impacted so many lives in the community, and people visited from near and far to offer peace and prayers for her. Now we were left only with the echoes of their vibrations. We prayed for the ascension of her spirit to the highest degree. We prayed that she would be among sages and gurus.

I felt lightness for the first time in ages. She was light. A calm came over me. I felt her warmth and love. I felt her tender voice, her kisses on my cheeks telling me I was going to be all right. I remembered the countless times she'd held me close, when I'd breathed in the scent of her skin, when she'd kiss me and promise we'd see each other again soon. I felt that comfort, but my mind wouldn't negotiate the fact that *I wouldn't be seeing her again, ever. She was gone.*

~

The distance between my parents and I had grown so far that I didn't know how to reconcile it without the confession that I wasn't willing to share. The pain ate at me because I felt I was counting my losses. With my grandmother gone, I was alone in the world. I was sure that true love did not exist. No one would ever be able to love me knowing the mistake I had made. I was in an exile of my own making. I decided my mistake would be taken to my grave.

CHAPTER 5

I was desperate for anything to numb the pain. I could not bear to face my parents for fear I'd reveal my mistake to them. A year after my grandmother's passing, I moved out of my parents' home and in with my friend Kate from Alor Star. She'd just moved back to Malaysia after her studies in England. We got a seventeenth-floor three-bedroom apartment in the suburbs of Kuala Lumpur. Our balcony view was of a beautiful aqua pool surrounded by palm trees and flowering gardens, a true oasis and sanctuary. Still, we spent our evenings after work at the gym in the basement of our building. We furnished the apartment a little at a time with every paycheck. The rent was a steal, yet we could still barely afford it. She landed a job at the company I was working for, and we got to work together. We were twenty-six, and our conversations regularly pivoted to romance, sex, and men. We talked about hooking up, as I no longer believed in the idea of a romantic relationship.

"I don't think I can do that, Kate. You can, I see that—you're so beautiful and cool. I'm just me." I did not think I was attractive enough to entice any man.

"You're just seeing everything with pessimism. You're beautiful, Amy. Any guy would fall for you. You just have an air of unavailability all around you," she said, trying to coax me out of my shell. I felt like this was a pity party, but she wanted so badly for me to feel good about myself. "If you just relax a bit, open up, and give yourself a chance, you'll see. It doesn't have to be a relationship—sex is sex. But who's to say you won't find someone?" She knew I'd given up on the idea of having a true relationship.

I wanted the guilt to leave me. It had been seven years since the night that changed my life and less than a year since my ex-boyfriend had left me on the side of the road. I was ready to change myself and the expectations I had about relationships, and Kate was keen to help me.

We structured an experiment. I was to land myself a hookup or at least exchange numbers with someone I found attractive. We were prepared to try this at a work cocktail party for the launch of a new lifestyle magazine. There was a guy at the party, Carter, who had all the girls' attention. He was Australian and had been working for the magazine for the past year. I'd heard through the grapevine that he didn't sleep with anyone from work, even with all these women so clearly vying for his attention. I was secretly hopeful, as I didn't work directly with him.

I joined the group of women surrounding him, listening and watching. Carter was by far the best-looking man there, and there were quite a few handsome men in attendance. He was average height. His shirt fit perfectly, just tight enough to show his chiseled chest and strong arms. His jaw was defined but softened by his sweet smile and dimples. The lines outside his beautiful deep-green eyes enhanced that sexy smile. His lashes were long, dark, and full. He stared straight at me, and his smile disappeared. His head cocked and he turned toward me. *Oh shit!* I was flustered and nervous.

"Hi. You're new. I haven't seen you before." He was talking to me. I tried to stay calm.

"Yes, hi. I'm Amelia." I held out my hand. I was giddy and beside myself.

"Carter," he said in a voice that suddenly seemed scandalously sexy. My heart was melting. *Take me now, please.* I wanted so badly to be wanted. His interest aroused a power within me. Is this really happening? He reached for my phone, which was sitting behind me on the bar. I watched him, mesmerized. My nose grazed his neck as he leaned in to take the phone, almost in slow motion. I felt tingling down my spine, as if I were about to float off my seat right there. He put his number in my phone and then called his phone. Who did he think he was—James Bond? We were engrossed in conversation about Australia. I had visited Perth a couple of years earlier for my graduation, a compromise trip from my dad after they pulled the plug on my going there for school. That trip came in useful for finding common ground with this sexy man. He was originally from Melbourne and shared what that was like. While we were chatting, his boss walked by and asked if we would like to join him for a media tour he was giving. Carter politely declined on our behalf. When the group moved on, he turned back to me. His hand gently caressed the small of my back as we continued our conversation. Somebody chose me over something else. Somebody chose me over other girls. Somebody found me interesting and attractive.

The next few days, we texted. Though Carter and I had yet to plan a night out, I saw my experiment as a success. I was nervous and talked it out repeatedly with Kate and with Carter. I did not want to stay the night, and he assured me that I'd be in control of how the evening played out. "You don't have to do anything you don't want to. My doors only lock from the inside. I promise," he had said in jest during a phone call. *Was this what respect looked like?* I had the power to engage or not.

We went out to dinner at a cute little Spanish bar near his apartment and had a wonderful time chatting and getting to know each other. Afterward we walked to his apartment for a nightcap that ended in his bed. I had not previously enjoyed sex the way I did that night. No thoughts of the past came to mind. A power took over me, and I was pleasured in a way I had not been before. That first time was not the only time. We had many future rendezvous that helped to instill in me something new, a sense of feminine power, something I had not known existed. Kate had been right, and she was excited to see my confidence grow. "You are so beautiful and intelligent and attractive. You don't have to think all those nasty thoughts about yourself. You're in charge, lady!" I didn't feel like dying anymore. I felt quite alive. It was electrifying to feel attractive and seen.

~

With the attention from Carter, something flipped in me. I no longer craved the protection and commitment of a man. Instead, I chased the high, the power I found in sex. The easiest way to find what I was looking for was at the clubs, and alcohol made it even easier. After a while, I didn't even need the company of friends. I was comfortable hunting on my own. I never went home alone. Sex became a power game. The goal was to smooth what felt like a dent in my sense of self. When I had a man within my grasp, I was worthy.

Each night I walked to the bar, where I had definitely become a regular. The same bartenders would greet me, and I imagined they judged me for what they knew was about to play out. Jack and Coke. Jack and Coke. I was always in a beautiful dress, classy but sexy, that showed enough of my silhouette but left some to the imagination. My hair, styled straight, would fall into my face as I danced. I knew my face was appealing, not striking. But thanks to my mixed heritage,

I was hard to place ethnically, and this made me exotic in the eyes of men. I felt empowered, intelligent, funny, and interesting, able to hold my own in conversations. I wasn't naive enough to think it was my conversation that led me to their beds, but in those moments at the club, I relished their interest.

Once I got my drink, I'd look around the room nonchalantly with my practiced air of confidence. I wore five-inch heels, and I loved the way the extra height made my body look lithe—I am slender but bite-size at five foot two. I loved the lighting by the bar, a dim orange light from the glass chandelier that made my chocolate skin glow. Part of the game was to pick out who I'd be leaving with that night, and they always acquiesced. It was a sea of charming smiles, intense looks, and bodies moving toward me night after night. I was in control. My whole being expanded, extending into a forcefield around me. However, a rip in the forcefield would emerge occasionally when I lashed out at a stranger or at the man I was with. At times, it ended with me being escorted out of the club. Triggered by the smell of cheap cologne, or the musty bar, or just the smell of alcohol, I'd be brought right back to the night at that disgusting motel. Yet, somehow, I craved both the power and the pain.

The same scene played over and over again. I saw them see me as I walked in. I saw them try to entice me, raising a glass, staring past their friend while smiling at me. I would excuse myself from conversation at the bar and grab a drink with the gentleman. I let loose on the dance floor, my body swaying and rocking, conveying that I wanted him to feel me. His hands would work their way down my waist, and I leaned in to smell the cologne on his neck. My breasts would rest on his chest, inviting him to take me. I felt my body send him all of my desire. It would be a fuck for the night. The ecstasy from the physical delectation had run out much earlier in the game, but I still chased the challenge of walking into the bar, making a mark, and being ravaged by a handsome stranger. They were always handsome. That was where my power lay, where my body grieved. I would be invincible until the darkness, like an acid fog, suffocated me. John, Nick, Miles, or Jack—they all did pretty much the same dance, to the same end. There was no release. It was repeated in a never-ending reel.

I was not ugly, as my ex had said I was. What a revelation. I needed more and more of the high, to the point that I had a booty call list for the weeknights the clubs were shut. I craved the company, the physical stimulation and appreciation of my body, and the love that I pretended existed in that bed, that night. It silenced the pain. It was warm comfort, without the words. I felt whole in those moments. I drank on booty call nights too. I stayed out all night, missed work, and broke all the rules that Kate and I had made about hookups. She became concerned with my recklessness. It had been eight months of this spiral, and I wasn't about to end it.

One night as I was coming out of the shower, Kate was sitting at the dining table, staring at me. I could see her eyes well up. "You can't keep doing this, Amy. You're going to lose your job. You're going to be in real trouble with all the drinking you do too. I'm worried." It was four in the morning, and she had been waiting to have this conversation with me because I was hardly home anymore. I only came home to shower and dress. Still wrapped in a towel, I sat next to her and took her hand.

"I'm absolutely fine. I'm here, aren't I?" I spoke with confidence, but inside I felt embarrassed at being called out.

"Boss is talking about your accounts. He's about to pass some of them on to me. I don't think that's a good sign, Amy." She'd always been a straight arrow, and I knew she loved me. But she couldn't fathom what a lifeline sex had become for me. It awakened me, made me feel alive. I needed this. I couldn't stop.

Eventually, my kamikaze style would lead her to move out and stop talking to me. In the meantime, we barely saw each other and only talked occasionally at work. I didn't realize that I was trying desperately to fill the void through my actions. But the more I pursued the high, the deeper the void became, swallowing me.

~

I'd been sleeping around for a year and was practiced in my form. For the most part, these were uneventful liaisons, but eventually I found myself in a precarious situation. There was a glitch in my flow of casual sex, because I fell in love. He was the drummer in a band at a club I frequented. Jean-Luc was from Montreal and supposedly in a committed relationship. This did not bother me. I had already seen how men did not give credence to these sentiments.

He was older than me, forty-two to my twenty-six, and he was kind, with sad eyes that went downward and some telling lines on his face. His face was captivating. I would get lost in his eyes, which sometimes shut as he played, brimming with an intensity I found immensely attractive. He had the muscular body of someone who worked out. As his wrists flicked his drumsticks, the sight of his forearms sent heat through my body. His sexuality poured out as he drummed on stage.

He'd occasionally look my way with a smile or a wink, sending shudders down my body. He'd jump off stage at the end of a set, grab my waist, and nuzzle his nose along my neck. Every movement he made was music to me. He had a deep, sexy voice and whispered sweet nothings in French. In bed, he did things to me that would melt my whole body, and he made me feel so loved. He would run his thumb and forefinger over my eyebrows as he spoke to me in French, intermittently kissing my forehead and my hair. We talked, and I shared everything with him, from how I grew up, to my work, to the night in that motel.

He listened intently. "I can't believe anyone would do that to you. You're too precious, my love." Tears ran down his face. He held me tight, allowing my pain to disappear into his chest. I felt safe. I believed I was in love with him and that he was in love with me. He knew I was hurting, and he wanted to be the cure. I wasn't filthy to him. I wasn't just another girl.

He started talking about future plans, about moving to Canada, but I was not ready for that. He had a partner he had been with for years and a son from that relationship. He talked to me about his relationship and how it was coming to an end. I loved him, but I didn't want anything more than what we shared. It was a capsule of romance that had an expiration, with no commitment, no expectations. In any case, I didn't believe he would stay with me long-term— no one would—so I said goodbye to him at the end of our blissful three months. But Jean-Luc gave me a gift, because for the first time in the past year and a half, I felt loved. I felt what I imagined love should feel like. I felt what it was like to love. I existed in someone's world.

We kept in touch, even though we knew we didn't have a future. He ended his relationship with his partner, for which I felt immense guilt. But he insisted that being in a loveless relationship was not worth it. With Jean-Luc, I had not felt used or dirty. I felt whole. I had discovered the possibility of something so special it was worth living for, even if I had to wait for the right person. I wanted a relationship again.

I still couldn't shake my need to have company in bed. I was deathly afraid of being alone. It wasn't logical. It was pure animal instinct, a habit by now, driven by a feeling so overwhelming that I could not fight it. I was reckless, not because I didn't care, but because I couldn't control myself. I would later realize the irrationality of my impulsive behaviors, but at the time, it felt like my brain would explode if I didn't indulge myself. I was not hopeful a change was in the cards for me. As much as I wanted to love and be loved, I also wanted to die. Though I didn't want to go to Canada with Jean-Luc, I did fantasize about running away to find a different reality. I could start anew and be the person I wanted to be—no history, no past, no dirt. I could trust someone fully, I could love entirely, and I could live absolutely.

~

A month after Jean-Luc left, I decided I could never recover from the loneliness and desperation for my demise. I thought of myself as damaged and tainted. I faced a conundrum. My sleeping around was proving to myself how nasty and disgusting I was. But at the same time, I was fueled by the conquest. The power was real, my confidence and strength a welcome counter to how I'd felt for so long.

I was running my life into the ground with my recklessness. I knew my reputation would catch up with me. Kuala Lumpur, with a population of two million, could get small fairly quickly. My lust for fleeing where I came from would soon come strong and urgent. Running away had always been easy. I belonged to nowhere, to no one. No one actually cared about my whereabouts. I had always been unsettled wherever I was—in my childhood home with my parents, in Alor Star with my grandmother and cousins, and at college after my life was turned upside down.

I had a secure job, and a TV production freelance job that paid even better, making it financially viable to plan a trip. Anywhere was possible, so I chose Shanghai, China. There was a Formula One coming up. This was an event I often covered, so I had become a fan. This seemed like a perfect excursion. My boss was not pleased but allowed me the vacation days. I had no plans and knew no one. The adrenaline rush was so high, however, I felt I could take on the world.

I stepped out of the airport in Shanghai and lit a cigarette as I peeked into the train station next door. It was like Grand Central Station I'd seen on TV. All the digitized pinyin characters streamed left to right, right to left, in every different color. There were loud announcements on the speakers in Mandarin and people rushing and pushing. I was paralyzed in the realization that getting out of the airport and finding my way into Shanghai wasn't going to be so straightforward. I didn't speak a lick of Mandarin except for the few words I had picked up from friends. I had hoped for some Roman letters to read or some broken English to help me, but looking around, the letters were all in pinyin. I had no way to figure out the trains. I knew how to say "please," "thank you," "hello," and "help me."

"Duibuqi, bang wo?" I repeated, "Excuse me, help me" to people passing by while holding out my hotel reservation.

I heard a young man shout, "Shanghai! Shanghai!" I ran to him. He was a random person with an unmarked van, not a taxi or shuttle of any sort. He opened the door to his van for me, but more young men got in as well. I felt nervous but also alive with that feeling of living on the edge.

I pulled out a cigarette in an attempt to ease the tension and asked if it was okay. "Ke yi ma?"

The whole van erupted in laughter. "Ke yi! Ke yi!" I passed around my pack of Marlboros, and they each had one. We puffed like a smoke machine all the way into Shanghai. We made it to my hotel, and the driver helped me check in. Along with the ride fare, I gave him a pack of Marlboros. He gave me his Chinese cigarettes, gesturing that they were better. We laughed and said goodbye. I had managed to survive on my own. I was on top of the world. It turned out to be such a sweet memory, my time with those twelve strange Chinese men in a van.

I spent the next couple of days exploring. I took pictures of the Pearl Tower from across the river, visited the city temples, explored the underground shopping malls, and finally attended the Formula One race. It had been three days since I'd heard any English, so when I heard a group of guys speaking, I was thrilled. I eavesdropped, looking for the right moment to drop into the conversation. I saw their flag—red and white.

"Hi," I said. "Toronto or out West?"

They laughed. "Vancouver."

"Malaysia," I said. "I would be lying if I said I haven't been enjoying myself here, but I must say your English is music to my ears! Do you guys speak Mandarin?"

"Joe here does, a little bit. Enough to get by."

They invited me to sit with them, and we watched the race together, cheering and screaming. We were on the edge of our seats. The driver I was rooting for, Lewis Hamilton, did not win. But it was intoxicating to experience the adrenaline rush with these strangers. I had found a troop to enjoy something together, and that was satisfying. I felt at home in a strange place. I didn't know these people, but I pictured myself free with them.

They invited me to dinner that night, and over traditional Szechuan cuisine and ridiculous conversation, we shared our travel experiences and talked about our home countries. I told how the previous day I'd found a long line leading up to a stall on the street corner, how the air was hot and steamy with a delicious scent—sweet and salty. I got in line without knowing what for. Once I got to the front, I motioned with my hands, pointing to whatever delicacy it was they were serving. The man picked up a bucket to show me some beetles that were to be chopped and fried in a sweet sticky coating. It smelled so good, and I was there, wasn't I? I tried them, swallowing before I could taste them. I was left with a sweet and spicy aftertaste that I rather liked. I was enjoying this crazy foreign world on my own, and I was present, living every bit of it. My Canadian friends found my story amusing. They took notes so they could find the stall and try the beetles the next day.

As luck would have it, I met someone I knew from the McLaren team out at the bar that night. I had met him once before in Malaysia. He was on the pit crew, and I had been working a press event at the Malaysian Formula One. I was delighted to meet up with him here in Shanghai. He was a handsome, strong black man who was hard to resist, so I left my Canadian crew to spend time with Bruce instead. Many shots of experimental drinks from the menu followed. I stopped counting.

"You want to get out of here? It'll have to be yours; I'm sharing a room with Thomas." I tried not to seem desperate and said nothing, but when he walked me back to my hotel, I didn't stop him from coming up with me. We had sex, as I had done in the past with the men back home. It was my last night there and the last time I would ever see him. Disappointment fell over me once it was over, for I had repeated what I was trying to escape. I had reunited with a bloke from home and reenacted what I would have done at home. *Was there no escape?* It seemed as though I did not know how to forge a path on my own. I could not be trusted with my own destiny. Tears of regret lulled me to sleep.

I woke up in the morning to find Bruce gone, and my shuttle to the airport had left without me. I ran down to the concierge and cried until she found me a taxi. I experienced another rush of adrenaline. I should have been distraught, but I relished this. I made it to the airport. I had a new sense of liberation and strength from being by myself and doing whatever the fuck I wanted. Bruce was but a blip in my adventure. There was no one to judge me, no one who knew my past, no one who cared about my past. The people I encountered accepted me as whatever I wanted to be. I was reckless, impulsive, and urgent. The escapade had exceeded my wildest dreams, and I couldn't wait for the next one. I had a deep hunger for the next adventure away from home, where I could be myself or disappear into thin air. But thoughts of Bruce diminished my sense of power. I regretted my night with him, but the rush of the solo adventure I had just been on pushed any negative feelings to the side.

~

I lived in those moments of liberation. It was emancipation from my life. I had to go back to reality in Kuala Lumpur, where everyone knew my business. I worried about what everyone thought. I imagined the things they were saying, just like what all those people had said about me in college. I felt trapped again. I rarely saw my parents or family anymore, as I knew what I was doing would bring them shame. It was just another secret. I could not be ruined more than I already had been. At least with my current expeditions, I was in charge.

I kept chasing the next high. An opportunity came in November 2009, about a year after I'd moved in with Kate. I got an invitation from Eric, a guy I'd met at a bar in Kuala Lumpur, to come to London. I decided immediately that I would go. My boss promised me I'd have a job when I came back, but I wasn't sure I would come back to it. I had a freelance writing job with my parents' production house that was paying me enough on the side to finance my travels. I wanted the high of living—of being present and in another state of being, which was not possible when trapped around all the familiarity and expectations.

When I arrived in London, Eric picked me up. We headed to his apartment, where I was to stay for the next eight weeks. Eric was kind, a little reserved, and polished. He was always coiffed, even for the casual occasion of picking me up at the airport. He was a year younger than I was but much more secure and grounded. We went out the very first night, and it was fun getting to know Eric's friends. I was captivated by their accents, which made them all sound so eloquent and sophisticated. It was amazing to be in the United Kingdom, a window into a new world. My time with Eric was glorious, and I scandalized my tight-lipped British friends with my crude jokes and witticisms. With Eric, I wasn't sure what we were doing, exactly. I wanted something like a relationship, but I didn't want to commit. I was there for the adventure. I wanted to find myself, even if I was exploring the dim possibility of a relationship. I spent time with Eric but also explored the city on my own.

Two weeks into my trip, I visited all the places my parents had taken me when I was younger, such as Trafalgar Square and Piccadilly Circus. I visited the amazing toy store from my childhood. My father had brought me to Hamleys, the best toy store in the world. As I walked in eleven years later, memories of my father's hand in mine flooded my mind. I missed the joy of being his little girl, how I had always felt safe with him. I felt the guilt, and my eyes teared. I remembered his laugh as we watched the toy airplanes and the clowns. This time I was alone, hoping to recreate that same feeling of wonder. But it was void of the love that I had shared with my father. I was hit hard by the realization that the detachment from my father was a result of my mistake. I would never be able to share it with him, and he would never be able to walk me through that pain the way he had through the flying toy planes, or the trains on suspended tracks overhead.

I found myself at the Tate Modern, off the Thames. I stepped in and was awestruck. I was not an art expert or even an enthusiast, but I was drawn in. I felt myself in every stroke, every shade and shape. I spotted Jackson Pollock's 1948 painting, *Summertime: Number 9A*. There was a long bench opposite the painting, and I sat down and stared into the colors and the strokes. Everything around me disappeared, leaving only Pollock's *Summertime* and me. I didn't know what intentions he may have had, but I was captivated by the interconnectedness of everything—the brightness of the blues and the yellows, the curves and strokes so light, just lifting off the ends. It made me feel intensely liberated. I felt myself in the painting. I was seeking independence. I watched the movements in the painting until I heard a man's voice. "Miss? Excuse me. It's closing time." I scurried to gather my coat and other items and realized I had spent my entire afternoon with Pollock, and it was glorious.

It was the first time in a while that I'd felt at peace. The last time I'd felt anything similar was when studying in Alor Star while Amachee pretended to stay awake in the other room. The peace was still there, if I could quiet the world and the pain enough to feel it. Mr. Pollock had given me a glimmer of hope.

I had a date that night with a Malaysian friend, Richard, at a club downtown. As soon as I got there, we ordered cocktail after cocktail, followed by shots. The bartender brought me a drink, indicating a man had bought it for me. I told the bartender to take the drink back and tell him, "No, thank you." The bartender laughed as he took the drink away. I saw the man still grinning at me. I switched places with my friend so I could avoid the man's gaze. It was ballsy of him, considering I was with a male friend. Richard was just a platonic friend from work, but that guy couldn't have known that.

On a visit to the bathroom, I chatted with a girl as we reapplied our lipstick. She gave me a card to another club and told me to come next weekend. "Just use my name at the door," she said. Richard and I said goodbye, as he had to work the next morning. He hailed a cab for me and jumped into the one behind it. Two seconds after my door closed, it opened again, and in jumped a ravishing young man. He had a tight body and beautiful smile. I recognized him from the bar where he had been smiling at me all night.

"Hear me out," he said. "I know you said no to my drink at the bar. Dodgy anyway, I get it. But here's my suggestion: we take this cab to my place and have some wine and see where the night takes us." He said this in that beautiful English accent. It was all so charming. I felt like I'd do anything for that smile.

"The name's Andrew, and I know that bloke you were with wasn't a boyfriend, or he wouldn't let you go home alone in a cab. Am I wrong?"

"And if I only want to stay for wine?" I asked, flattered but still puzzled by this man in my cab.

"Then we have wine, I get you a cab, and you ride home," he said, seeming confident I wasn't going to change my mind.

The cab driver advised against it. "Miss, it's not safe. Let me take you home." He was getting agitated with the young man in his cab. "This cab only goes one place. She was here first. No sharing—please get out!" he said angrily.

He was not leaving. He looked at me and said, "We're going to the same place, aren't we?" I decided to take the chance. After all, it was quite flattering to be pursued so persistently. He looked decent, and we had just left a very nice club. I weighed the risks and decided he was safe.

The cab driver said, "Here's my number. I'll be driving around here. If you want to go home, you call me. If in a half hour, you don't call me, I'll call you. Okay?" I exchanged numbers with him. He had a worried scowl on his face as I stepped out of the cab at Andrew's apartment building.

It was a posh apartment, all very well kept, probably for these kinds of weekly shenanigans. Being in a stranger's apartment didn't faze me at all. I'd been in plenty of strange apartments in Kuala Lumpur—living out the night with a stranger, exerting my power, giving my body over to someone for the night. I figured this wouldn't be much different.

We had wine and chatted. He was incredibly witty, intelligent, and very sensitive. The nightcaps inevitably led us to bed. I stayed the night.

The morning after, I left Andrew's on a long walk of shame back to Eric's place. I knew I hadn't been entirely honest with Eric. I saw the relationship as casual, and Eric saw it as more. I explained that I had stayed at my Malaysian friend's apartment. He wasn't pleased, but he trusted me.

The next weekend, chasing another spontaneous experience with strangers, I went to the club to meet the girl who'd given me her card. It was an underground, exclusive club. I used her name, and the bouncer led me to her table. There was bottle service, and someone immediately poured me a drink. I spotted her right away, making out with someone on a velvet chair. She managed a smile and a quick wave. Then a striking young man with his shirt unbuttoned walked toward me. He put his arm around me, pulled me toward him, and just lightly grazed his lips on mine. The vodka on his lips led to me downing two shots with him. A second later, I was pulled away by another man salsa grinding on me. I could feel his hardness on my lower abs and the side of my hips. It felt good; I wanted more. The previous guy came up behind me, and I felt his breath along my neck. He grabbed my arm and tried to pull me upstairs. I wasn't quite sure what type of club this was, but I felt out of place.

"I need a smoke," I said, pulling away. It was clear that everyone in there was high, and I was overwhelmed by it all. As I took a drag of my cigarette alone on the sidewalk, my thoughts went to poor Eric. He was willing to give me love, but I didn't have feelings for him. What he had to offer didn't speak to my heart. The countless meaningless hookups left me feeling empty, yet my experience was like driving in thick fog. I couldn't picture what lay ahead, no matter how hard I tried.

~

Some four weeks into my stay, with Christmas approaching, I found myself wandering around Spitalfields Market. In these moments alone, exploring a foreign city, I felt relaxed. The markets of London were my favorite. There were flea markets with old-fashioned things that I had never seen before. I purchased trinkets and took photos to remind me of my experience. I scoured Camden Market and played with my camera. I walked the streets of London, photographing anything that caught my eye, such as couples playing and kissing, or children running and crying. I saw old vinyl records, original oxfords, and beautiful vintage stuff. I was a wanderer in my thoughts and my photography, and I enjoyed every bit of it.

Eric had invited me to spend Christmas with his family in Derby, and I was excited, though I knew he thought of me as his girlfriend. His mother was welcoming, hugged me often, and introduced me to all her friends. We had a lot of fun in Derby, visiting his old stomping grounds and meeting his friends. They were warm but in a skeptical way, as they should have been. I wasn't the real deal, though I pretended to be.

"So are you staying, Amelia?" asked Adam, one of his best friends.

"I'll have to go home and figure things out first," I said, evading the question.

"But eventually we'll find her something here in London. Won't we, baby?" Eric said with confidence.

"That ought to be the plan!" I said, trying to sound agreeable.

I felt utterly out of place. It wasn't that I meant to hurt anyone. I was just as hesitant as ever about a real, committed relationship.

Upon our return from Derby, I thanked Eric for everything and cut my London trip short at six weeks. My conscience caught up with me after the holidays. It was clear he was getting more invested. To soften the blow, I told him I was still in love with Jean-Luc, the Canadian drummer. We had spoken about our past, and he knew about Jean-Luc. Of course, I wasn't leaving him for Jean-Luc. I was just leaving him.

"Why are you hanging on to something that cannot be?" Eric tried his best to persuade me to change my mind. His stare burned, and I saw tears in his eyes.

"How can I ever love someone else when my heart is stuck with another?" I asked, trying to get out. Holding back my guilty tears proved to be difficult, though, and I let them out.

"I want all of you, love. How can I not be enough? Tell me, and I'll do it, baby," he said, squeezing my hands as he kissed them.

"Perhaps we can talk about it again, if I can deal with my feelings for Jean-Luc?" I tried to convince him. It was more guilt, which I'd have to deal with in time.

He conceded, but not without trying. In the end, I returned to Malaysia after experiencing so much—liberation, excitement, and exhilaration, along with guilt, pain, and shadows from my past. I desperately wanted to get rid of the pain, but I didn't know how. I wanted everything that would give me a glimpse into ecstasy, euphoria, and pure uninhibited joy. I needed more, but it was never enough. I needed the newer challenge, the better-looking guy, the harder-to-get guy. Old habits die hard.

～

A little over a year to the date that I had started my "sexcapades," I met a guy at my regular club in Kuala Lumpur. It was the usual routine, but I didn't go home with him that night. Instead, we agreed to meet up for dinner the next night. The restaurant he chose was exclusive, and he'd apparently reserved the entire place just for the two of us. The chef cooked us dinner as his guests. We enjoyed the meal and wine, and as expected, I chose my high. We ended up in his apartment. We started kissing, and the urgency turned up a notch. His mouth was rabid on my neck and my breasts. His arms were strong, grabbing me and pressing me against the wall. He placed his knee under my crotch, holding me up against that wall, and put his hand over my neck. What had started out being adventurous had turned violent and scary. I couldn't breathe as his thick hands grasped my throat tightly. His hard knee on my crotch was hurting me. I kneed him repeatedly on his thigh, and as if waking up from a state, he released me. His eyes widened, and an expression of surprise and annoyance appeared with the redness in his face.

"What the fuck, Tom?" I screamed when I found my voice again. Blood rushed back into my limbs as I fell to the floor, gasping for breath, shaken and frightened.

"I thought you liked it," he said argumentatively.

"*No*, not like that, I did not. Fuck, you were going to kill me."

"I thought you lived on the edge, and I wanted you to have that. Come here." He grabbed me, pulling me onto his lap as he sat on the edge of the bed.

"Not like this. That was fucking mental," I cried, still shivering in fear.

"So are you. You're so fucking hot." His hands stroked my body, enticing me back to the bed. We did the deed. I was not into it anymore, but I was afraid of what might happen if I resisted. I held back my fear and allowed it to happen, my eyes wide open as my body bounced on the bed. I had my eyes locked on the bedroom door—my exit. Immediately after he was done, I got dressed and rushed out, without looking back.

My wont for urgent sex waned after that. It was too familiar to me, even though eight years had passed since I'd woken up in that motel room. I felt sick. I was in pain and afraid. I had never pondered the possibility that I might change my mind during a situation or that any of these men would ever turn violent. I realized how lucky I had been all this time. I had always been in charge and a fair judge of character. I was in control, until I was not. Any power I once had seemed to have been erased in the brief encounter with Tom.

The experience with Tom woke me up, in a way. That was not how I wanted to die, at the hands of another demented asshole. I started thinking about what I truly wanted. I wanted the romance—the dinners and conversations. I wanted the love beyond the soiled sheets. I wanted something real. I imagined I wasn't going to find it, that I was incapable of finding it, given how I had played this game. I was practiced in the art of casual sex, and I didn't know how to get out. I knew I wouldn't find love if I didn't find the escape hatch.

CHAPTER 6

"We're at the large intersection by McDonald's," said David, Sophia's friend from America. David and three other friends were on a great Southeast Asia adventure, stopping in Kuala Lumpur for a few days. I had just gotten off work and was not looking forward to showing them around as I'd promised Sophia. She was in America and had extended them the offer of her best friend showing them around her home country. The plan was street food and a bar.

David described himself as "a black guy in glasses and shorts," who was with "three white guys." They were easy to spot because not many people hung out at that busy intersection between roads going in four different directions. Nevertheless, it was a good landmark in chaotic downtown Kuala Lumpur. David jumped into the passenger seat and introduced himself. He then introduced Matthew, Daniel, and Patrick. They each called out their names along with hellos and slid into the back seat of my car. They had an upbeat vibe, excited to be exploring a foreign destination. I looked in the rearview mirror and saw beautiful blue eyes looking back at me. I turned around, and there he was in the middle seat, smiling sweetly. His eyes were wide, and he wore a gray baseball hat with a star on it. He was happy to be there, and my sour mood lifted.

I drove them downtown for a definitively Malaysian gastronomic experience. We walked down a street neatly lined with countless trucks loaded with fruits. People walked by and made their purchases right from the drivers. The durian, a green thorny fruit called "the king of fruits," got a lot of attention from my new friends. When people tasted the yellow custardy flesh of the fruit, they reacted one of two ways: they either loved it or gagged. I was tickled by the guys' reaction to the smell, which could beat your worst milk fart. I called out the names of the local fruits as we walked past. They were nice, well-mannered guys, and I liked their accents. There were two Brits and two Americans, all of whom worked for the same company in Japan. I got goosebumps whenever Daniel, one of the Americans, caught up with me to ask something. His voice was honey, and we had an immediate chemistry, an attraction so strong I felt butterflies in my chest. This was something I hadn't experienced with other men. Perhaps it was the fact that I'd told myself these guys were off-limits. They were Sophia's friends, and I didn't want to tarnish her reputation by being loosey-goosey with them. However, the taboo only made the attraction stronger. Daniel wasn't just interested in the city and the food. He was curious about what I did for a living, where I lived, and how I knew Sophia. He knew a little bit about everything as he described Japan and living in Nagoya. The world melted away. I felt the isolation, but this time he was in the bubble with me.

We had a good Chinese dinner on plastic tables outside. My guests were amused by the red plastic chairs right there on the street and how the cars and motorcycles whizzed past while we slurped our noodles. We talked about the next few days, and I was excited to be part of their plans. I wanted to spend more time with Daniel.

The five of us enjoyed a night of drinks, shots, dancing, and more laughing. We dropped Daniel's friends off at their hotel, and I couldn't resist the pull. I asked Daniel if he would spend more time with me that night. Thoughts of Sophia dissipated.

It was, at first, just another fling as I'd have with any man at a club. But I saw something more in him. I really liked him, and I allowed myself to fantasize what it would be like to be with him. I knew he would be leaving in a few days, so I decided to just enjoy the next two days with him. We explored Kuala Lumpur, and I basked in his charm. I had been telling myself to live in the present, so I vowed to enjoy any time I had with him entirely. But I knew there was something special about him, about how I felt when I was with him. He was not like the other expats or travelers; we were connected by my best friend. He was someone who'd been vetted to some extent, through Sophia. He was a good guy, one of her friends, not a total stranger or some pickup at the bar. I wanted to be with him in a real relationship, but I didn't know how to make that happen. I had done the same thing with him that I had done with those other men. I hoped that our night together would not change his interest in me or cause him to view me as just a fling. There was still a possibility this could be something real, but I dared not indulge too deeply in the fantasy for fear of being hurt.

The second night they were visiting was also the night I was to move out of my apartment and back in with my parents. Kate had left a month earlier, and I couldn't afford the place on my own. My mother had hired movers, and she was delighted I was moving back home. My parents had not approved of me moving out, though they tolerated it because they had no choice. My relationship with them had distanced, and we had settled into something cordial. I called every so often to check in and let them know I was all right. The weekly coffee dates with my parents had to be enough to pacify them.

My mother was eager for more time together, so she jumped at the chance to spend the day with me, even if it was moving day.

That morning, I waited anxiously for the movers. I was supposed to be going out with Daniel that evening. When they arrived, I was shocked and annoyed at my mother. I asked her what she was thinking when she hired them. They were a husband-and-wife duo in their eighties.

"I couldn't see them on the phone when I spoke to her," my mother responded, trying very hard not to laugh as we both watched them move around the room.

The wife hunched over, her bony fingers wagging at all my stuff. The husband was more spirited but was skin and bones. He walked around, nodding and mumbling to himself, as his wife pointed and shouted. She called out instructions and yelled aggressively in Hokkien for her husband to move the fridge. There were no trolleys or back straps—this lady was planning on pushing the fridge onto his back. My mother and I exchanged a wide-eyed look. This was unreal. The wife then walked to my room, pointed at the dresser, and shouted at my mother and me to carry it.

Suddenly, I was overcome by an incredible laughing fit. I couldn't hold it in. My mother asked the couple to go relax and wait in their truck while we figured out what to do next. As soon as they hobbled out the door, my mother laughed so hard she cried. She told me that she had just called a number from the paper and had no idea what she was getting. We laughed together for the first time in a long time. I longed to be in this space with her just a little bit longer, free of the guilt and shame that had been heavy on me for so many years. I made a quick list of people I could call to enlist some help. I called up my friends, but not a single person was available. Out of desperation, I called Daniel. He arrived at my apartment within the hour. We carried that refrigerator to the elevator and down to the truck. We did the same with all the furniture until the apartment was empty. I said goodbye to the apartment that had been my home for the past year. Daniel came with me to my parents' house to unload the furniture. We were both drenched in sweat. I changed quickly out of my sweaty clothes, skipping a well-needed shower so I wouldn't hold Daniel up. I took him to a tapas bar downtown, as he fancied a beer after the manual labor. "This one's on me," I said when the bill came.

He smiled. "You really don't have to. I was entirely happy to help. I did say you only had to ask and I'd be there." He was so lovely and kind. How was it possible someone could be so genuinely nice? I wasn't taking no for an answer and took care of the check. He was joyful through it all, and that drew me to him even more. I was compelled to stay in that bubble with him. I had never met someone so steady, stable, and kind. I desperately wanted all of that. I wanted it to rub off on me.

The next leg of their trip would be backpacking and trekking across the Javanese island, ending in Bali. I listened with envy and sadness. This would have been the end of my short time with Daniel if he hadn't invited me to meet them in Bali. I didn't even have to think about it. I accepted immediately.

～

In Bali a few days later, Daniel and I broke away from the group and got our own hotel. We rented a moped, which Daniel insisted he knew how to operate. As soon as he revved the engine, we ran into a wall, which made me laugh very hard. I was discovering joy that had been hiding deep in the darkness. I hadn't known how to access it, but with Daniel, it surfaced. We did all the touristy things together.

I held tight to him on the moped, my body against his, the Balinese wind in my hair. I pressed my face up against his back, and I could hear his heartbeat, soft and calm. After watching the traditional Balinese *Kecak* dance at the famous temple in Uluwatu, we went back to our room. He listened intently as I shared the great love story of Rama and Sita, a story I knew from my childhood. His eyes were so soft, and it didn't feel uncomfortable to stare straight into them. I felt safe in his gaze; I felt whole. I willed myself not to future trip about the inevitable end of our fling. I reminded myself to live in those little heartbeat moments.

On our third afternoon in Bali, we got in from the beach and relaxed in preparation for a night with Daniel's friends. We chatted as he folded his dirty laundry and repacked it. I watched this in amusement, enjoying how he was constantly in motion but also perfectly calm. I had never met anyone like him. He paused and then said, "My mother is everything to me. She's everything I've got, and I love her more than anything in the world."

Who is this man standing here? He must have been born of the angels. I wanted in on that kind of love he had, how he had no inhibitions in declaring his feelings about his mother. I asked him to tell me more about her. He shared some of the challenges she'd faced as a single mother and how she raised him to be the man he is. *Oh please— love me back. Please love me back and be with me. Please love me.*

That night, we hopped from bar to bar with Daniel's friends, who had also become my friends. The clubbing scene in Bali was out of this world—we drank fishbowls of Long Island Iced Tea, beers, and shots. We saw people dancing in human-sized birdcages, a fire-eating man, and drag queens in their magnificent dresses and makeup. There were live bands and DJs, and music blared out of the clubs, bars, and restaurants. We walked past street performers. In front of the businesses, we saw the little baskets woven from coconut leaves and filled with offerings of flowers for the Hindu gods.

Daniel's hand squeezed mine as we walked. The next day would be our last together. My heart sank a little lower with each squeeze, made worse only by his smile. We wandered through the streets, taking in the beautiful night sky and music booming around us. That night, as we were dancing under the Balinese moon, Daniel pulled me close. As his soft lips pulled away from a deep kiss, he whispered, "I love you."

I met him with another kiss. "I love you." My heart knew the familiarity of his love, as if we'd been two souls in this world looking for each other, finally found.

I told him about that night at the motel eight years earlier, certain he would think I was damaged. I wanted to see if he would still accept me, if he could really be so good. And even when he was that good, I couldn't understand his acceptance of my rotten indiscretion.

"It's not your fault," he said. "What happened was awful, and it is not your fault." It was a shock to hear that. He held me tightly. Though it would take me years to believe the truth, his reassurance brought a quiet to my soul. I was not as pure as he was, and I didn't feel worthy, but I allowed myself to want him. I was damaged goods, and I blamed myself for what had happened. I had been stupid enough to make a mistake that had destroyed everything. As much as I wanted to be loved by Daniel, I struggled to reconcile whether I even deserved that kind of love.

As the night progressed, we drank without any limits. It got harder for me to maintain my composure. Bars often triggered my trauma of that night, but this time it was different because of Daniel. It had been eight years since the incident, but it stuck to me like starving leeches on an open wound. The musky smell of one of the clubs brought back disgusting flashbacks. I lashed out and lost control, breaking into a rage about something incomprehensible. No one understood, but Daniel was steady and loving. He walked me back to the hotel, comforted me, and tucked me in. As I lay in bed that night, I felt disappointment in myself and embarrassment. I believed I'd ruined my chances of ever being with Daniel, no matter how much I wanted it.

The next day we went sightseeing. It flew by, and then it was time for us to part. Leaving Bali would prove to be agonizing for both of us. The realization that we would be apart indefinitely was more than I could bear. We sat at the airport, hands clasped, having our last coffee together. Was this the end of our love affair? I was besotted with him. The intensity of the love I felt was something I didn't understand. We'd only spent six days together, but the world around us had disintegrated when he looked at me. I had lost my way for all those years, and now I was finally here. I'd found home in Daniel. How were we supposed to leave each other? We locked in a tight embrace. I sunk into his chest to breathe him in one last time, and we parted ways.

~

I was still skeptical about an actual relationship. I wanted a relationship that I could feel loved in and share the love I had to give. I wanted to be myself entirely. I had never been in a relationship like that. My last long-term relationship was with a man who hit me and berated me. Daniel and I both wanted to see each other again, but we didn't know how to proceed. We called and texted each other after he left. We agreed that I'd come visit him in Japan.

About three weeks after Bali, I boarded a flight to Nagoya. I stayed about two weeks and absolutely loved it. We enjoyed being in each other's company in the same house. He had a roomy, Western-style, three-bedroom house to himself, which meant there were amenities common to a Western home as one would find in America or Kuala Lumpur. He had a full-size dishwasher, full-size stove, full-size oven, washer, and dryer, all of which were uncommon in Japanese homes. He used the master bedroom and had the other two rooms for closet space. I thought he would get sick of me, but he didn't. He introduced me to all of his friends, a network of expatriates living in Nagoya.

On my first weekend, we celebrated Daniel's friend's birthday with a picnic at a park. It was a beautiful sunny day. Some of his friends had biked to the park. They began "throwing the ol' pigskin" around, which I tried, even though I had never seen an American football before. There was music blaring from a speaker next to a grill manned by some of Daniel's friends. I felt welcome and included. I craved this kind of friendship, being part of a group like this, which was something I hadn't experienced since being abandoned in college.

All of Daniel's friends were curious about me and asked lots of questions about Malaysia. It was beautiful and surreal to be part of the group. I could feel their love for each other, a strong connection that's often forged by expats living away from home. They were easy with each other and welcomed me. I was so grateful, and I didn't want to risk losing this. I watched them like a scene from a movie—a good old American cookout. Everyone was smiling and drinking beers around the grill. Some of us sat on a picnic blanket on the grass, sharing sandwiches.

One of the girls, Sara, introduced herself to me. She invited me to have coffee with her the next day while Daniel was at work. I liked her immediately, and we set up a meeting point at a little café in downtown Nagoya.

The next morning, I went on the train and managed to find my way to the café. Navigating Nagoya with no knowledge of the language was possible, and I felt proud of myself for figuring it out. The café was cute, with an elaborate cake display and only three tables. I walked in to find Sara already there, and I was immediately nervous. After Kate left, I hadn't hung out with any girlfriends. I realized how much I missed having a friend like this. Sara and I launched straight into conversation as if we were old friends. We talked about Shanghai, where she had visited several years ago. We talked about all the sights in Nagoya, my family, and my background.

Over the next few days, I met up with Sara every day while Daniel worked. Her husband worked as an engineer at the same company as Daniel. She kept busy during the day, exploring and taking ikebana classes, the art of Japanese floral arrangement. She showed me around Nagoya, and we became fast friends. I hadn't trusted many people and been open to new friendships since everyone had turned on me. Even Kate, my closest friend, had ultimately left. With Sara, I felt acutely conscious that I was waiting for the other shoe to drop. But as the days passed, I realized she had no hidden agenda. We had dinners with the rest of our friends, and I felt like part of the crew. In the meantime, I fell even more in love with Daniel. When it came time to leave Japan, I realized I was going to miss more than just Daniel. I was going to miss Sara and the group of friends I had come to love.

I returned home to Malaysia feeling torn. It was torture to be apart from Daniel. I'd stepped into a life I wanted. After Japan, Daniel visited me a couple of times in Malaysia. He stayed in a separate room at my parents' house, and the visits exceeded my expectations. My parents loved and accepted him because I was so happy. "He's a good boy, raised well," my father remarked. My father's approval made me even more invested in the relationship. But I still held on to each trip as if it would be our last. Finally, after about three months, Daniel asked me to move to Japan to live with him. There was no question in my mind that I would accept his offer.

Still, it was scary as hell. I had travelled since I was a child and had always wanted to live abroad, but the prospect of moving in with Daniel proved to be nerve-racking. There was so much at stake, and I wanted it all to be perfect. I did not want to lose him. I was afraid that living with him would bring to light all the ugliness in me and he would change his mind. But at the same time, the choice to leave Malaysia wasn't difficult. I loved my family dearly, but I had distanced myself from them. I hated being around my family because of how I acted when I was around them. I yearned for things to go back to how they were, but I was powerless to be different. Going to Japan seemed to be a way to redeem myself, to be rid of my past and create a future on a clean slate.

The thrill of being with Daniel called loudly. With Daniel, there was none of the desperation I'd felt in previous relationships, none of the emptiness that trailed every one of those nightly engagements. There was a peace, and everything just made sense. Right from the start, I felt it was meant for me and that was to be my home.

~

Daniel and I spent many nights on Skype with me in tears. "Are we doing the right thing?" I asked.

He was always calm and confident. "Of course, we are. We're taking a chance. I understand your hesitation, but we have to try. Don't you think?"

"What if you find me dreadful, and I would have upended my life to be there?"

"Well, what if you find *me* dreadful? But, baby, what if it's beautiful, like we've imagined? We'd miss out." His words warmed my heart, but I was still apprehensive, much more about myself than about him.

"Okay, how about we give it a go, and if at any point at all you change your mind, I'll make sure you get home safely? I promise I'll never keep you here, stuck in something you don't want, and I won't just abandon you." In reality, not much would have changed in the worst-case scenario. I would live with my parents again. I would have a job with my parents waiting for me, a job they had been trying to convince me to take for years.

I pondered this for weeks while waiting on my visitor's visa approval. As much as I wanted to be with him, the idea of screwing everything up still ate at me. One night, I was at a club in Kuala Lumpur when an acquaintance offered some wisdom.

"Why are you afraid?" he asked.

"What if it doesn't work out? What if everything I was dreaming of falls apart?"

"Come home. This is home. Your family is here. Don't be afraid. Don't miss out on trying something because you're afraid. If anything should ever go south, you come home. Enjoy your life; you only get one." He said it so plainly, and I knew what he said was the truth. I could take the leap of faith, knowing I had a safety net.

~

Two months after that trip to Japan, I quit my job, tied up loose ends, and packed my bags to give our love a chance. I said goodbye to my parents as if I were leaving indefinitely, and they were happy for me. My father assured me that everything would be all right and made me promise to keep in touch. My father had let his guard down. He was making a huge concession in his support of me living with Daniel.

This was unheard of in my family. None of us had lived together with a partner unmarried.

But I had been miserable for so many years, and they saw it. They saw a spark in me when I was with Daniel, and it made them reconsider their conservative views. They liked Daniel and trusted he would keep me safe and, more importantly, keep me happy.

I didn't yet have a job in Japan, and I would need one to secure a working visa, which allowed for a longer stay than a visitor's visa. I didn't speak Japanese, so I figured I'd try to teach English. Everyone warned me that it would be difficult to get a job, much less a visa, unless you came from a country where English was the native tongue. I told myself I would just try, and I prayed to the powers that be to ease my way. Within a week, I had lined up interviews with jobs that I found online. The following week, I had an offer that came with sponsorship of my working visa. With that, I was able to unpack my bags and claim closet and counter space. I was officially in this relationship.

I settled in. I got used to our weekly hangouts with the big group of expat friends. While I was getting assurances from my friends, Daniel was getting warnings. At a bar one night, I overheard someone advising caution: "Be careful. These kinds of girls, they only want you as a ticket out." *Ticket out of where? Have you seen where I come from?* I loved everything about the home I'd left behind. Kuala Lumpur is a metropolis and melting pot of international cultures. I had a great life that had afforded me travels around the world. My family was a wholesome one, even though I had taken a step away from them. I found myself feeling defensive, but of course this person knew nothing about me. He didn't know what I was running away from. But his words did bring about a realization. I *was* running away—from myself and my mistakes.

Some cautioned Daniel because they were sure he was falling too hard and too fast and that I was going to break his heart. This was a different picture than what I had seen on my short trip before. They were all so kind and welcoming then. Now that there was serious commitment in our relationship, it felt like I wasn't deserving of a place at their table. I was hurt but held it inside. As much as it hurt, there was a benefit. In light of people's reaction to us being together, Daniel and I had more clear discussions about what we wanted. He knew what he wanted, and he was certain that he loved me, even before I understood what that meant. The caution from his friends had little effect. He just carried on being himself with me as he had been from the day we met. I would learn that about him in time. He was a man of few words, but he showed his feelings tenfold in his actions. His friends couldn't help but witness this love we had for each other. In a short time, any doubts they had were erased. This was the real thing.

Daniel introduced me to his mother via Skype as soon as I moved in with him, and we became fast friends. She was accepting and loving, welcoming me into the family and even sending gifts for me in her care packages from America. Sometimes she called just to speak to me while Daniel was at work, and we chatted like old friends. She gave me the assurance I longed for, as I knew she was the only one whose opinion Daniel cared about. The love from his mother lessened the sting from his friends' doubts. She offered the kind of warmth I had always longed for from my mother. I had kept so much from my mother that our relationship was strained beyond comprehension. She missed me and I missed her, but I couldn't be myself around her. With Daniel's mother, it was always easy. She accepted me for who I was. I took comfort in her nurturing. The love that she had for me felt real. She treated me as if I were her own, just because her son loved me.

Daniel and I spent more time with each other alone. I discovered more of myself, free from the influence of expectations, reputation, and perceptions that had once plagued me. Here, next to my Daniel, I was myself. We enjoyed time together doing mundane things, such as watching TV. I was happy to discover that we both liked *Chuck*, a hilarious TV series. It was about a geek from an electronics store who had the whole national intelligence classified files downloaded into his mind, and he suddenly possessed spy skills. I did not know another person who watched that geeky show. We had this early connection as we were figuring out our new life together.

We traveled every chance we got, exploring Japan. On a drive up the mountain in Gifu on a snowy day, I realized the last time I had played in the snow was as a child on a trip with my parents to Gstaad in the Swiss Alps. That was a fond memory, and when I mentioned it to Daniel, he pulled over right away so we could get out and play. He made snowballs and laughed at me as I stuck my tongue out to taste the snow. It brought back childlike feelings of rolling in the snow with my brother. My heart was full as I took in the frozen flakes on my nose and the glistening white fluff all around us. I welcomed everything that I was experiencing with Daniel.

Of all our Japanese adventures, my favorite was about six months into my move. We drove up to Nagano to see the snow monkeys. Along the way, Daniel introduced me to old-school country music. Some of it I knew—my father was a big Dolly Parton and Garth Brooks fan. I thought about all those afternoons listening to music with Daddy on the couch, singing along, snapping our fingers. Here in the car with Daniel, I felt the same love. We laughed and sang together, and then he listened to my Florence and the Machine, and Corrine Bailey Rae, with no complaints. We both listened to Nirvana, Green Day, Sum 41, and Oasis. We relished in learning more about each other. We'd grown up across the globe from one another, and there were so many memories from our childhood that seemed to have the same sentiment. The things we enjoyed and our experiences growing up in the same pop culture drew us closer.

~

We also traveled outside of Japan, and on one of these trips, we discovered how truly aligned our values and belief systems were. It was New Year's Eve 2011. I'd been living with Daniel for almost seven months. We were about to celebrate our first New Year together and had decided to go to the island of Palawan in the Philippines. We had made friends with a local girl who worked at the bed and breakfast we were staying at. We asked to join her New Year's celebration in her fishing village. She was puzzled, but Daniel and I wanted to have a local experience. We rode in a *tuk-tuk* as she conversed in Tagalog to the driver. We were headed to get a roasted pig for the celebrations, as we were informed this would be an adequate gift for the host. It was a little unnerving to be at the hands of someone we'd just met, who was arranging our travel with another local in a language we couldn't understand. We had no idea where we were headed, and no one from home knew exactly where we were. But Daniel and I craved adventure, and we trusted our judgment.

We arrived at the village, which was a network of little wooden huts connected by long platforms over the water. It was large, the size of a little suburban neighborhood, with huts as far as we could see. It was like a whole other place, compared to the town center. We walked past huts on the platform, the sound of waves crashing, toward our new friend's house. There were unlit portions, and we had to use the light from our cell phones. People were busy getting ready for the New Year's celebrations, and we waved hello.

Some were wrapped in bath towels, coming out of the communal bathroom.

It was fascinating how they lived this communal life, and I watched Daniel being friendly, respectful, and sweet to everyone. I had never been in a village like this. The wooden huts seemed tiny, with worn wooden boards making up the weathered walls. Something was striking, though. There was a warmth in the air and smiling faces everywhere we looked. Children ran sure-footed on the two-feet-wide platforms, rushing to their friends, cheering and laughing. Everyone seemed to know everyone, and there was pure joy and elation in the air amid the humble, worn surroundings. I could smell the ocean and something savory, which was coming from the house of our new friend. She went inside to inform her parents that we were there. Once we were invited in, I took inventory. There was linoleum lining the floors, and we sat in a small love seat to the left of the entrance. There was only one little bedroom in the house, with a curtain hanging in place of a door. Behind the drawn curtain, there was a bunk bed, a cupboard for clothes, and several futons stacked against the wall. Over to the far end of the room we were sitting in was a square table for dining.

When our friend came back to the front of the house, she said that her parents would be a moment. She went back to give her parents our gift of roast pig for the New Year celebration. I asked to see them, to say hello and thank them for having us. She walked me back to steps that led outside the house, and there was a very friendly, sweet, olive-skinned man. He had dark wavy hair that reached his ears. He smiled with a cigarette in the corner of his mouth, revealing the gap where a tooth used to be. Daniel said hello and Happy New Year to our friend's father. "Manigung Bagung Taun!" I called out to him, showing all the Tagalog I had learned to impress the locals. He laughed, surely amused at my well-wishing. He grabbed a dish and motioned for us to go back in the house. We were offered some local delicacy, and Daniel tried it without a beat. The gesture impressed me. He didn't hesitate to eat something that we had no idea about, so that we didn't offend our hosts. In my book, his show of respect earned points. He was a traveler like I was, trying to feel at home and to learn about other cultures outside our own. This openness to humanity is what I had longed for in my own explorations. I loved learning about others beyond the stereotypes. I looked to understand our differences and the beauty of our similarities. I loved that he felt the same. Later during this same trip, he would join me in eating raw woodworms that the locals were smoking out of the wood. I was a huge Andrew Zimmern fan and liked trying peculiar food. I was impressed when he even ate worms without hesitation.

We had the best time. We trekked the platforms to another part of the village and danced under the moonlight on the basketball court with the children. We sang karaoke out in the courtyard. I couldn't remember the last time I'd felt this much joy, especially watching Daniel dance and laugh with the children. The next day, he talked about how grateful he was for that experience, to be with that community, free from our material notions.

Our constant pursuit of lofty material gains, which were supposed to constitute happiness, was so far from what we had just experienced. Unclouded by material pursuits, with so little at their disposal, the villagers welcomed us in joy. Our preconceived notion—that to have more possessions would equal more joy—was beaten flat by the generosity and warmth of the villagers. They included us in their celebration as if we'd known each other all our lives. Daniel and I bonded over this revelation, and we'd come back to this precious moment in the years to come. We wanted the same thing: a life of gratitude, joy, and appreciation for each other.

~

We had so few notable cultural differences other than our specific cuisines. I loved cooking, and he enjoyed everything I made. My Malaysian food appealed to him. He was from Louisiana, so he was accustomed to spicy foods, thank goodness. I attempted to make some classic Southern food one night, but what was supposed to be meatloaf looked and probably tasted like canned dog food. I failed at that first attempt, but he just smothered it in ketchup and finished it.

Daniel and I hosted friends a lot while we lived in Japan. When I dressed up, he whispered, "You look lovely." He would kiss my fore-head, and I felt like I was the most important person in the world. After a dinner party, we'd sit on the couch with a beer. He'd comb my hair with his fingers and smile. "I think that went well. You did great, baby." It was the kind of love that I had only seen in movies or books, the kind that people fantasize about. I was living a fairy tale with him.

When we were together, I felt powerful. He challenged me to be adventurous. When we climbed Mount Fuji together, he stood by me as I struggled to meet the mental and physical challenge. Sara, my closest friend by then, and her husband came on the climb with us. I hadn't been very active in those years and I'd also been a chronic smoker, so the climb proved to be a challenge. We joked, and he allowed me moments of whining and a few curse words. But then, three-quarters of the way up, I found the drive to get to the top. Once we'd scaled the side of the mountain and I realized I'd done it, I felt invincible, playful, and adventurous—all the feelings I had forgotten. As we sat on the mountaintop staring at the horizon, with the red sun sinking into pink and yellow clouds, gratitude washed over me. I thanked the mountain for this experience. I was slowly gaining back my confidence and strength, one experience at a time.

We went skydiving, something I thought I'd never be brave enough to do. It was comical but scary. Before we reached jumping altitude, our tandem divers attached themselves to us. I looked around the plane. We were seated in a row. I was the farthest inward, my back against the pilot's seat, and Daniel was next to me. We howled, cheered, and laughed. The higher the ascent, the quieter we got. All we heard was the hum of the propellers and engine. I was getting nervous every time I looked at the gaping hole in the plane. In a few minutes I would somehow will myself to jump. The tree canopy and the concrete jungle below us looked like a child's train table, miniscule. I turned to look at Daniel but was distracted by his tandem jumper doing the sign of the cross over and over. I stared at him.

'Why are you doing that?" I asked sternly.

"I'm Christian," he replied nonchalantly.

"But why do you do it over and over again like that? Are you afraid?" I was starting to get concerned for my boyfriend.

"Yes," he answered.

"What? Why? Isn't this your job? Don't you do this every day?" I was genuinely worried now.

"Not every day. But I have jumped 846 times. Today will be 847. I pray like this every time."

I appreciated his explanation, but I also found it overly cautious and overly religious. It didn't instill the kind of confidence I needed for Daniel to be strapped to him.

My turn came. As soon as I looked out the door, my heart dropped. I tried to hold onto the airplane but was pushed off by my tandem jumper. A bloodcurdling scream came out of me. A year earlier, I had wanted to jump off a building. Today, I did not want to die. I wanted to be in Daniel's love forever. Once I jumped, I was overcome by the experience of free falling, but I wasn't falling; I was flying. I was floating and gliding in the sky. I was free. I was whole. That scream was a release, one of many I needed to free myself. I was living every moment. I was letting go of all the things that had held me back from experiencing this beautiful life.

Sometimes you fall into something you never expected, only to realize that it's everything you ever needed. This was my new life with Daniel. There was now "before Daniel" and "with Daniel." I was finally alive. I was seen again. I was treated with respect, reverence, love, and kindness.

I believe in the universe responding to my calls. I had never felt such a love. I can recognize lust, I enjoy infatuation, and I require adoration in romance. But Daniel—he was all these things and something I couldn't put my finger on, something unique to us, for which I would be forever grateful. I had been longing for this feeling of being whole, with no tattered ends. I could finally imagine what my future might look like. No one had ever offered me this possibility before, and now the path was clear. There was hope on the horizon.

CHAPTER 7

The bleakness followed me like a dark shadow. No matter how good my life was, a sense of dread haunted me. Daniel's presence put a lot of it at bay for me with the calm he brought. But I still couldn't escape the hollow grief. By the time I'd been in Japan a month or so, it led to incessant suicidal ideation, which I was helpless to control.

Daniel didn't know the extent to which I was detached from the world, but that year he bore the weight of my pain. He watched me break down so many times. My choices pushed him into a corner, making him unable to deny the pain I was going through. I romanticized the notion of disappearing to the point that it began to fill my days. Like a weightless zombie, however, I carried on.

For the previous eight years, I had toyed with the idea of making good on my intent to disappear. The first time, I'd attempted to hang myself near campus with my pashmina. The second incident had occurred when I stood at the windowsill of my seventeenth-floor apartment.

This was before Kate moved out, and I was home alone. I was ready. I had one last cigarette. I flicked the butt out the window to watch it spin down seventeen floors with the wind. It was pretty, like one of those spinner leaves. I watched it disappear, my mind a complete blank. A peace came over me, almost lifting me off the windowsill. My right foot stepped forward, but just then my bedroom door opened, and I jumped back and landed on my bed.

"What is happening, Amy? Are you okay? Are you not okay? Are you okay not okay?" That was something Kate and I had come up with to say, "It's okay not to be okay, but I have it under control."

I was definitely not okay. "Yeah, I'm fine. Why are you home?"

Kate started sobbing. "I can't do this. I'm worried about you. I can't work. I can't be at peace. I'm so worried about you."

I stared down at her black pumps while she spoke, avoiding her gaze.

"You've been out of control, and I don't know how to help you. You're so sad all the time. What is going on?" She tried to engage me, but I didn't know what to say.

"I don't know," was all I managed, tears in my eyes.

It was divine intervention that she was even there. My heart was racing. I was trying to breathe. I stared at her as she turned around to set her purse on the kitchen counter. We talked, for what seemed to be forever, about my misbehavior and her concern.

"I'm okay, just a little down. I needed some time to myself is all." I saw a look of disgust on her face, blaming me for how this whole stint had gone to shit.

"You're always locked in your room, skipping out on work so much lately—what are you going to do? You can't be drinking and partying to no end. This is real life." She was scared. I could see it in her eyes.

"I don't know."

Living with me was the worst idea she had ever had, she said. I had no doubt that she was right. A few weeks later, Kate ended the lease to our apartment, packed, and left without a word. She had to look out for herself, and I was poison.

I comforted myself with the reminder that this was best for me too. But in other moments, I hated her. I didn't have a say in ending the lease. She had come to pick up her stuff and left me in a lurch. But I couldn't imagine the constant strain she had been living with, watching me waste away. She had lost respect for me. *Why am I still here? Why did she have to come home? Why didn't I just fall forward instead of back when that door opened? How did I lose that perfect opportunity to leave all this pain and certain future pain? Why am I being punished?* Because I did terrible things. It was me. I was forced to trudge through the quicksand, which kept sucking me in but never suffocated me.

~

In Japan, though I was oceans away from home, I heard the same call to death. Kate had watched me descend into pain and self-destruction as Daniel now was. Living with me, Daniel got ringside seats to watch me battle my demons. I recognized the weight of it all on him because I had already seen Kate go through it. I wanted what I had with him to last forever, but I couldn't help the destruction that dragged me from the pain of my past.

During the year since I'd left home, I stayed in contact with no one other than my parents and Uncle Bala. I talked to Uncle Bala to try to understand why my life was so messed up and how I was supposed to live through the pain. He never directly addressed the source of pain but treated it for what it was. With him, all that mattered was that I was upset, and he wanted me to feel better. Uncle Bala was a spiritual man. He believed in karma, meditation, and divine life. We talked about higher purpose, the scar to the soul if I took my life, and karmic hurt.

He assured me, "Don't dwell. The universe has a plan for you, ma.

None of us are insignificant. We all are precious, but how will you use your presence here? You will find it."

I felt like a child again every time he said "ma," an endearment from when I was a little girl living with my grandmother.

"I can't," I said, sobbing.

"Maybe now what you need is rest, ma, just rest. It will be okay. Take a break and reconnect with your inner self. Meditate." He had always sought peace in solitude. He believed you could hear your inner voice if you could free yourself of noise.

I didn't yet understand, and the noise from my self-loathing was like a jackhammer to the brain. I was alone and suffering, and though Uncle Bala was lighting the path, I could not see it. He would tell me he was praying for me. He would encourage me to meditate. He said I was going to be okay. *Why would he pray for me?* Prayers are for those who ought to be helped. But I was rotten to the core, and the pain I carried was a penance.

I wanted to believe what he told me, that I just needed to hold on. "Hold on. You're okay, ma. Nothing is wrong. You're okay." Sometimes he would talk to Daniel. He knew the toll my state would take on people who cared for me. He assured Daniel of his support and asked for him to hang in there, promising I was a good girl and that it would be worth it. Daniel promised him, as he had promised my father, that he would take care of me no matter what.

Many times, I thought the pain would leave now that Daniel took up such a big space in my heart. I was convinced that, because of Daniel, there would be no place for the pain to live. I was wrong, however—the pain *was* me. There was nowhere for it to go. It was relentless. The thoughts of escaping into the next world took hold of me sometimes. Daniel was on edge, and though he was steadfast in his commitment, I could see him wearing down. He wanted to be the cure, but he didn't know how, and this strained our relationship. We were constantly fighting. Each time, I imagined that whatever silly thing we were arguing over, usually instigated by me, would end our relationship.

~

The first month I was in Japan, we went to a party at David's apartment downtown. We were drinking. I'd had a cocktail and was nursing my second one. I was hanging out with Patrick, Matthew, and Daniel's other friends, and we were planning to go to a bar. I found comfort in Patrick's company. He was one of the few who had made me feel welcomed and seemed truly excited about me moving there. It was 9:00 p.m. when something came over me. My head was so heavy, and my heart was pounding. My eyes darted around the room. Everyone was staring at me. Everyone knew my darkest secrets. A huge wave of heavy emotion came over me. It was guilt and shame. I was going to be found out. They were going to know I was rotten. My eyes went wide, and I stumbled my way to the first door I saw. It was hard to put one foot in front of the other when the whole world was spinning. I didn't know what was on the other side, but I walked in anyway. It was the laundry room. My chest was tight and I couldn't breathe. I was so scared. I wanted to yell "Help!" but couldn't speak.

"Amy, baby, can you hear me?" I could hear the voice, but he was so far away. I was crying, but I didn't know why. It took a second for me to realize where I was. My eyes opened to his thumb moving over my cheeks.

"Are you okay? What are you doing here? I've been looking for you." It was Daniel, and he was speaking so softly. I was on the floor in a fetal position. I got up and fell into his chest, my face pressed desperately against him. His warmth covered me.

"Breathe," he said. I did.

"I'm sorry. I'm so sorry." I instantly felt humiliated. What was wrong with me?

"I embarrassed you. I'm so sorry."

"No, you didn't. I was worried when I couldn't find you."

"I want to go home to my parents. I can't do this. I know you don't want to be with me."

"Don't say that. I've never even thought that."

I glanced at his phone—11:30 p.m. That couldn't be right. Patrick's voice was clear in my head. *We'll leave at about ten, ten-thirty, yeah? 'Bout an hour?*

Daniel verified this. "I went to the club because I thought you headed out without me. Then someone said they saw you here, so I came back for you."

Someone saw me here? I did it again. Everything was going so well, and here I was, destroying everything. I was Midas with a shit touch.

"Amy, tell me what happened? Do we need a doctor?"

The mention of that was enough to make me scream, "No! No doctors! I am absolutely fine. You just want to call doctors so you can get rid of me. Just tell me if you want me to leave. I'll leave."

I recognized his look of disdain. He surely wanted out, but he was a good guy, and he wasn't about to abandon me. He didn't take the bait and didn't want to escalate the situation, so he walked me off the fight train.

"All right. Let's just call it a night and get some rest. David said we can sleep upstairs." I followed, still sobbing. I didn't know what had happened, but at least this time I didn't wake up to the smell of sweat and moldy carpet. That was the first time I could recall blacking out, losing a full two hours. It's like I disappeared and left my body.

This was worrisome, but I didn't need anyone else worrying about it. I kept my worry a secret, buried with all the other nasty secrets.

~

On my own, I often went into that zone of emptiness. About two months after the first blackout, I was at the subway station. I was subbing for another teacher in a town about an hour away. It would take two trains to get there, and it was not a very popular stop, so the platforms were quiet. I looked around. I took in the smells, sounds, and the rush of the wind as trains zoomed past. My body swayed, and my eyes locked on the katakana in the poster on the other side of the tracks. "Bee-koo ka-may-ra," I whispered. I was remembering more and more characters. I had to learn it all myself, with a little help from our friend Takeshi.

I stumbled a little as the next train left the platform, until I was standing beyond the yellow line, too far. *Back up,* my mind said. My feet were planted firm. I looked up and saw the guy with the flag that instructed everyone where to stand. He was at least three hundred feet down the platform. *He wouldn't get to me in time.* I looked down at the lightning bolts in the tracks—a voltage warning. If I timed it just right, it would be over in a blink. I would be done. I looked at the digital screen hanging ahead: Fuso 11:26. That was in six minutes. *This is it,* I thought. Everyone would be free of me if I just fell into the subway track.

My phone rang. I didn't want to answer, but I checked anyway. It was Daniel. I should say goodbye. That was the right thing to do— one decent thing before I left.

"Hello? Babe?" he said. My heart melted.

"I love you so much, more than I have ever loved anyone," I said, to make sure he knew.

"Well, I love you too. Where are you now?" he asked.

"I love you." I said, sobbing. "I'm sorry."

"I love you so much. Please talk to me. Please. Talk to me. Where are you? Please." He pushed on with a heavy desperation.

"I'm going—goodbye." I was looking at the screen: 11:25.

It was time. I heard the roar, the whistles, and the loud whooshing that preceded the train. I could hear Daniel's voice and felt my pulse slow down. Everything slowed down. My body was light, and I felt liberated, my eyes fixated on the tunnel. I saw the light on the tunnel wall. There was a loud ringing in my ear, and I stumbled backward, landing flat on my ass. *What the fuck was that?* There was the flag guy, whistling at me, flags in hand. He was flailing every which way, motioning to the yellow line, his eyes angry. *Did he know?*

The light on the phone screen was on. Daniel was still there, frantic and in tears. "Where are you, Amy? Please! Where are you? Please answer me. Please, God, please. Please don't do anything stupid."

"I'm here. I'm here," I said, crying uncontrollably. My body sunk onto the tiles of the subway platform. *How am I so bad at this? Why am I here again?*

"I didn't do it. I'm going to catch the next train," I told him. I looked up at the screen again: Fuso 11:36. What a fuckup.

I wasn't dead, and now I was late. I would be in trouble when I finally got to work. Daniel was still on the line, and I felt uncomfortable and humiliated. What could I say? Most would consider what I had just attempted really dumb, dumber still that I didn't manage it.

"I'm sorry. I'll see you at home." I tried to rush him off the line.

"No, I'm going to stay on the line with you 'til you get on the train." And that's what we did, in silence. All the sounds of the subway station came through the phone to let him know that I was

still standing and not decimated on the track. I boarded the next
train.

"I love you. Bye," I said.

"Bye," he said.

Click.

~

The day came when I was sure it was happening. I'd pushed him so
far that I knew he would throw his hands up and leave. We'd been
living together for almost four months and learning more about each
other's habits. We were arguing about dishes in the sink, the laundry
piled in the bedroom, and my clothes all over the bedroom floor. I
was embarrassed and angry because I hated being called out. He was
furious, but his version of furious is firm, calm, and never shaming.
I was the opposite, and you best believe I was an overachiever in this
arena. It was almost like his calmness was a trigger. He didn't have to
shout or be vulgar; when he spoke, his words stabbed twice as deep,
with jagged edges.

I stormed out of the house and got on the subway. I didn't know
where I was going. I texted David. He lived downtown, and we had
become good friends. I met him downtown at our regular expat
bar. We sat and chatted. He asked me to call and let Daniel know I
was safe. I refused, wanting Daniel to worry about me. I was testing
him again, to see if he really wanted me. When David pulled out
his phone to text Daniel, I was disappointed and angry, but I kept
it together. We chatted over beers. I told him everything about the
fight but omitted the part where I had not done my part in the house.
I instead listed things that showed me in a favorable light, such as
ironing Daniel's clothes and his boxers. We talked and laughed. I was
just buying time because I wanted to be as late as possible. *That will*

make him worry more and be less angry at me, right? It was a school night, and David had to be up early. Beers and wings finished, we hugged, and he walked me to the station.

I ruminated and started hyperventilating in the train. I was startled when I heard over the loudspeaker, "Hongo, Hongo." It was my stop. The doors opened, and a gust of wind filled my lungs. As I walked down the stairs, I saw Daniel's car. He was sleeping in the driver's seat. I knocked on the window and got in. No words were exchanged. I knew David had updated him on my whereabouts.

I got changed and into bed. When he joined me, he just lay there, staring at the ceiling, hands clasped and resting on his chest.

"I love you. You know that." His voice was low and raspy.

There it was. I knew this was the moment he was going to break up with me. He sat up.

"We can't go on like this. You need help." When I looked into his eyes, they were not cold or angry. I was confused because I could see warmth. "I want you to get help. Talk to someone. Please."

Should I stay or should I go? Snap, snap! The Clash tune came into my head briefly and I started to nod but then stopped abruptly. This was not funny. My world was about to end. He was my last chance. If Daniel left me, I'd have nothing left to live for.

"You want me locked up? Because that's what's going to happen," I said with conviction.

"Get help, or you're going to have to go home." He turned over.

Tell me you love me. Please—I need you to say you love me. I was waiting for it. Silence. My cheeks were warm, and there were more tears. My heart raced, and my legs shook uncontrollably. My fingers gripped my palms. A gentle pressure was on my knee, easing the shaking. "I love you," he said. "We're going to get through this. Now breathe."

A calm came over me for a moment before the guilt set in. I knew what a burden I had become. He shouldered the responsibility of keeping me safe, even from myself. This was despite all the things I did that pushed him away. The harder I pushed, the stronger he pushed back, reassuring me of his love and care for me. But I could see how worn out he had become in the past few months. He was trying to do right by me, but he didn't have the strength of a titan. It would take that amount of strength for him to carry my pain and the burden of my suicidal ideation. I was willing to get help. I knew something needed to change if I wanted to be with Daniel.

I repeatedly asked myself why Daniel was with me. Why did this amazing, ridiculously good human invite me to walk in his journey? He'd been nursing me ever since I arrived in Japan. He knew my darkest secrets. I had told him all of them to see if he really wanted to be with me. He repeatedly assured me, "I want to be with you, not your past." He told me some variation of this statement almost daily. I wanted to believe him, as much as I believed he would eventually leave me. The idea that I would eventually be abandoned came naturally to me. I had full certainty that it would happen.

～

It would be weeks before I found a doctor. The pain was relentless. I found myself in situations I didn't realize I was getting into. After the subway incident, Daniel was on guard. He alerted our friend Takeshi to be on standby in case I needed help, and that turned out to be pretty often. Takeshi's family had adopted us, and with that came all the love and concern of family. It felt almost perfect. I had family I could rely on here. They were concerned about me as if I were their own. Daniel had shared the dire state I was in and how worried he was. Takeshi promised to check in on me. All Daniel needed to do was call him. I was grateful but thoroughly embarrassed.

Meanwhile, there were days when everything seemed fine. I had a steady job I enjoyed and a weekly schedule. On my off days, I slept late. On one of these mornings, I woke up at a quarter to eleven and walked downstairs into a welcomed silence. Daniel was already at work, but he had left me coffee. I sat on the couch by the window, watching the crows nip at the garbage. I pondered my current situation. Like a broken reel that kept getting taped back together, thoughts of the past appeared in my mind. I kept a steady gaze on one crow that had managed to pull out a plastic bag. I wanted to get out of my head, but like the crow, I was pecking—pecking at my brain. Finally, I gave in. My chest tightened with thoughts of what a failure I was. I imagined how it would feel to have the bag that the crow tugged at wrapped around my head. I started crying.

Once I came back into my body, I looked up, and there was Takeshi on the armchair. Daniel and Takeshi somehow knew I was in trouble, and they had decided it was time to descend. Daniel knew because he had seen me like this at the party a few months ago. Takeshi knew because he had found me by chance in this state last month. I was sobbing at our doorstep when I arrived home from work one day. I had no recollection of even sitting down outside the house. Takeshi found me because he was driving past that evening to make sure I was all right. I had lost an hour that day when he found me, and he stayed with me until Daniel got home from work.

I eyed the clock on the wall. It read 12:05. I lit a cigarette. "Amelia-chan, daijobou?" he asked, wanting to know if I was okay. I was embarrassed. My middle finger, my cigarette finger, stung. The butt of my cigarette was smudged red. It was bloody. My left palm was stinging from my nails digging into my palm. I wiped them off quickly and said, "I'm so sorry, Takeshi. I'm so sorry."

He smiled, showing the kindness he had toward me. I was sobbing, and I kept apologizing. Takeshi was special. He had an understanding and empathy that knew its place. He knew I had a dark past and still loved me. He made me feel like a person, despite having to come to my rescue.

That evening, Daniel came home and retold the story of us talking on the phone and me scaring him. "I want to just jump in front of the subway. It will be quick and fast. I wish that when I was walking, a lorry would just run over me. I want to die so badly. I just can't bring myself to do it, Daniel." *Click.* These were my words that he relayed back to me, none of which I remembered.

He worked an hour away from home, so he had called Takeshi to come see me and stay with me to make sure I didn't kill myself. Takeshi got there and found the doors unlocked. He rang the bell, but I didn't come to the door. He let himself in to find me in the fetal position, shaking and sobbing furiously on the couch. My eyes were bloodshot. I'd been crying a long time, he told Daniel. He just waited it out and called to me until I responded. He texted Daniel when he got to the house and called him again to report on my state after lunch.

This was my life. People just found me sobbing in the fetal position. I lost time, again, like losing two pennies out of my pocket I wouldn't get back. It would later be explained to me by a psychotherapist that these "disappearing acts" were a trauma response to triggers causing the psyche to dissociate, hence losing time. But to others it just seemed like I was sobbing uncontrollably and nonresponsive, as if in a trance. I never knew where *I,* or rather my consciousness, went in those times. What I knew was that I was consistently embarrassed coming out of those fits of "disappearing."

~

I finally agreed to see a doctor. Even if Daniel wanted to be rid of me, which is what I thought would happen if I went to therapy and possibly the psych ward, I could not be without him. We found a general practitioner on a friend's recommendation. We figured it was a start—at the very least we could get a referral. He didn't speak perfect English, but it was something we had learned to adapt to. I could kind of guess what people meant by the look on their faces and the direction of the conversation. It was a very animated interaction. However, things got complicated for the medical portion. The doctor asked me no more than three questions and wrote a script for what we would later find out was a tranquilizer. Something to help with the panic attacks, he told us. He explained that my "disappearances" were panic attacks, and that the medication should help.

"For calm down, slow down, it's good," he said, not very convincingly.

Okay, I was finally getting help, and that's what Daniel wanted. I was of a different mindset—that all I needed was time to get my shit together. I was dealing with a lot, but I felt I was getting better since I had gotten to Japan. The drinking every day and the sleeping around that I'd been engaging in back home had halted. I wasn't self medicating. I wasn't crazy, so I sure as hell didn't need a doctor. But I knew this would pacify Daniel's concerns, and I obliged. On the bright side, I would have a whole bottle of pills to off myself if the time came.

For now, though, I wanted to stay with Daniel. I had never been with somebody like him. His kindness and tolerance were unreal. If I was going to live this life out, I only wanted it to be with him. He was my safe place.

But the challenge remained that I often wanted to die more than I wanted a life with him.

~

The suicidal ideation functioned like an answer to all my grief. I had a threshold of pain I was willing to wear like a cloak of nails. All I needed was to be pushed an inch, and the nails embedded into my flesh, forcing me to think about death. All I wanted was for Daniel to stay, to love me, but I didn't know how to accept that this was what he was already offering.

Most times, my intentions to die were kept in check by guilt. I felt guilt that it would bring pain to Daniel, and this kept the fight in me. The grief and pain were unbearable. Sometimes it came about unannounced, but other times, situations directly invited suicidal thoughts. I never realized how easily it would happen.

Several weeks after starting my new medication, Daniel and I got into another fight. Trivial arguments about the slightest thing— the coffee mug in a different spot, the glasses on the table instead of the sink, clothes left in the dryer—seemed to dominate our days. This time it was because he'd put the clothes away, and I was enraged because I couldn't find the shirt I wanted to wear to work. Daniel came home that evening to find all of our clothes strewn across the bedroom as if the closets had violently vomited them. He was furious, and we got into a heated shouting match. He had an unspoken expectation that I would magically bounce back with the new medications, but I had not. I was irritable all the time. I was angry, and I hated everything, and I hated myself more than all of that.

One weekend afternoon, I watched a whole season of *The Sopranos*, and I didn't want to stop. I needed to finish it. I didn't want to do anything else.

He wanted to go out. "Let's go for a hike or at least a walk at the park."

"Let's just hang out at home. Please, I really want to know what happens with Tony here. Please."

He stood up from the couch. "I can't do this. I don't want to just veg out like this all day every day. I don't want to be partying all the time, either. Why can't we do something normal?" He was so frustrated.

I didn't want to talk to him. But I did, and the words exploded out of my mouth, with no restraint. I was cursing, sobbing, and screaming. He fell silent. I stormed up the stairs to our bedroom and locked the door. The moment I clicked the lock, I heard his feet pounding the wooden stairs.

"Amy, open this door! Open it now!" he shouted.

My chest swelled up. My ears got hot, and my head filled with pressure. I couldn't breathe because of the fierce crying. I was not thinking anymore, but my feet made their way to the bathroom. Now he was pounding on the door. The next part happened so fast that I missed the communication between my head and my limbs. I swallowed all that was left in my bottle of meds. By my estimation, there were about eight pills.

Suddenly Daniel was there. He had used the second door to the bathroom. He saw the empty bottle on the counter, and his finger was immediately in my throat. He dragged me over to the toilet and banged on my back, crying with me.

"No, Amy! What did you do? What did you do?" His sobbing was desperate and frightening.

I was frozen. I was watching this happen from above. I sat there, sobbing, as he held my hair back. The pills plopped into the toilet. They were easy to see—thankfully, I hadn't eaten anything in two days. I'd survived solely on coffee and cigarettes. "One, two, three, four, five, six, seven." He counted out loud, then let out a loud sigh and punched the wall. He knew exactly how many pills there were in that bottle. He grabbed me and held me. I didn't know what to say or do. He cleaned my face off with a wet towel and took me to the bed. There were no more words. I fell asleep to his voice talking to the doctor. He was helpless and clinging to the doctor's words to keep me alive. His shoulders held the burden of my life. Those shoulders were slowly but surely caving.

I had marched up those stairs on a mission. It was like a knee-jerk reaction to any added ounce of pain I had to bear. I couldn't bear being without Daniel, and our fights always led to the fear of him leaving. I had nothing left if he didn't want to be with me, and my mind knew only one place to go. I was a problem and had been way before I was with him, way before living with Kate. I had been a problem ever since my life was turned inside out by that bastard. This problem had an easy fix, if only I could see it through. I was useless. All I did was cause worry, irritation, or pain. Daniel would be better off without me, especially now, because the meds seemed to be having no effect.

$$\sim$$

We found an American psychologist, Dr. Jacobson, licensed to practice in Japan. He agreed to see me over Skype. Our first appointment arrived. He wanted to be called Tim. I was present, but Daniel did most of the talking. He listed all the issues. I felt like the delinquent at the principal's office. The whole litany of my offenses was brought out for us to dissect. Daniel was looking for an answer—a magic spell that could take away all that troubled me.

I hated everything about that appointment. We all knew

everything that was wrong with me. I felt attacked and refused to respond to questions. I felt like an unstable nutjob. I honestly did not know how he expected me to react. I was afraid, embarrassed, and defeated. I didn't want to be hospitalized. Though this had not been mentioned, I felt certain hospitalization would be the outcome.

For the first two sessions, I kept silent while Daniel talked about the subway incident, the many nights I wept about wanting to die, and the pills. He even spoke about the initial incident eight years ago in the dank motel. I wanted to disappear. This was degrading and humiliating. I wasn't in control of my own story. These men were deciding things without my say.

By the third session, I finally lost it. I shouted at them both, "I am not crazy! This bullshit therapy is not going to fix fuck all!"

Daniel was taken aback and softly said, "You have to see that how you've been behaving is not normal, babe. It's not healthy. I'm worried, and I don't know what to do."

I locked into my defense. "I've had a lot of things happen, and I need time to process." Tim listened intently to us.

"I can't stand watching you suffer while you disappear in a fetal position, sobbing in pain, and I can't reach you. I can't do that, baby. I'm helpless at those times. We can do something about it. It doesn't have to be this way, please."

My tears came again, and I lost my voice in embarrassment, knowing what he was saying was true and unfair.

Tim said, "From what Daniel described, it sounds like you're having dissociative symptoms, which is a common trauma response. We can talk through that and find a way to process them in a productive manner. I need you to be on board, Amelia. Can you do that?" I felt defeated, but a glimmer of hope made me nod. I agreed to be more present in the fourth session the following week.

In that next session, I kept my silence but was more present in the conversation. I generally was okay with Daniel being in charge, but the inescapable thought still crossed my mind: *What if he was doing this to get me out of the way so he could come out of this looking like the good guy?*

On my end of things, what if I was in too deep? I couldn't shake the remnants of filth that smothered me. I was not only worthless, but I was a coward. I needed to snap out of this. My father said I just needed to focus on the good things in my life, that the bad was in the past. But he had no idea what the bad was. He would disown me if he knew. His heart could not handle what a disappointment I was.

"Amelia? Amelia," Dr Jacobson said.

"Yes."

"If we are to proceed with treatment, then we have to talk boundaries and expectations," he explained.

"Yes."

"You will have to keep our appointments. Can we be clear about that?"

"Yes." I said this even though I missed the next three appointments, paid for them, and then rescheduled.

"We talked about possibly beginning drug therapy, but you'll need to be compliant with that, too, and keep the appointments with the prescribing physician. Can you do that?" He had kind eyes but a perfect poker face. I no longer felt like a child, as I thought I was being treated in the beginning. When I paid attention to him, his voice was commanding but gentle.

He looked like he cared. I needed that. He sounded very professional. He didn't give a reaction to any of the bizarre, stupid things I had done. Daniel was sad, frustrated, and concerned. His head was cocked to the side occasionally. But Tim's face remained stoic through it all. He was expressionless, nodding in understanding. He was validating, acknowledging the information.

Next came the hardest policy in this treatment plan—the course of action if I tried to kill myself again. "What should we do if you have thoughts of hurting yourself or you act on those thoughts?" Tim asked.

"I won't!" I said this before I even had time to think. I knew where this was going. I knew they were going to tie me up, tranquilize me, and lock me away, *Girl, Interrupted* style. I would be in a straitjacket, bouncing off the walls because no one other than these two goons would know I was admitted. No fucking way. I'd seen this in the movies, and I'd heard about mentally unstable people all my life. They always ended up in hospitals. It was a prison for the insane. I didn't want that.

"Are you having any of those thoughts now?"

"No."

"Have you had them at any point today?"

"No." It was true. I had been too worried about this appointment to think of anything else.

"All right. We don't want you to stress about this. But it would make Daniel feel comfortable and safe if we have a plan. Doesn't mean at all that we're going to have to use it. It's just good for us to have a plan that you're in control of and that you feel comfortable about."

"Okay," I said, crying. Deep down I knew—*who was I kidding?* It was obvious I wanted to die. He had me at "control." I would have a say in something, and it sounded like they were willing to listen. I couldn't bear watching Daniel suffer.

"If there comes a point you feel overwhelmed again, and you act on it, we need to get you medical attention. At that point, it's not safe for you. You should be examined by a doctor to ensure you're physically well, or the doctor will be able to treat you, should it be needed. Can we agree on that at least?" He sounded like he had my best interest in mind. *Or did he? He just wanted to cover liability; no shrink wants a suicide on their watch.*

"What does that mean? See a doctor? The last one we saw prescribed me a tranquilizer. It didn't help *shit*. It only made things worse." I challenged him, because that's what I did, to see how far I could get. I needed assurances that this was going to actually make things better for me.

"Well, what that would look like," Tim explained, "is Daniel picking up the phone and calling ambulatory services. You'll be taken to the psychiatric facility we choose. But the priority is to keep you safe and alive. That's what we want for you." He was serious and staring straight at me. How was he doing that over Skype?

I believed him. He was agreeing to work with me to change my views so I could enjoy life again. I decided I would give this a shot.

"I don't want to hurt myself again, but I also do not want to be in an insane asylum. Please don't lock me up."

"We don't want that for you. We want you healthy and safe. Hospitalization is a last resort. This is a safety plan, to make sure we all know what to do if we should ever get there. The plan with treatment is not to get there." He was reassuring, and I felt more at ease.

~

There were three basic rules: safety, boundaries, and honesty. He talked us through them, and we both nodded, accepting that these were reasonable, no matter how angry I was.

In following sessions, Daniel was only to be there if he and I agreed there would be value in it. Otherwise, these were my sessions and mine alone. A boundary was set up for me to take charge of my own treatment. I started to see how this could allow me to, as Tim put it, "experience and even enjoy life." For the first time since shit hit the fan, there was consistency and steady care from people who cared about me, though my own accountability during treatment would prove the greatest challenge. I was up for it, knowing I wanted a real life with Daniel. I wanted to be with him as *me*, not the wounded me constantly posing a threat to our happiness. I was ready to share my secrets. I wanted to be unafraid, to no longer be at the mercy of my memories and my past experiences, to be strong enough to see my life through.

CHAPTER 8

I'd been in Japan for nearly six months when I began treatment with Tim. The first few sessions were a challenge. I struggled to show up on time. Instead of a fifty-minute session, I would get a thirty-minute session or miss the session altogether. I would then feel stressed and flustered the next time I'd see him.

"Would it help to have a reminder on your phone?" he asked me more than once. "Would it help to have a Post-it on your fridge, or by the bedside, or on the TV?" He never passed judgment, nor did he ever say, "It's okay." He was setting boundaries gently. I was worried he was going to stop seeing me, though he never indicated that. We worked on simple things to start getting me into a rhythm.

The first few weeks were spent talking about doing typical, benign things, such as setting daily goals. I had to reset my mind, organize my thoughts, and put my dirty clothes in the laundry basket. Ever since the fight over my misplaced top and the subsequent rage that followed, I decided that I should put away my own clothes. Daniel did the dishes and the laundry. He retreated into silence often. I took it as the resentment he felt in having to do the most trifling things, which I could not manage. In response, I retreated into silence too. I was struggling. It became clear that I couldn't even do tasks that used to come easily to me—household chores, grocery shopping, running a simple errand. It seemed that more than one thing at a time overwhelmed me. I felt I was always wrong, and every time I asked Tim a question, my head started buzzing. There was tension, as if I were taking a test, expecting the answer to reveal my inadequacies or incompetence. He helped me stay the course by reminding me of the errors in my thinking.

The new medication was working. A selective serotonin reuptake inhibitor, Lexapro, was cutting-edge stuff. I felt hopeful that the sessions with Tim and the meds would make a new reality possible. It was like I was being rescued from an invisible monster.

One night, about six weeks into therapy, Daniel and I were invited by friends for a night out barhopping. I had just gotten home from work and was excited to go. Daniel phoned me on his way home from work. "Sounds like a fun time. I think we can, if you feel up to it?" We had been abstaining from partying, but I felt stable.

"I think I feel good. I'd like to see everyone. I think we'll have a good time," I said. I'd also started feeling guilty for having him stay home with me all the time because of my unstable mental state.

We took a train into downtown Nagoya. The streets were buzzing that Saturday night. We saw a group of people facing the dark, glass building of the subway station, dancing. They seemed to be practicing a routine to the music blaring out of a stereo nearby. As we turned the corner, we ran into a group of girls in costumes. One was dressed up like Little Bo-Peep, with ribbons in her curly hair and a shepherd's stick. "Where are you going? A party?" I asked.

"We walk, meet our friends, and walk," she answered in her best-managed English. This fascinated me, the idea of dressing up just because they liked to. It felt like a fog had cleared in my mind. I was fascinated by things again. I saw the beauty around me again. There was a bounce in my step.

We met up with our friends at a tiny bar, which had a small space for dancing. It had been weeks since we'd gone out, but I reverted right back to how I had always been. I was the life of the party, jumping up and dancing on the bar. All of our friends were cheering and laughing. I enjoyed being the center of attention. I drank too much but never thought it was too much. I went too far, but I didn't know until it was too late. I felt numb, so I kept drinking to feel the joy I was supposed to be feeling. How I had missed drinking and partying without a care in the world. We had a great time, partying until closing time. Daniel was laughing along and smiling all night, and I was glad he was having a good time too. He held me tight as we walked out of the club and said, "I love it when you're happy." I could hardly put one foot in front of the other and held onto him. His happiness was an anomaly, and I blamed myself for that.

As soon as we got into a cab, I recalled something our friend D had said back in the bar. Any guilt I might have been feeling a minute earlier disappeared. I turned on Daniel in an instant. The woman he'd been holding, whispering his happiness to, suddenly lashed out at him. There were hurtful insults and accusations that he didn't understand me, that he was only with me because he was stuck, because he didn't know how to get rid of me. "I heard D say you were pussy whipped. I knew they'd blame me when you didn't go out with them!"

"Don't pay attention to him. Who cares what he thinks?" His voice was soft, trying to pacify me. I hated the way he sloughed things off, as if nothing I felt mattered. It mattered to me that I was being blamed for his choices. I couldn't articulate this at the time, that his friend's comment was an affirmation of what I already believed. I had to get angry at Daniel to distance myself, to rail against the guilt. From where I stood, I felt I was offering him mercy, a way out from this dreaded path we were on. He could step off and resume life as it was before I invaded. Words kept rolling out of my mouth, on and on, a rage rising in me.

"Calm down," Daniel said as I kept pushing. I should have shut up, but I couldn't stop. Daniel was arguing with me now. This was as combative as he got, but I couldn't even make out what he was saying. There was a buzzing in my ears, and I spewed words in such a rush that I was barely making sense. I was clearly upsetting him, but I didn't know how to stop. After a while, as was always the case, I was fighting by myself, with myself.

Abruptly, he stopped talking. He leaned forward toward the driver and in Japanese said something to him. I saw the driver nod and point to the sat-nav screen. It was in kanji, but I saw the familiar numbers of our address. The cab pulled over. Daniel got out and slammed the door without a word, and the cab driver drove off. I was frozen in my seat. I stared out the window in silence until I got home. I let myself inside our home, which was dark and quiet. I undressed and lay in bed. I saw myself as if from above—naked, all alone, staring at my phone.

After two hours, Daniel was still not home. He wasn't answering his phone. *Is this the end? Is he leaving me?* I didn't have energy to get the sleeping pills I needed. The truth was, I didn't even know where they were. Daniel had been the self-appointed "dispenser royal official," and I was only allowed to handle the ibuprofen. Even the ibuprofen had only a few in the bottle, because Daniel was regulating that also. God forbid I find a way to kill myself with Advil. I just lay there, lifeless, crying. I was so full of pain. I didn't want pain anymore—Daniel's or mine.

After what felt like hours, I heard the jangling of keys and the front door unlocking. Daniel had come home. He was exhausted and surely still angry, but he said nothing as he undressed and got into bed next to me. My heart sank for him, but my lips refused to part. I just stared at him.

"Are you okay?" he finally asked. I was practically despondent, but I also felt guilty for ruining our night. I didn't know how to get better or whether I *could* ever get better. No, I was not okay, but I nodded anyway, and I saw his face relax. I turned away and saw the stripes of light coming through the blinds. Morning had arrived.

He put his hand on my forehead. "Get some rest." I didn't speak to him or anyone for the next few days. Daniel and I carried on as we had done after our fights in the past, without speaking a word on the matter.

~

The next person I spoke to was Tim, three days later. I explained how everything had started out okay until I ended up upset and hysterical. I didn't know how I'd gotten from point A to B, but Tim did. He introduced a new concept to me: triggers. Drinking excessively was a trigger, as it brought on maladaptive behaviors, such as not being able to control myself. Being at a bar was a trigger for me to repeat maladaptive behaviors, such as being out of control and reckless as I had been in the past. Until I was able to control my behaviors, I needed to abstain from triggers. Not abstaining from my triggers had brought us to the point of me verbally assaulting Daniel for no good reason. I now had more reason to feel guilty. But Tim assured me that it was a logical reaction to the situation I'd put myself in. By identifying that and being cautious with my choices, I could avoid this kind of thing happening.

After that revelation, Daniel and I stopped drinking excessively. He wanted to support my recovery. Though I had guilt about his distancing from friends, he seemed sincere when he said he preferred the quiet times with me, that he had grown tired of the hangovers and the unnecessary spending on those nights out. It also was temporary, we believed, just until I could get a handle on my mind. We could then take baby steps back to the life we'd had before. Tim got me a new prescription for a different antidepressant. Daniel and I fell into a new routine. In the mornings, he handed me my drugs along with a glass of water. I would swallow and open my mouth to show him the pills had gone down. Once he left for work, I went back to sleep. We did the same thing at night. I hated swallowing the pills, but I did it for Daniel. I stayed on track, and when I had hard days, I reminded myself *this too shall pass.* I was to do things that made me feel better and stay out of situations that could trigger me.

For the next two months, I listened intently to Tim in my sessions, took notes, and played the role of compliant patient. He had answers for all the things that confused me about my own behavior. It made sense and gave me hope that I could be a better version of myself. Tim was calculated in his approach. He talked methods, data, and science of the brain. I had always been fascinated with psychology and how people think and behave. He answered my questions, and sometimes I felt like I was in a private psych class with him as my teacher. We talked about my "disappearances," which were still happening, though less frequently. He explained to me how this was part of a trauma-response mechanism in the brain—a skill to cope with extreme pain. I was escaping my body to avoid the pain.

A few weeks into our one-on-one sessions, I felt ready to address the assault that Daniel had already disclosed on my behalf. I divulged in detail my history for us to examine. Every single dirty detail was to be blown up for scrutiny and processing, as Tim called it. He was the first person in eight years to give it a name. "Rape," he said, unequivocally. It was a violation, he said confidently, and I'd done nothing to bring it on, nor could I have prevented it. I tried to refute and reject this claim. If I hadn't taken that drink, gone out that night, or trusted the wrong people, none of it would've happened. I rolled out the whole shitshow as stemming from my dumb choices. But Tim was adamant. He matter-of-factly reminded me that all the things I had mentioned were things young people in my stage of life did routinely. It was terrible that the rape happened, but it was not my fault, he reminded me over and over.

Over our next few sessions together, Tim gave me an additional diagnosis beyond my major depressive disorder. Now I also had PTSD. I felt like I'd been loaded with lead jacket over lead jacket, heavy and painful to bear but made to be mine. The medication stayed the same—antidepressant, antianxiety med, a sleep aid—but the new diagnosis led to a new game plan. With Daniel's help, I identified triggers, and we avoided those scenarios. We paid more attention to the roots of my problematic behaviors and found many of them to be the result of a trauma response. Daniel assured me that he wanted nothing more than for me to get better. We were isolated, but I felt that I would come through it. He was more mindful of our conversations and made additional efforts to show he was committed to me and not going anywhere, allowing me to ease into healing without the worry of abandonment. He made conscious efforts to make me feel special. With that, my confidence grew so that I could get through this, and he'd still be by my side. I was beginning to feel whole and empowered to take my life back.

~

Three months into my treatment, I started looking forward to my sessions. One morning, I got ready for my Skype session with Tim. I'd been charting my moods, and I shared with him that morning that I seemed to have constant depression. My Beck Depression Inventory (BDI) scores stayed consistently over forty, which was categorized as "extreme depression." Tim showed me a chart he'd printed. I felt myself cringe when I saw what he'd pulled up to share. The chart looked like the vitals a doctor might print out at the emergency room. The lines were jagged, like shark teeth. Every week since we'd started together, I had filled out the BDI chart among other questionnaires and worksheets. I had charted my good days, feeling satisfied when I did, as if I had won a prize at the fair. Not realizing how many good days there were, I never once would have thought they'd be cause for concern. If anything, I thought I was winning points by being such a model patient.

"That's not normal, right?" I asked. I felt panicked by what was coming, afraid Tim was finally going to deliver the news that I was indeed crazy.

"I think we need to explore another possibility here. It looks like you have been dealing with rapid mood cycles. And if you look at these really high peaks over here, the dips seem to fall even deeper. I think we should watch these transitions and try to address the mood changes." He was calm and collected in his delivery, as always. From that point, we increased our meetings to twice a week. The urge to better understand those jagged lines initiated Project Me. The data I tracked was precise and showed a picture of something I hadn't ever fully understood. An overachiever by nature, I was all in. Tim needed me to closely monitor my moods and start journaling my days, hour by hour. I also filled out daily questionnaires, and I didn't miss a single day.

A month later, he pulled up the chart again. He pointed out the dips and peaks along with the dates and what was happening during those times.

"Have you heard of bipolar disorder?" His eyes squinted ever so slightly, the smallest break in his otherwise calm demeanor.

"Yes, but I'm not crazy." All I knew was that bipolar people were extreme. They were the ones in the asylum. They were the ones who cut themselves to feel something. I'd read about this. Shit. My biggest fear seemed about to come true. Tim and Daniel were conspiring to have me hospitalized. "I'm not crazy," I repeated, as if it were of significance.

"Bipolar disorder is an illness," Tim said. "Just like depression is, just like anxiety is, just like diabetes is." Later I'd find out how common bipolar is. According to the National Institute of Mental Health, in the years 2001–2003, 2.8 percent of US adults had been found to suffer with bipolar disorder. But at the time I was diagnosed in 2010, I had no idea about the prevalence nor any fundamental insights on the diagnosis. All I knew was that I did not want to have it.

I climbed down from the precipice. Daniel was not waiting in the wings to cart me off to the mental ward. Tim was explaining the situation, as always, in a measured, kind, nonjudgmental way.

"There is a genetic component," he said. "There's evidence that points toward intense trauma as a cause for it to surface in some cases. We can't say for sure what happened in your case—if your trauma caused it—but I believe we can manage this condition."

He helped me stay focused on what mattered—treatment. "Figuring out where it came from won't be useful to us," he said, reading my mind. I felt fixated on where it came from, because then I could fix it. But Tim knew better. It's not something that can be fixed, but it would take me many more years to come to terms with this.

〜

Over the next few days, I thought about my experience, my past, my moods, and my highs and lows. It seemed like hypomania always came to visit when I got mentally stimulated by something. It was like that asshole friend who calls for another shot when you've obviously had three shots too many. For me, I'm fucked the minute this friend is in the room. My hypomania friend—let's call her Haddy Maddy—is Wonder Woman, Hercules, and Joan of Arc. With Haddy Maddy around, I am invincible, with superhuman courage and strength, all fiery passion and excitement—the life of the party, exactly where I want to be in the center of it all.

The problem with Haddy Maddy is that when she drags me higher and higher, I can't stop her even if I wanted to. It's like watching from outside my body. Haddy Maddy wears leather chaps and thongs, stiletto Greek sandals, and balloon-sleeved cotton shirts. She doesn't care if there's spilled red wine on her chest. She's all kinds of wonderful and ridiculous, brave and confident. She gets what she wants. She brings me all the way to the top of a cliff, and like a defenseless puppy on a leash, I keep pace with her. I know it's a bad idea, but there's nothing I can do to stop it. When she pours me shots, I open my mouth. When I'm with Haddy Maddy, I'm not in the driver's seat. If I see something I shouldn't be doing, I throw caution to the wind. I know better, but I keep going. I keep pace with Haddy Maddy the whole time, with her as the puppeteer.

But then she's gone. When Haddy Maddy leaves, it's as if she'd never been there, and then I'm like a skydiver with no parachute. Then I find myself deep in darkness. I am overwhelmed with guilt, shame, and pain. Haddy Maddy is gone at the very moment the descent starts. In this state, there is no friend, just complete despair.

Through my work with Tim, I finally began to understand who Haddy Maddy was. I was able to give her a name to separate her from me. I started to understand my patterns relative to my episodes. I rarely sat in the middle portion of the ride, which ought to be the calm after the storm. I was mostly in the ravine, until something switched, and I'd be catapulted to the fancy world of hypomania.

Once I understood these episodes and that Haddy Maddy was part of me but not all of me, I had to be honest with myself. A whole new world opened up to me. All those lies I'd believed, including that I was unworthy of love, were becoming a self-fulfilling prophecy. I was convincing Daniel of my unworthiness of his love. He didn't know that I was sick when he met me. He didn't sign up for this. Now he was carrying the burden of my sickness, which clouded our life. But I was seeing a path forward, and I was more conscious of how I shouldered the blame. I was ready to forge ahead, growing through the treatment. We could have a life together that was different, without the bickering, the knockout fights, and the blackouts. I could be present. I could handle Haddy Maddy, I could handle the depression, and Daniel could have me, all of me.

Tim and I worked out being more in sync with the cognitive behavioral therapy (CBT), which focused on recognizing thinking errors and automatic thoughts. He helped me to reframe my self-judgment and catastrophizing. I'd challenge him occasionally, and he would punt back to me, identifying thinking errors. In time, I would learn to identify the thinking errors myself.

Simple things would wind me up. Someone at work invited me to lunch, and my mind raced. *Why did she invite me? She's not going to like me.* Filled with anxious thoughts, I leaned toward rejecting her invitation off the bat. *Thinking error. Jumping to conclusions. I have no idea how this lunch will turn out. It's just lunch,* I reminded myself. Recognizing the error allowed me to step out of my comfort zone, bringing a favorable outcome. We had the lunch and I made a new friend. I practiced consistently in those months. Recognizing my thinking errors and making more mindful choices became second nature and helped a lot with my processing stressful situations or identifying my descent into either end of the pole.

Over time, I learned to modify my thoughts. When a triggering thought rose to the surface, rather than moving to anger—or worse, dissociating—I learned to reframe the error with the facts. "Feelings are just feelings. Feelings are not facts," Tim reminded me. I understood that not giving in to my feelings all the time often allowed me a renewed perspective. I understood the workings of my mind, and I was learning to take control. I was peering beyond the horizon to a different reality that I wanted for myself, without the burden of pain, loss of control, and—most importantly—guilt and shame.

~

There had been times when Haddy Maddy had clearly ruled my life, convincing me with certainty of all the anxious thoughts my already-feeble mind could endure. So many times, she'd dragged me into reactions that exacerbated my feelings of worthlessness and loneliness. She led me enthusiastically into a game of Russian roulette at the hands of strangers. "Recklessness" was the word used by Tim to describe my nightly shenanigans at the time. Haddy Maddy would take over. I remembered the times this had happened and how I took a back seat to my life when she showed up:

1. The time Haddy Maddy almost got me sexually assaulted
While living with Kate, I had been partying for nights on end. Haddy Maddy had taken over, and I didn't even have a chance at taking back my body.

She went drinking every night, even the weekday nights. One

night, she was there with a couple of friends and met a guy, someone I had known from my shitty college days. Haddy Maddy was blasted drunk, and for some reason, my friends just left her there at closing time with this guy. She only remembered flashes, like blinking lights, of this night. She was so drunk that she wasn't able to walk to her car on her own, but she made it to the car. All I know is that Haddy Maddy had been downing shot after shot and passed out. I awoke to a furious banging on the car window. When I opened my eyes, it was Carter—sweet, sweet Carter—my first-ever conquest. Haddy Maddy had left me in that car with the stranger, and I was about to face the humiliation of her unruly escapades. *What the fuck was he doing here?* I unlocked the door. I was in the passenger seat. The door swung open, and Carter grabbed me. My chest was on his, but I was like a rag doll, so sleepy. He was shouting angrily and shaking me. There was someone in the driver's seat. I tried as hard as I could and managed to see the asshole I used to know running off as he was zipping up his pants. Carter was banging on the car and shouting vulgarities at him. Then he looked at me. I was limp in his arms. Haddy Maddy was down for the count. That bitch left, and now I had to face the firing squad. Carter was so angry that he looked like he was going to cry.

He put me back in the passenger's seat. "What is wrong with you? Why are you alone? Where the fuck are your irresponsible friends? Why, Amelia? Why are you doing this? *Fuck, fuck, fuck!* You know what he could've done?"

Carter took me to his apartment, gave me a shower, dressed me in his shirt, and tucked me into bed. I was a fucking invalid. I didn't have the language or the understanding that it wasn't me who'd ended up in the car with that guy—it was Haddy Maddy. In the morning, I thanked him for helping but was completely humiliated.

2. The time Haddy Maddy dragged me into a drug deal

I had gone out in Kuala Lumpur on my own after Kate refused to party with me anymore. I met a new friend at the bar, and he asked if I wanted to party some more. Haddy Maddy took over and enthusiastically said, "Sure!"—because *fuck yeah!* She wouldn't have to go home and drink by herself—that's just sad. Never mind the fact that I'd been drinking every single day for the past month in the same bar. She knew what he meant when he said "party some more." There would be drugs involved, and Haddy Maddy was game, not caring about the implications. She got into her car, already drunk, and drove to his apartment. Haddy Maddy held steady through all this excitement, chasing the next high. When offered a cigarette "laced with the good stuff" by the host of the party, Haddy Maddy took it. She didn't even care to know what "good stuff" was. She lowered herself onto a beanbag or ottoman of some sort.

Haddy Maddy sat up, laughing from the "good stuff," and saw her friend grabbing a white packet and tucking it into his jeans. The host set money on the table. She took another drag of the joint she had been handed. She was laughing, but her head was still. Haddy Maddy was high, and whatever she was talking about seemed to anger the host. My new friend helped Haddy Maddy, still high, get up and leave the apartment.

Somehow, Haddy Maddy found her way home that night. Again, she had made a stealthy exit. By the time I was conscious of what had transpired, there was too much to even grapple with. In Malaysia, the penalty for drug dealing or possession of a certain amount is *death* by hanging. We don't mess around with drugs where I come from. I had risked everything and was feeling the rush from alcohol and psychotropic substances. Haddy Maddy had dragged me into a state and left me to face the consequences.

3. The time Haddy Maddy spent money I didn't have

Haddy Maddy spent frivolously. I'd taken an interest in the paranormal, escalated by Haddy Maddy's intensity on the topic. She was convinced that there was something wrong with my energy and that psychics had the answer. She called one of those online psychics one night while I was in Japan, ultimately spending $250. But she didn't let it end there. She sought out a medium, because what if my grandma was watching over us? Maybe she'd tell us the right thing to do. She spent $120 on the medium and then another $150 for a tarot card-reading psychic only to find out she had a beautiful, green energy about her. Whatever she was about to embark on was going to be a huge success.

I fell asleep on my computer that night. When I woke up, I realized I'd been in the throes of some sort of trance. Because I didn't recognize Haddy Maddy yet, I couldn't explain to Daniel what had happened. When he woke me, he said, "There was more than $800 charged to my credit card in the middle of the night. I just want to know if it's actually yours and not fraudulent."

A giant fight ensued. "Where is the money coming from to cover this? I can't afford surprise bills like this every week!" he yelled. This wasn't the first time I'd racked up outrageous expenses I couldn't pay for. I didn't have an answer, as Haddy Maddy already spent my biweekly salary on clothes and accessories she was convinced were needed. *Fuck! Fuck! Fuck!* This was not including the five new card decks she had bought. All of this totaled up to $1000 in one night.

4. The time Haddy Maddy earned me money for writing

When I still worked in Kuala Lumpur, I had a side gig freelancing for my mother's TV productions. Haddy Maddy would spit out six-episode scripts with very few flaws within two days and then the rest of the thirteen-episode season within the next few days. That specific TV program would be stuck in her mind, and she would not leave the computer when the ideas flowed. With Haddy Maddy in the driver's seat, I imagined countless concepts for television programs, which my mother has brought to television: children's educational programs, cooking shows, travel documentaries, and women's magazine programming. Haddy Maddy handled all genres like a pro. However, it was a problem when she left and I was required to keep that pace— impossible to do when not under the spell of hypomania.

5. The time Haddy Maddy kicked ass at work

Before I left Kuala Lumpur for Japan, I was in the public relations and marketing field, which I had entered upon graduating college. Haddy Maddy jumped in at my job a time or two. She could be very creative, full of great ideas. Every time the boss listed what needed done, she would be on it in a second. She would suggest grand ideas and get started on them right away, such as the time she offered to take the lead for three events happening in the same month. Her ideas were great, and my boss agreed to them. However, when my boss criticized any of the ideas, Haddy Maddy took offense and left, plunging me into a depression. I subsequently failed to deliver. The projects got redistributed, and I was on probation. I was stuck with the fucking commitments Haddy Maddy made while acting like Wonder Woman. The expectations didn't change just because I got fucking depressed after she left. But for some reason, Wonder Woman finds shelter somewhere in my brain and gives no access to Haddy Maddy's powers. I'm then like Jabba the Hutt, immobile and incapable, but still fully accountable for all the promises made by Haddy Maddy.

~

Despite how she failed me, Haddy Maddy had a glorious side to her. I rather liked being in that hyper-focused, creative state. I loved how Haddy Maddy flowed with incredible thoughts and ideas. She could be queen of the world in certain situations. The recognition of who Haddy Maddy was and how she showed up in my life was helpful but terrifying. I couldn't control whether she came or went, but the awareness of her presence would become a powerful tool for me to fine-tune my behaviors.

My father called weekly to check in. During a Skype call with my parents, about a year into my time in Japan, I had a panic attack. I had learned in treatment that my father's criticisms triggered my sense of hopelessness and unworthiness. We always started off cordial. Daniel stayed with me during these conversations, because it was hard for me. He convinced me that I needed to talk with them, even if it was just to let my father know I was okay.

My father always found something to criticize. This time it was about my car, which I had left behind, and how he had to take care of it. Haddy Maddy took over. In the grip of hypomania, my anxiety became uncontrollably high. She whispered about my failures and what a piece of shit I was. She berated me, but my response was to scream at my father, "I can't take this anymore! You're always doing this to me! Always something I've done wrong! I know I'm useless and a pain in the fucking ass for everybody! I know! I know! I know!"

I stomped off screen and lit a cigarette. Daniel took over the conversation. I heard my father pleading with Daniel to be honest with him. "I don't know what just happened. Why is she so angry? I'm so sorry. How is she doing? Is she okay? You know you have to tell me if she needs anything. Take care of her for me. I cannot do anything right now." My father was at a loss as to how to find his way back to his little girl.

Haddy Maddy whispered, "Look at you, a fucking mess Daniel now needs to clean up."

Daniel tried to appease my father. "I promise I'll do my best. She just needs some time. She's doing so good at work. She loves her job, and she's happy. We'll see you soon."

While he promised my father a visit, Haddy Maddy had me in her grips. "You're a fucking waste of space. Everyone has to make allowances to clear up your shit!" I didn't really want that. I wanted a good distance from my past. "You ought to get on a plane home. Maybe it will crash, and everyone will survive except you. That's what you deserve!" She was screaming in my brain. I'd inhaled four cigarettes by then. My inhales got deeper and deeper—I was desperate for that heat to go deep down, to kill the buildup of grief and guilt. Even though I'd been away from home for nine months, it hadn't gotten easier. Haddy Maddy's voice, clearer than ever, was a fucking menace in my brain. "You're such a failure. You ran away and left all your problems for your parents to clean up, you douche." This time it was my car, before that it was my furniture, and before that it was the necessity of explaining to the rest of the family what I was doing in Japan all of a sudden.

"You take, and you take, and you take from your family. What do you offer them except for headaches?" Haddy Maddy was convincing. I took another deep drag, trapping the smoke inside. And then, as if seized by some unseen force, I couldn't breathe out. The tears poured out. Daniel hung up and looked at me, alarmed, then ran upstairs. It was panic attack time.

He brought me my medication. I swallowed the pill, crying profusely, and then it hit me. *Whoop-whoop.* I was feeling light. I heard Daniel talking to me, but I couldn't exactly reply. My thoughts didn't match my words. "Sky forest in the bicycle gate fire," I said as I fell into a deep sleep. The panic attack medication worked the same way tranquilizers did, which was not very practical unless I was having a panic attack at home. Once I came to, Daniel reminded me to discuss this with Tim.

The hardest lesson was that so many things I grieved were manifestations of this illness. I struggled to know what was real. How much joy was normal, and what was over the top? How much sadness was acceptable before it counted as depression? Were my uninhibited ways my own, or were they Haddy Maddy's? She was discreet in her role in my brain, sometimes brainwashing me, sometimes taking over my limbs entirely. I paid more attention to surviving and waiting for the episodes to pass. In time, the shark teeth were less jagged as the cycles got shallower and wider. Sometimes there was even a plateau of blissful balance. The dips weren't as deep, and the peaks weren't as high. On the bright side, I had a new kind of clarity. I enjoyed my life, and I started recognizing when Haddy Maddy showed up. I had the coping skills to catch her before she started. Sometimes she filled my mind with fucked-up thoughts that paralyzed me; other times, she took over my body.

Two months into my official diagnosis, Tim started talking to me about a healthy, productive life. Everyone talks about the light at the end of the tunnel. Finally, I was starting to get what that might mean. I saw a dim light far in the distance. I didn't know if I could make it all the way there, but I was starting to believe there was something more than pain and struggling. Perhaps I could walk through this dark path to the other side, where clarity and a normal life awaited me.

In therapy, I discovered the pieces I needed to make myself whole: the love I had with Daniel, and the family I had. They'd held fast to me for so many years, keeping my head above water. I had security with Daniel and a job I loved. On the good days, I would be lonely. I was alone in a world filled with humans. I craved connection, but making friends and keeping up relationships were too daunting. My anxiety and volatile moods would make it hard to maintain any kind of relationship without divulging my condition. But what I had with Daniel pulled me through. He held my hand through therapy, medication, and real-life episodes. This gave me the strength to face the illness and grasp the future I now wanted. My changing demeanor did not deter his commitment to me and my healing. I held on tighter.

~

Six months of treatment gave me answers and also helped me to forgive myself. Daniel took it all in stride. Our fights were less frequent and less volatile. We no longer threw objects, screamed bloody murder, or stormed out of the house. He understood the work was mine to do, and his contribution was to be a support, my safe place.

One Saturday afternoon as I was reading, I watched Daniel busy folding laundry. I couldn't understand the nonchalance he showed in the burden of all the tasks he'd taken on. As I watched him neatly place the folded piles of clothes back in the basket, I was consumed by guilt for the grief I'd caused him. "Do you resent me?" I asked.

"No, baby. Why would you say that?" He put down the basket and looked into my eyes.

"We don't fight anymore, but we don't talk anymore, either. You just carry on, almost as if you're numb and stuck." I wanted to stop myself, but I didn't. There were some things medication was never going to cure completely. I hated to threaten leaving, but I worried about his future. I worried that I'd sucked the spirit out of him. "I'll go home," I said. "You won't be a bad guy. This is too much for one person to bear. I know it's not fair."

He stayed where he was, his shoulders slumped as he set the scrunched-up T-shirt back into the basket. "You know, pain, grief, helplessness, and dysfunction—none of that's entirely foreign to me. I've been here before—not exactly this, but the same sense of help-lessness." His voice became a whisper. "I lost my dad when I was nine. It was just me and my mom. I missed my dad so much, but I missed my mom too." His voice was shaky and he had tears in his eyes.

I started to cry. I realized we were eight months into our relation-ship and I didn't know about his dad. I was so wrapped up in myself, I had smothered our lives. I took up all the space, and he never had a chance to share his life with me. He had been private, but I was the asshole who didn't even know his dad died. My chest swelled in pain for the selfish prick that I had been, all while he learned everything there is to know about me.

"I'm sorry," I said softly.

"It was just us, but in her pain, she had me to care for. We'd spend some time together after school, and each of us found solace in solitude, locked in our own rooms afterward," he continued. "I knew she was hurting, but there was nothing I could do but keep myself busy. Thoughts of my dad killed me inside. I buried myself in baseball cards and whatever collectible I could find. I couldn't do anything for my mom, even though I knew she was hurting. I wanted to. I needed her. She needed me, but we got by the best way we knew how." He wiped away his tears.

This crushed me even more, realizing the pain he carried. My pain was not the only pain worth anything. With all his pain, why should he have to bear mine? It all seemed unjust. I was unworthy of it all.

"And now you have to care for me while I'm lost. It's not fair. You deserve better. I'm sorry," I said.

"That's not what I'm saying. I couldn't help anyone back then. I was a child. I didn't know anything about anything. I just couldn't then, but I'm not a child anymore. I know how I can help you, because I need you, and you need me. It's hard sometimes—I won't lie—and I'm only human to feel frustrated and resent this situation. We're figuring this out, and I'm not going anywhere." He pushed the hair away from my face. I put my book down, and he hugged me. I still felt guilty but also reassured. If I could get better, we would be solid.

I had found more peace. All this time, I thought I had to carry the burden of the mistake I made to my death. But now I saw that wasn't the case. I didn't have to carry it alone. With treatment, I saw a dimly lit path to a more bearable life.

One day I watched the crows on my porch again. I noticed how they flew away after they were done pecking. As they flew overhead, one of them looked knowingly at me, as if to show me the way. It let out a loud caw and kept flying. I imagined letting it carry away the rape, the bipolar, and the guilt. The bird could leave it all behind. I wanted to have that kind of freedom. It occurred to me that maybe treatment was my path toward flight.

I had it in me to fly. I didn't have to peck incessantly at my own life, causing a mess to appear, fearing the triggers that would entrap me. I did not need to be chained to the ground anymore. I could find freedom in this new path.

CHAPTER 9

We packed our bags about a year and a half after I moved to Japan. We were going to Woodstock, Ontario, a town about an hour west of Toronto. Daniel had accepted a reassignment to the Canadian branch of his company. Having spent time in Japan teaching elementary kids, I decided to go back to school to get a degree in human ecology so I could work with children. It was easy to feel at home in Canada. I had watched enough TV and movies that the realities of living there matched my expectations. The stereotypes of Canadian politeness and warmth were accurate, and the weather was even colder than I thought it would be.

I'd been in school for about a year when I woke up to Daniel crouched on one knee beside the couch where I'd fallen asleep. It was a frosty winter morning, and I struggled to open my eyes. I looked at the French doors that led out to the deck and noticed the frosted morning dew on the plants. The fireplace was still going, and I felt the warmth on my cheeks. There was snow on the porch. I took Daniel in but was momentarily distracted by the loud panting. Our dog, Morgan, whom we'd adopted together shortly after we arrived, sat next to Daniel. Morgan was holding a sparkly ring around the bow tie on his neck.

Although Daniel was speaking, I wasn't taking in his words. All

I knew was that I wanted to be with him for the rest of my life. *"Yes! Yes! Yes!"* I said, crying. I had no reservations other than that he might have doubts about me. For years, he'd proven his love and devotion to me. Every hurdle we faced, he was the steady one—always patient and always comforting. We'd been together for a little more than two years by that point, and I couldn't imagine a life without him.

The ring was simple and understated, a Canadian diamond to mark this time of our lives. Even though I'd thought about marriage, Daniel and I rarely talked about it in detail. This was due to my fear of jinxing what we had. I was terrified that I'd built up false hopes, and I worried incessantly that Daniel would decide one day he'd had enough. But here he was, showing his resolve and commitment. I was euphoric.

~

We called our best friends and family. My mother squealed in excitement. She loved Daniel and had always championed for him when I complained or worried about our future together. My father was most pleased, though. He, more than anyone, saw how Daniel took care of me. Daniel had made clear his intentions to marry me the last time my father had come to Canada, and my father had given him his blessing. But both had managed to keep this a secret from me. Daniel was so pleased when he told me what my father said: "You have to be patient, always, with her. Hold her always. Marriage is forever. It is not something to play around with." Daniel had assured my father that he was prepared to do that.

My father had never approved of other men I had dated. Never had he welcomed another boyfriend into our home the way he did Daniel. That he was okay with us living together from the get-go was a testament to how highly he thought of Daniel. Cohabitating before marriage wasn't something people in my family did.

The first time they'd met, about a month before I moved to Japan, it was a true family affair. There were fourteen people at dinner that night—my parents, aunts, uncles, and cousins. Everyone was curious to meet Daniel, and I felt pressure for the evening to go well. My family had assumptions about him as a foreigner and were skeptical about his intentions. I laughed at their teasing to hide my nervousness.

Daniel brought an exquisite red wine, which he had researched because he didn't know much about wine. When my father casually remarked over dinner that he didn't drink anymore, Daniel was mortified at his faux pas and that I hadn't told him. But I had no idea that my father had quit alcohol for health reasons. I tried to assure him later that my father was grateful for the gesture, which I knew to be true. Poor Daniel thought our chances were blown due to that wine blunder, but my father beckoned his brothers and Daniel into the main room while the women stayed in the kitchen.

I watched in eager anticipation from the kitchen. I had seated myself as close to the living room as possible to hear what was going on in there. I strained to hear through the short hallway between us, but I was in a prime spot that afforded me a good view of everyone. Most importantly, Daniel was in clear view. My father sat with his back toward me. My uncles and cousins sat around on the floor and the sofa. Daniel was on the floor next to the coffee table. I was glad he remembered this about our culture. The elders were always given preference in terms of where to sit. If he got a chair, his legs were not to be crossed, and feet should never point toward an elder. Daniel was doing well. I imagined it couldn't be easy. My father poured the wine for the men sitting around the table as he grilled Daniel about his credentials. My sweet boyfriend won over my father and my uncles that night just by being himself and honest about his feelings toward me.

One of my uncles tried to put him on the spot. "So, Amy says you're an engineer—what specialization?" he asked once the wine was poured. All eyes were on Daniel.

"Mechanical, and now I work in manufacturing, my first job out of college," he answered with poise. I could tell he was nervous by his eye twitch.

I could see his head spinning as the questions came at him rapid-fire. "What does your mother do?" "How many siblings do you have?" "Where did you grow up?" Then came my father's pointed question: "How many times a year can I expect to see my daughter once you take her away?"

I saw Daniel blink, then glance at me, before mustering his courage to respond. I tried to listen to the conversation while keeping up with the women in the kitchen bombarding me with their own line of questioning. "I'll try my best to make it as often as possible, sir."

My father's eyes widened. "That's not good enough for me, my friend. She is my baby, you know. I need to see her and hold her."

Daniel sat up, straightening his back, and said, "I can promise at least once a year if I'm being realistic, but of course we can come more often as long as we're in Japan." My father was seeking assurances from Daniel as he already knew of my intention to leave Malaysia. It was important to both Daniel and me that we got blessings from my parents. This was excruciating for me to watch. It was Daniel's first time meeting my family, and here was my father already forcing him to make promises. But Daniel was steady, even as he wiped sweat from his forehead.

After that, my father regaled him with stories of his visits to America. He was interrupted by my uncle, who apparently wasn't done holding Daniel's feet to the fire. "How can we trust you're going to take care of our Amy?" All eyes trained on Daniel. I was shaking. I couldn't interfere or I would make him look like a ninny. He had to hold his own. "I can't promise you more than that I'll try my best, sir, and she knows I'll return her home safely if ever she chooses."

My uncle nodded and said, "Fair enough." He then raised his glass to Daniel, in approval of his response.

My mother and I sat with the women in the kitchen. She occasionally smiled at me, knowing I was nervous. My aunts and cousins carried out their own interrogation excitedly. They wanted to know everything about Daniel, our relationship, and our plans. Everyone in the room was impressed. I was reassured by the loud laughing and exchange of stories, which was unlike the interrogations I'd witnessed with my sister's boyfriends.

When I left for Japan a month after that gathering, my father confirmed what I already knew. "This boy is raised well. He's respectful and good. I hope he makes you happy." Daniel had come home with me to Malaysia several times by the time we moved to Canada.

My father was always worried about me. I was the child he lost. He knew I was in pain, though I couldn't, and wouldn't, ever tell him why. As he was my defender, I purported to be his too, and I held up my end of this by keeping my secret. He had cared for me all those years and presumed that a good man would come along so I would be happy and settled for life. Our engagement gave him great delight and relief. The relationship had been strained since he and my mother had gone to Africa, but the resentment had dissipated. I had effectively distanced myself from my parents, and my father must have known that he couldn't protect me. I imagine he saw that Daniel could. It was more than he might have dared to hope for me during all those years in Malaysia when I was suffering in silence and acting out, though he knew nothing of those episodes. I imagine he thought I was lost; and through Daniel, he'd found me again, at least a part of me.

We finished up our conversation over Skype that morning, the joy in my father's face showing through his huge smile and tears. I knew that with this news of my engagement, he was releasing his worries about me. I had found the happiness he had wanted for me all these years.

We said goodbye. Daniel left for work, and I ran over to my neighbor Joelle's. She was my closest friend at the time, and she'd been sure Daniel was going to pop the question. I played it cool, waiting to see if she'd notice the ring. We chatted for a bit, and I waited the whole time for her reaction. It took fifteen minutes before she caught a glimpse of the sparkle on my finger. She screamed, I joined in, and we jumped for joy.

~

On the outside, I was elated. Anyone who knew me would have said that this was all I wanted. But inside, a louder shout often threatened to overwhelm my happiness. *Why would he want to marry me? We'll never make it to the altar.* We were not without our struggles, nor had we ever been. The year leading up to our wedding would prove to be filled with more of the same. Was it due to the fact that I found it hard to believe he was really going to marry me? Would we have found contentment if I'd been able to take him at his word that he loved me?

A couple of months after he proposed, Daniel came home from work one night and asked an innocuous question. "What are we having for dinner?" He set his backpack down in the living room. "Should I order takeout?"

The loud voice inside me erupted out of nowhere. "Why are you even marrying me? I can't even have dinner ready for you! What do I do for you?"

I was screaming these questions at him as I thought of something

my mother would say: "Always cook for your husband—it'll make
him happier at home." She would say this often when I was a child
and when I was a young woman dating the wrong men. Her advice
for being a good wife was beyond what I could do, and this failure
contributed to my self-loathing.

Daniel wasn't such a saint that he could always stay perfectly
calm. He often defused my reactions, but when I came at him out of
the blue like this, it was hard for him not to get defensive. "I was just
saying that if you're studying, we can do takeout or go out for dinner.
What the fuck, Amy?"

I was shrunken and angry at the same time. I had convinced
myself that he didn't want to go through with the marriage. I was
sure he was going to leave me as soon as he realized how useless
I was. I escalated the situation, screaming at him and grabbing
my keys. I left in a blind rage as he shouted at me to come back.
I backed out of the driveway, and he ran after the car to no avail.
As I drove down the dark interstate, my mind vibrated with all the
indignities of my past and even present self. I was soiled by that
bastard years ago, and it was a kind of filth I could not wash off. I
felt invalid due to my bipolar, which was not going away. I couldn't
see how Daniel could choose me when he could have someone
without all these problems. Surely, he wouldn't want to be with
me forever. The thoughts simmered to a low boil as I headed back
home. When I got home, he held me as he always did. He gave me
the reassurance I needed. I wondered whether I could stop putting
us in these situations. I had to keep fighting to get better, for both
our sakes.

I had begun seeing a local therapist in Canada. Sheila brought
to my attention that my hotheaded behavior had to do with a trauma
response. She wondered if the engagement itself had triggered an

irrational perception of the risk of abandonment and disappointment. I heard her words but found it hard to believe. I wanted more
than anything to be with Daniel, yet the evidence was clear. How
many times was I going to force him to prove he wasn't going to leave
me? The CBT and all the skills I had learned in therapy the past few
years were hard to put into practice when I was in a rage. I was physically sick from this tug of war in my brain between what I knew I
wanted and what my brain would not allow me to believe.

For months following our engagement, I provoked Daniel into a
fight almost weekly. He conceded every single fight to calm me down.
But this didn't leave me satisfied. I wanted a fair fight, I wanted to
lose, and I wanted to be proven right. Treatment continued, though
I struggled to comply. I started drinking and smoking again. Daniel
hated these behaviors and saw them for what they were—acts of
rebellion—but was powerless to stop me.

I stocked up on wine and drank during the day and into the
night. Daniel would come home from work to find me drinking and
smoking. "Shit, how much have you had already? It's six o'clock and
there's already a bottle and a half gone. Amy, this isn't normal." His
face would quickly redden with his anger. I'd feel a touch of ire, but
often I was too checked out to care.

That time, I guzzled down a whole glass of wine and stared defi-
antly. "I am not normal," I said. I reached for the bottle, but he lunged
forward and poured it down the sink.

"Enough is enough. What are you trying to prove?" His voice was
no longer calm. He couldn't look at me.

I felt his disgust as I heard the last of the wine going down the
drain. My anger popped up like a jack-in-the-box. "That you can't
handle me! You already can't stand me!" I screamed so loud I was
sure our neighbors could hear.

"It's not you I can't handle. It's this bullshit with the smoking and the excessive drinking. This is not you. This is you acting out. Be a grown-up, and figure shit out!"

I waited for him to say he would leave me. My eyes stung but before a tear could fall, I grabbed another bottle of wine and the corkscrew and left him standing by the kitchen sink. I went out on the patio to sob because, despite what he'd actually said, all I heard was that he was growing weary of me. I was pushing every button I could to make him leave me. I believed it would be better if he left me before we got married so he wouldn't have to confront the decision later, after we'd promised ourselves to each other forever. Sheila would call this a defense mechanism. I called it the truth.

We were encouraged by Sheila to attend marriage-preparatory counseling, which we both agreed would be good for us. By the third of six sessions, the counselor had gotten to know us well enough. "In marriage, there's messy stuff to deal with, so let's talk about how you're going to handle that as a team."

I awaited Daniel's list of all that he wanted changed in me, but never once did he express anything like that. He said, "We figure it out, we talk, we talk, we fight, we talk some more, and we figure it out together." I was caught off guard, but I believed him. I felt ready to conquer my irrational fears and maladaptive behaviors. I vowed to work harder in my therapy to counter the trauma responses for the sake of making our marriage work.

The ghost of trauma past did not leave me, but I was mindful of my thoughts and actions. I stopped my excessive drinking and sparring with Daniel. I recognized that my trauma responses were detrimental to this marriage, which I wanted with all my heart.

∼

After two years in Canada, and one year after he'd proposed, we moved to Kentucky for Daniel's job. We rushed to get married at the county clerk's office before a judge and two of our best friends, Sophia and David, for the sake of speeding up my green card application. We had been in the immigration process for more than a year. Though we had ninety days to do it, we wanted to clean up our paperwork and get my green card process underway by obtaining a marriage license and certificate.

The judge recited beautiful poetic affirmations, and we followed with our vows. Neither one of us were prepared for this. It all seemed so official, so final. When we said "I do" and kissed for the first time as Mr. and Mrs. Zachry, a void deep inside of me finally felt a little less bottomless. This was our forever. Any doubts I had about him wanting to be with me or of this working out dissipated. We didn't have our rings with us because we hadn't expected any kind of ceremony. I hadn't expected to feel such fullness in my heart, given all the pain and doubts. But a peace found me, and I prayed I could hold onto it.

Our actual wedding day was a few days later, two weeks upon our arrival in the States. It was simple and lovely. It was August, and the weather was perfect. We held the ceremony in Cincinnati, in a small church with a barn, about an hour from where we'd just bought a house in Northern Kentucky. We had been through hell to be here, and I promised myself that this would be my new start. The wedding was small and intimate, with fifty of our closest friends who came from all over the world to be with us. We had guests from Malaysia, Japan, Canada, and America. Lori, Daniel's mother, and her husband, Dewayne, came from Louisiana, as well as Daniel's half-brother, uncle, and several cousins.

My mother, father, sister, and little brother made the trip out to celebrate us. My aunt Devi Atthey and Uncle Bala also endured the long flights, and it was a blessing to have so many of my immediate family stand with me. In their exhaustion, they were intent on being present and giving us their blessings.

Daniel's mother had come a few days early to help with the preparations. At one point, she pulled me aside and handed me a box. Inside was a lace garter with a little blue ribbon on it. She teared up as she told me, "Here's your something old, baby; it was the one I used when I married Daniel's daddy, and now it's yours." I was touched and embraced her as she said, "You're mine now. Not my daughter-in-law—my daughter. Welcome to the family, my dear." We had bonded, and I felt the love. She had been my confidante ever since I met her on Skype a few years before. Now we'd officially be family.

My new mother-in-law busied herself with the rehearsal dinner she insisted on preparing, Cajun fare for my family. It was elaborate, with gumbo, jambalaya, étouffée, corn-and-crab bisque, and other delicious bites. She was proud to share her culture, and food was a bond we'd already forged. When she came to visit us in Canada, I'd shared Malay cuisine with her. I had spent the whole morning cooking a dish called *lontong*, which is rice cakes in a coconut-turmeric vegetable gravy, eaten with a bit of chili paste called *sambal*. We all sat to eat, and I warned her, "The chili paste is very, very, very spicy. Try just a little first. Daniel and I are used to it."

But she was excited and couldn't wait to dig in. "I can handle this. We like spicy in Louisiana," she said as she took a large spoonful of *sambal* with her *lontong*. Within seconds she was sweating and crying and downing water. Once she felt better, we laughed, and later this dish became known as the "firebomb *sambal*."

My mother was pleased because she was also an avid foodie. She engaged in deep discussions with my mother-in-law about the recipes and history of the dishes. At the rehearsal dinner, my mother pulled me aside, gift in hand. I opened it to find a necklace that my mother had worn for as long as I could remember, a rectangular gold pendant on a gold chain. "I want you to have this. You're going to another family now, but Mommy will always be with you. You're always going to be far away from me now. This you can keep, as a part of Mommy, with you always." I hugged her so tightly, but nothing could make up for the time we'd lost from her going to Ghana in my childhood and my pulling away from her in the aftermath of my assault. It was time lost that I regretted, and this gift seemed to offer some sense of finality. I would not be coming back to Malaysia, and we both knew it.

At the wedding, I gazed around the barn banquet room. Against the red brick walls, guests smiled, laughed, and hugged. It was like a fairy tale, one I hoped to remember in times of hopelessness. I felt overcome by love and support. They had loved me through hard times, giving me a sense of purpose and will to carry on.

My parents took it all in. They got acquainted with my friends they had only heard of but never met. My father thanked everyone graciously in his speech. He knew that everyone had played a role in my survival, and he cried as he finished thanking them. "Everything she has done, she has done on her own. I only ever have supported her from the sidelines," he said, reminding me of all I had been through. I was contrite for the secrets I had kept so carefully from him. Earlier that day, when he'd walked me down the aisle, I'd noted his proud chest puffed up and that he was holding back tears. When he handed me to Daniel at the altar, he put my hand on Daniel's and whispered, "You're going to be okay, baby, okay." He kissed my cheek and walked away. I was about to embark on another life.

Daniel and I exchanged vows attesting our love to each other. I held his hand to help him through the tears and words, and I felt

strong. I was his and he was mine. It was not for ceremony, the theatrics of wedding celebrations, or the sake of family and friends. It
was for us, for each other. We supported each other in this life we
were choosing to walk through together. Haddy Maddy did not show
up that night. I was fully present, awake to life on my terms. As we
had our first dance together at the reception that night as husband
and wife, I held on to my husband. Our love wrapped us in our own
bubble, just the two of us.

~

I found a psychotherapist in Kentucky, as neither Sheila nor Tim
were licensed to practice in America. The first therapist we met was
informed in bipolar disorder and post-trauma processing, and initially I was delighted that she had an opening. At the first session, we
discussed my family dynamics and my newly married status. I told
her I was excited to start a family soon. The jovial woman who greeted
me changed her demeanor. She bent over in her seat with her elbows
on her knees and hands clasped under her chin. "You know you can't
ever have children." She stared at me as she cleared her throat in what
I supposed was discomfort in delivering such jarring news.

"What? Why? I'm not following," I said frantically.

"You shouldn't have children, given your condition of bipolar.
It will be impossible for you to manage," she said with a sigh as she
straightened up in her cushy chair again.

My heart dropped. I couldn't believe what she was saying. "Isn't
this why we have therapy? To help me cope? To figure it out?" I asked,
desperate now and trying to sort out the impact of what she was
saying.

I went home that day and broke down as soon as I saw Daniel,
who held me and without a beat said, "Fuck that. We'll manage, baby.

You and me, we'll manage. One person's opinion is not the be-all and end-all." It was so soothing to have an ally. I wasn't ignorant. I knew it wasn't going to be easy. I knew I would need professional help and support at home. But I believed I could manage it with the right help, which this woman was obviously not willing to provide. I decided not to see her again.

I called Tim in distress. I knew he couldn't treat me, but he was willing to help. He assured me that people with bipolar have children and go on to have fulfilling lives. He encouraged me to keep searching for a therapist. He gave me an analogy: "Let's say your car made a dreadful sound, and you know it needs fixing. So, you take it to the first mechanic, and he tweaks the car and hands it back to you, but it keeps making a sound. Now you don't trust the first mechanic, so you bring the car to a different mechanic. He fixes it, but the dreadful sound is still there. You know something is wrong. Do you keep driving?"

I smiled, knowing what he was getting at. "No."

He looked at me seriously. "No, you don't. You keep looking until you find someone who works for you and can work with you. It's not easy, but you have to keep trying. Find someone you like." I knew he was right, so I set out making phone calls and meeting doctors. Finally, I found my Goldilocks therapist, Natasha. When I told her about Daniel and I planning for a baby and our intent to manage without medications, she was supportive though cautionary. I was to manage my triggers and work hard to avoid any situation that would present triggers. I was to keep up with therapy sessions and treatment plans. I was more committed than ever, and Natasha was on board to support me.

I was almost thirty-one. I wanted to have two children, and I was starting to feel impatient. I made the decision to go off the meds before our trip to Malaysia for our second wedding. I wanted to flush my system and start trying to conceive as soon as we got back. Daniel agreed with me. I'd been doing so well, and we were on the same page about timing.

What I failed to consider was just how triggering Malaysia and my family dynamics would be. I didn't realize that going off my meds right before this trip was probably the worst possible time. I was so focused on my future with Daniel and how well we'd been doing that I flung myself into the lair without armor or shield.

$\sim$

A few months later, we traveled to Malaysia for a second wedding celebration with my family that couldn't make it to Cincinnati. I'd been away from home for almost three years, returning only for a few weeks once a year, as Daniel had promised my father when they first met. I had only a few friends who I kept up with on Facebook, and I'd been losing touch with extended family for some time. I hardly spoke to cousins, and coming home turned out to be an exercise in facing my demons. I was excited for Daniel and his mother to celebrate with my whole family, but my inner voice reminded me I no longer belonged to them. I never heard from most of them, save Uncle Bala and Devi Atthey.

We arrived two days before the wedding, jet-lagged but excited, to a house filled with people. I had never been close to my mother's family, as most lived in Borneo and we hardly ever saw them. My father's family, whom I grew up with, were all there. They were all busy getting things we needed for the wedding. It was so festive and wonderful.

Lori was excited to be there, to see where I came from. We did our rounds, greeting everyone. I introduced Daniel and his mother to them all. It was hilarious with the language barriers. I only spoke English and Malay, but my mother's family originated from the Cocos Islands. They spoke a dialect of Malay, which I didn't speak and understood only very minimally. I would begin speaking in Malay, and they would respond in their dialect, which my mother would translate. My mother's family were besotted with Daniel's fair skin and blue eyes, and with his mother's blonde hair. I was reminded of a conversation I had with one of my mother's sisters when I was a teenager.

"When you grow up and look for a husband," she'd told me, "be sure not to find one that's dark like your daddy." She suppressed a little giggle.

"Why?" I'd asked.

"You are already dark, and if he is dark, your child will be ugly—too dark." She laughed hard, as though this were a punch line. Clearly, I had missed what was funny about any of it because I ran out of the room crying.

On the night of the rehearsal dinner, I overheard my father say to one of his friends, "She doesn't work now. He's got a good job to take care of her. Lucky girl."

Later that evening, he said to another relative, "She's okay now. She doesn't have to worry about anything. Got a good husband."

I was *okay now*. The words reverberated in my head. Of course, intellectually I understood that my marriage had released him from the burden of worrying about me. Emotionally, I understood that my father had long suffered because of me. It was true—I was not okay. But I was sometimes. And I did have a job. His disappointment in what I had made of myself showed. He had always imagined me as "successful" in a big corporate career or heading some big firm. I was a preschool teacher at the time, and he knew that. That was not up to his standard of success, and so he made little of an achievement I was proud of, a job that brought me so much joy.

His words buzzed in my mind. I was highly irritable.

"Babe, where am I supposed to be?" Daniel asked me urgently.

"I don't know!" I snapped, a decibel short of yelling.

"Why are you mad? How am I supposed to know anything?" he replied.

"I don't know! I don't know! Asking me again and again isn't going to change that!" I yelled.

"You're embarrassing us. Stop it," he said, mortified.

My mind went blank, right there in the middle of the wedding rehearsal. The fifty people present stared at me. I got up to leave. My mother-in-law looked shocked but stayed silent through it all. As our eyes met, I felt regret for having caused a scene.

I found a silent spot at the hotel to smoke. I turned off my phone and sat in silence, the smoke entering my lungs and meeting the fury in my body. I wallowed in the embarrassment, but it was too late now. I was angry and sad. I was in a mixed episode of hypomania and depression. Going off my meds had started a degradation. I was triggered by being home because I was in constant anxiety over bumping into someone from my past. The wedding was stressful, and my insecurities were creeping up. I had no meds to fight Haddy Maddy. It would all have been fine if we were back in Kentucky and I could see Natasha. But I proved naive in thinking I would be able to handle being back home with none of the professional support or meds. I couldn't find my way through the triggers. I was at a loss about how to handle this, and it made my anxiety worse.

Daniel found me in my secret smoking corner and held me for the next hour as I sobbed. He knew. As we were walking back to our room, we ran into a cousin of mine who was on the way to another cousin's room. Apparently, my entire family was gathering to drink in celebration. Great, a celebration of me without me—I had never received an invite. I no longer belonged as things had been going on without me when I was gone. Daniel comforted me, assuring me it was better we go to bed anyway. When I woke up to the wedding preparations the next day, everyone went about business as usual, thankfully. I received a silent absolution from the embarrassment of my outburst the night before.

~

The next morning, I was surprised by the early arrival of a good friend, Alia, who had flown in from Brunei for my wedding. She sat with me and chatted away as I had my hair and makeup done. She helped me feel better, like a warm blanket on a nippy morning. We had gone to the same university, the second one I attended. I never told her about my condition, but it was as if she always knew there was something going on with me. Still I did not reveal anything to her, not even knowing where I would start. I was just glad she was with me now as Daniel could not be with me during the wedding preparations. She was calm and patient. Her bubbly personality was perfect for this moment of darkness. I'd never known her to have a worry in the world, for if she had any, she masked it beautifully. She kept me company and kept me sane, giving me comfort in all the anxiety that remained from the night before. I was still unsettled, but I had to be still for the makeup.

Mask on, I was ushered to the ceremony. It was quick. My mother-in-law fit the ring on my right finger. I put her hands on my forehead and asked for blessings, and she kissed me on the cheek. She said nothing to me about the night before. I kept my regret to myself. Daniel held my hand. I held his hand to my forehead, and he kissed me on my forehead as instructed by an aunt calling out the procedural rites. We posed for photos and returned to the hotel to grab a quick lunch before the reception. This came with another outfit change. Alia accompanied me through it all. Had she not been there, I would have had no one but the makeup artist with me. I was a loner in a festivity with hundreds in celebration of me.

The reception itself was glorious, with 350 people. Many of them were my relatives. There were traditional dancers, and the whole venue was decorated for a traditional Malay affair. Jasmine garlands adorned the entire hall. There was a whole lamb on the pit and twelve different dishes for the meal. We were escorted into the venue by a troop of drummers playing the Malay hand drum, the *kompang*. It was so regal and ceremonious. At the head of the troop were my cousins carrying the *bunga manggar*, an artificial version of the palm blossom, signifying marriage and fertility. We walked into the hall to be seated at the *pelamin*, a raised platform with thrones on it. This was tradition as we were royalty for a day. The dances and performances ensued as we sat awkwardly on our thrones. My brother and cousin kept us cool with large hand fans and brought us drinks. After enough time had passed with us on display as the newly wedded couple, we were escorted to the head table to finally have our meal and watch even more performances. My cousins' children put on a traditional South Indian dance, the *bharatanatyam*, an homage to the traditions that raised us.

The whole festivity was my mother's show of love for me. She had always been shy with words, showing her love in acts of service. She meticulously put together the show, celebrations, and three outfit changes for Daniel and me, for us to feel like the king and queen of the day. She did so brilliantly, and we felt it. Still, I felt like an outsider at my own wedding. I was fading away already from my family picture, fading away from the place I called home. It was inevitable but painful nonetheless.

~

When we left Kuala Lumpur to return to our new home in Kentucky, my father's words rang in my ear. I knew he was proud of his son-in-law and was bragging about him. Self-doubt and insecurities refused to let me believe this. I was embarrassed for not having achieved anything that my father could brag about. I was a disappointment.

I called in a crisis session with Natasha, and we processed the episode that had begun in the three weeks I was in Malaysia. She confirmed what I'd suspected. "What you're in is what we call a mixed episode, with both hypomania and depression presenting simultaneously." It explained my irritability and anxiety climbing higher than it had in a long time and the recurring thoughts of worthlessness and sadness.

"Is this what it's going to be like for the next year or so?" I was reconsidering what the first therapist said about me having children.

"No, episodes don't last. They always pass, and you'll get through them one at a time," she explained. "But it sounds like your trip to Malaysia was exceptionally stressful. Here at home, you'll have more control, and we can manage the episodes as they come. You can do this." It took a few weeks for me to get back to baseline once the stressors were removed. I realized how much harder it was going to be without the medications, but I was determined to have a healthy baby, drug-free. Even though Natasha said there were drugs that have been proven to be safe with pregnancy, I was not willing to take any risks. I gathered all my strength to power through the next year or so without my medications. I was scared as hell knowing the anguish that the episodes brought, but I wanted a baby.

Daniel and I began trying for a baby as soon as we got home from Malaysia. It didn't take long. My period was late on my next cycle, and the double stripes on the pregnancy test confirmed that we were going to become parents.

CHAPTER 10

The doubts cast by the therapist about having children were slow to die. But my desire to have a family won. Now we were joyfully expecting our firstborn, a baby girl. I quit my job during my first trimester to become a stay-at-home mom. The pregnancy was a dream, and my episodes were rare. Daniel and I attended hypnobirthing classes, where we learned about pregnancy and birth. I took prenatal vitamins and did prenatal yoga. I meditated, went on long walks, and took breastfeeding classes. I dreamed about a natural birth. My two absolutes were that my body was made to carry this child to birth and that birthing was an absolute natural process, which I should be able to perform with no interventions.

One of the books on hypnobirthing I read said that women in Africa had babies, then went into the fields to work immediately. My mother in Malaysia had four drug-free births. I wanted the same for my babies. Any kind of medical intervention meant subjecting my child to drugs, and I had worked to wean myself off prescribed drugs in order to become pregnant in the first place. Breastfeeding was an extension of this idea. I wanted to feed my child from my breasts, the most natural way for a baby to be fed. All the antibodies and nutrients were in my breast milk. I learned that breast milk strengthened the baby's immune system and digestive system, lowered risk of infections, and even lowered risks of sudden infant death syndrome (SIDS). I had struggled in the past with so many bad decisions in my own life. This time, with my baby, I was going to do things right. I would put her first and do everything in my power to keep her healthy and safe.

I prepared for birth and motherhood the whole nine months that I carried her, whispering to her all the wonderful things we would do together when she arrived. When she finally did, it took two long days of labor. I was confronted with decision after decision, but I made them all with surety. I had the newly discovered power of a mother making choices for her child. Due to complications, I had to abandon my hypnobirthing plan for an emergency C-section. While I was disappointed, I knew it was necessary. Her pulse had been dropping, and all that mattered was that she was safe. Daniel was by my side every step of the fifty-one-hour labor and delivery, but I did not feel an absolute reliance on him to make the decisions for my baby. I spoke to her while she was still in my belly and assured her of my strength and ability to bring her into my arms. The moment the doctor held my nine-pound baby over the sheet, I was in love as if for the first time. It was the kind of love that was unfamiliar and intoxicatingly possessive.

Nursing my sweet baby Mandy was all I had imagined it would be. It was a deeper connection than I'd ever known. I learned in my birthing and breastfeeding classes that breast is best for the baby, a sign of the primal intuition between mother and infant. It sounded magical to me, and I wanted that natural connection with my baby. Mandy took to the breast almost instantly. I felt as if I were born for this role, and nothing could stop me from doing right by baby Mandy. Within a day of nursing, watching her on my breast brought me power. I was the only person in the world who could give her this gift of life and love. She was mine, as I was hers. I watched as she suckled my breast, her eyes blinking sleepily. For the first time in years, I felt full, whole, and no longer broken. I was utterly smitten by her.

Our first few months together were intuitive. We were in sync in all we did. We played, and I cooked as she cooed softly at me. Her bath times were the best. She smiled and laughed as I read her the bath books. She opened her mouth wide to kiss me when I lowered my face.

When Mandy was six months old, I met Jenny, the woman who'd become my best friend. I was in a checkout line at Babies "R" Us, nipple cream in hand. Mandy was fast asleep in her Ergobaby carrier on my chest. It was the best carrier known to man; I would never be persuaded to try any other kind. In front of me was a couple about my age with a baby about Mandy's age. They were using one of those baby slings I could never figure out. The mom looked really nice. I didn't know what they were talking about, but she laughed a little, and my heart answered. I liked her, and something in me compelled me to talk to her.

"Hi. Do you like that sling?" I asked.

"Hi. Yeah, I love it. It's really comfortable. . . ." She said more, but I was too busy trying to think of what to say next. I wanted to continue talking to this lovely woman for as long as I could.

But we were just two moms checking out, and each of us had to be on our way. I berated myself later for not asking her for her number, but maybe that would have been weird.

About a week later, I was at Mandy's music class, wiping down the drumsticks she'd been chewing. I looked up and there she was, the Babies "R" Us mom.

"Hi!" I exclaimed.

She stared at me for a few long seconds, then said, "Babies 'R' Us, right?"

I nodded, and we chatted through the whole class. We did not pay attention to anything that was going on, engrossed in conversation. We kept up with our friendship, meeting up regularly after that day. I didn't know it then, but the universe had presented the exact kind of friend for some of the challenges that were in store for me.

It was just Mandy and me, and motherhood was a dream. Even as an infant, Mandy and I traveled together, as she was easy and adaptable. We went to Colorado, Texas, Louisiana, and Malaysia together within her first ten months. I felt like a champion mom, as other moms commented on how hard it was to travel with children. I was in charge of decisions that seemed to have made Mandy agreeable at every turn. I stayed true to my intentions of staying off medications while I was nursing, and by the time we were closing in on a year, I felt absolutely confident that we could handle baby number two.

~

Daniel and I wanted to have two kids not far apart in age so they would have a close relationship growing up. We thought it would be months of trying as I had read about secondary infertility. Instead, I got pregnant again almost immediately. I was eight weeks pregnant at Mandy's first birthday party. I was once again fully resolute to be pregnant and nursing with no medications. I figured my second baby would benefit from everything I had learned was best for Mandy. But from the get-go, this pregnancy did not go as well. I was sick through the end of my second trimester, landing in the emergency room three times for dehydration. Then I was in physical therapy for pubic symphysis, which made it impossible for me to stand or walk without a stabbing pain in my pubic bone. I was in and out of the chiropractor's office for the pain in my tailbone and had to wear a support belt for the rest of the pregnancy. I started to resent the baby and the whole experience with all the physical pain I had endured. The depressive episodes started to slip in.

Two months before Allison was born, we moved to Lexington, a city about an hour south of our first home. Once again, we found out the gender, so we decorated the nursery in anticipation of a second girl. I went into labor two weeks early. I had been cleared for a vaginal birth after C-section (VBAC). I also planned to go with no medical interventions this time. Unlike my birth with Mandy, there were few issues. The VBAC was successful, and I was elated when she was delivered. I held her on my chest, tears running down my face, triumphant and grateful about what we'd accomplished together. It felt like an auspicious beginning. But I only had five seconds with her before the nurses grabbed her, lying her on the tray next to my bed. I hadn't noticed, but she was quiet when she came out. A stern nurse was slapping Allison's back. "Come on, baby. Come on, baby. Come on." The whole room froze. I watched Daniel glued to his spot, staring at the nurse. My midwife's eyes were wide. Two other nurses stood by her side with their chins dropped.

"What's going on?" I asked. "Somebody tell me what's going on." I was now terrified. I prayed hard for my baby. Everyone in the room avoided eye contact with me. Then a sharp shriek filled the room, followed by loud cheering. From the instant she was born, she had me on edge.

When we got Allison home, she always seemed to be uncomfortable and crying. She had colic, eye infections, and ear infections. It seemed like each day melded with the next, and rest was not part of our routine. During the day she cried all the time, never settling in my arms. She cried herself to sleep and did not find comfort on my skin or my breast. They say oxytocin, the hormone responsible for contentment, flows when we breastfeed. Now that she wouldn't breastfeed, I was uncertain about how to keep her or me happy. Everything seemed hard with Allison in contrast to Mandy. I started to doubt myself. I felt like a failure, always at a loss for how to soothe her.

Now that she was here, I yearned for when it was just Mandy and me. It was not supposed to be this way. I wanted a relationship with Allison, but she would not have it. She pushed my breasts away. She cried when I picked her up. But she was not this way with Daniel. He soothed her on the nights she woke up screaming. One night when she was about a month old, I tried to soothe her as I'd seen Daniel do. I carried her carefully with her head on my chest like he did, hands cupping her back and tapping slowly while humming to her softly. Every time he did this, she calmed down. When I picked her up, it was like my skin burned hers—it only made things worse. She stared at me as she cried bloody murder. I put her in the cradle and rocked her gently, but she only cried more. I tried to nurse her, and she screamed, looking away from my breasts as if they disgusted her.

When I looked up through my tears, there was Daniel, watching with pity. I could tell he felt sorry for me. The judgments came into my head. *She doesn't love you. You are rotten. She is repulsed by you. You are an unfit mother.* Daniel brought a bottle to me. I tried to give it to her, but she was crying so violently, she couldn't take the bottle. In despair, I handed her over to Daniel. "Shh, shh, shh. . . ." He lulled her to sleep after feeding her, and I watched the whole thing unfold, this confirmation that I was an unfit mother. Resentment welled up inside of me. The sight of them together, wrapped up in their love, clawed at my heart. How could she prefer him? How could my own child not like me?

~

When Allison was three months old, I made an appointment with the midwife to talk about the difficulties I was facing.

"Postpartum depression." The midwife threw the assessment out as if it were the common cold. "It's very common with the hormonal changes after birth to feel a little out of whack. There are many drugs out there that are safe while nursing."

Okay. I smiled and nodded. I hadn't had any drugs throughout the pregnancy. I had done my best to keep my body healthy despite my emotional pain. Surely, I did all the right things, so why was I being punished now that she was finally in my arms? Even though I knew I was in the throes of a mixed episode, I refused to get back on drugs. No, I was already a shit mother. I was not screwing up this child. I would take *no* risks. She was going to get the healthiest food from my breasts, even if it was delivered through a bottle. No drugs. I thought of my inability to connect with Allison as karma for all the terrible things I had done in my life.

The thought of everything I had to do in order to get back on meds was overwhelming. I already had a diagnosis. I dreaded the impending sessions and questionnaires verifying my hypomania and depression. I knew I should be medically treated—I had been all those years—but I wanted to wait until I was done nursing. I wanted things to be as easy as they had been with Mandy. Putting my baby first was all I could think of, and I had read somewhere that formula punctures little holes in the baby's intestines. That this might be untrue didn't matter, as I was not willing to take any chances. I was willing to bear down on my pain while my daughter got what she needed. I'd done so many shitty things, but raising this baby was one thing that was in my control. I could get this mothering thing right.

But I was struggling to keep either of my children happy, because I was depressed and detached. I wondered if that therapist had been right, that I wasn't capable of having children.

I was holding back tears as I saw the midwife's lips moving. I wanted to leave, to disappear into thin air. She handed me a paper with "vitamin B" and some advice about mindful relaxation written on it. Fuck that—I hardly had any energy to breathe. I'd come there because I needed the baby to stop screaming. I would have gone to a therapist if I wanted help with my state of mind. I needed the midwife to give me an explanation for what was wrong with my breasts and why they repelled Allison. I wanted this midwife to fix me, to help Allison see me as a worthy mother.

But she'd already been examined by her pediatrician, lactation consultants, and nurses, all of whom had said, "She's perfect," every time. "Sometime these things just take time." That was the universal response. No dice—I was the fucking problem. I left the midwife's office disappointed, screaming baby in tow.

A few days later, I found a new therapist in Lexington. Her name was Hilary, and she was not insistent that I start drug therapy, although she encouraged it. She said we could take it day by day. After several sessions, Hilary confirmed my diagnosis and treatment plan for bipolar disorder, type two. Allison continued struggling to latch and was constantly hungry, but I pumped milk and fed her with a bottle. Finally, after four months, I gave up pumping altogether and conceded to the formula. I resumed drug therapy and waited for the balance in my brain to take place. I was prescribed a new drug that was the latest in treating bipolar and was assured of its efficacy and manageable side effects. I had come to a conclusion that playing martyr was not what was best for my children. My irrational obsession with breastfeeding and its connection to me being a good mother took a back seat. The pediatrician also debunked the rumor I'd heard, assuring me that formula did not result in punctures to the intestines. I saw right away how absolute my thinking had been and how detrimental it was for Allison and me. I started taking medications again, hoping to quiet my mind.

Therapy with Hilary got off to a slow start. Two months in, I wasn't feeling any better. I'd stay up all night watching Allison breathe. Daniel woke up twice to feed her and once more to comfort her. He was such a good father, the kind who just knew what to do. I was feeling less resentful. I appreciated everything he was doing. My connection with Allison hadn't improved significantly, but I was glad for the comfort she found in Daniel. The sinking feeling in my heart came from not being able to give her the same comfort. From the time we had our first child, he was always ready to jump in. He was also a solid husband. He had almost all of the responsibilities because I was struggling, and I was no help when it came to Allison. He saw the signs of my depression, asked me to confirm, and swooped in to keep the train moving. He cared for the children's and my every need. Daniel was relieved that I was back in treatment as he had urged me to seek it after Allison was born. He knew I needed support, but I had been adamant in proving I could do it on my own. I found relief now that I was seeing a therapist again.

Therapy and medication helped me come to terms with the fact that my illness was back. Hilary explained that I could have been in a stable baseline during my pregnancy with Mandy and the year that followed. Peaks and troughs are part of the experience of bipolar. Some episodes might last a few days, while others go for months. To be considered hypomania, according to the American Psychiatric Association's *Diagnostic and Statistical Manual of Mental Disorders* (DSM-5), the mood must last at least four consecutive days and be

present most of the day, almost every day. Presentation of depressive symptoms in two weeks can be diagnosed as a major depressive
episode. This last episode I had been in had lasted more than a few
months.

Apparently, I'd been in a healthy place with Mandy. For someone with bipolar, this means somewhere in between, a baseline, when
the illness is under control. Now Haddy Maddy was back, screaming
in my head. At the same time, I had fallen into depression without
even realizing it. The best way to combat this mixed episode had been
through medication all along, but everything felt slow to take effect. I
wasn't even close to getting back to that healthy baseline.

"Mommy, Mommy, I want susu." Mandy was standing next to
my bed, asking for milk. I looked at my toddler, at a loss to help her
with this simple request.

"Mommy, can you please get me susu? I'm hungry." I shut my
eyes, hoping she'd go back to her room. She was so articulate, like
a mini adult. She was well ahead of her years with speech, so much
so that we'd recently had her assessed. But she was having night terrors and acting strangely at home. Ultimately, we discovered that
our two-year-old was suffering from anxiety. The assessment also
revealed that she had an abnormally high intellect. I kept that information tucked away. I didn't know what to do with it, especially given
the issues I was facing with Allison, who was fast asleep next to me.
I looked at my older daughter. She needed me to get out of bed, but I
couldn't. She turned around and left, and a few seconds later I heard
her bedroom door slam shut. I just needed a little more time before
Allison woke up.

I considered the two relationships. Allison and I struggled. I
couldn't ever be settled with her because she was never settled with
me. We seemed not to like each other at times. She had made my

body sick during pregnancy. The two years before she arrived had been bliss. Mandy breathed life into me. But Allison had managed to surface all that sadness and grief, shoving it down my throat. *What kind of mother cannot connect with her own baby?* And now I was pushing Mandy away because of her. I wondered if Allison hated me because she knew the truth about me. She could see that I was rotten to the core. Maybe it was as simple as that.

~

I kept seeing Hilary. The days turned into months. Soon Allison was ten months old, and things were not significantly better. Daniel arrived home from work one evening to find Mandy playing in the playroom as I was rocking Allison to sleep in our bedroom. I heard him through the open bedroom door.

"Hi baby. Are you playing with Kion?"

"Lion Guard, defend! Mommy's crying in the room, Daddy."

My heart was crushed. I felt embarrassed that my two-and-a-half-year-old understood the deplorable state I was in and was concerned for me.

"I see," he said calmly. "Mommy is feeling bad and won't be able to get out of bed, so we need to help her, baby. You can help by playing in the playroom or on your iPad, okay?" At times like these, I willed myself to believe she would be better for my issues, that she would be independent, strong, and compassionate. She already knew to get her own water, fruit, and snacks. She was more self-sufficient than other toddlers, which made me feel both pride and guilt.

I tried to put on a smile for Daniel, who was coming up the stairs. He walked in to kiss Allison gently on her head so he wouldn't wake her. Then he sat on the bed next to me and gave me a peck. "Babe, I'm not pushing you to feel better, but maybe we should consider new medications? I hate seeing you suffer like this." This reminded him of our days in Japan.

"I am on medications, and I am better than I was before them. It just takes time." I didn't want to try a new set of drugs only to suffer side effects. I dreaded the trial-and-error method of figuring out the right medication. I longed for a one-size-fits-all drug, but that did not exist.

"We can't go on like this. Mandy understands something is wrong. The children need you," he said as he stared out the bedroom door. We could see Mandy in the living room now. I was so sick and tired of being so sick and tired. I was tired of having to continually revise treatment *plans*. But Daniel was right—the children were suffering. I hugged him and promised I would find answers.

"I know you will, baby. You always do," he said, smiling as he went to take a shower. The next day, I made an appointment with my doctor to ask about new medication. She agreed to put me back on the regimen that had worked, and now I had to wait for it to build up in my system. All of us hoped that this would lift the fog that obscured everything I had dreamt of but that I now seemed incapable of being present for.

Two weeks later, I felt the weight lifting. Mandy kissed me goodbye and went to spend the next four hours with friends at the preschool. I saw this as a blessing for her, a time to be away from my pain. Allison seemed content in the back seat, and soon enough we were back home together. I placed her on the floor on a play mat. I watched her as she gnawed on toys, looking up whenever a chirping noise came from the window. She didn't seem to detest me as much anymore. I was aware that my depressive episode had made things harder. I routinely identified my thinking errors and made efforts to redefine them as I had learned in therapy. I pulled out some bananas, carefully slicing them into bite-sized pieces for her.

The pain, which I was consistently told to think away by everyone around me, was a stubborn motherfucker. I wished I could
think away things like Daniel did. It seemed effortless for him to set
his mind on something or change it. Though the fog lifted, it was
replaced by incessant guilt for being a terrible mother, terrible wife,
and waste of space.

~

By the time Allison's first birthday rolled around, she and I were
finding our footing. I was starting to feel better emotionally, and the
medication was helping. Allison demanded my attention, but I felt
like I'd earned my way into her inner circle. I was so excited to plan
her first birthday party. I hired a petting zoo with an alpaca, a sheep,
a goat, and some rabbits. She loved the animals in her books, so we
had a barnyard-themed party. It turned out that she did not love the
live animals as much as the still art in her picture books. But she sure
enjoyed friends at the party and cake.

That afternoon, as we were cleaning up after the party, we
received a call from Malaysia. It was my brother Adik telling me my
father had suffered a stroke.

I acted fast. The first flight I could find was the next morning. I
booked tickets for Mandy, Allison, and I to make the trip to Malaysia.

We got there thirty nine hours after my brother's call. My father
had suffered paralysis to his right side. This was the man who had
walked miles with me and traveled the world. His speech was affected
by the stroke, creating intense frustration for him. The prognosis was
weak—he might regain some movement in his limbs, and chances
were slim that he would walk again. I tried not to stress him with
conversation, and he indulged in time with his grandchildren. They
were thrilled to play with him.

On the second week of our visit, my father wanted to leave the house. He'd regained his strength and had been growing restless. He insisted that we were keeping him captive. My brother conceded and said he would take him for a drive to grab some takeout as long as he stayed in the car with my mother.

While I was putting the children to sleep, not twenty minutes after they had left, my brother called for me to rush to the hospital. My father had lost consciousness in the car. I got the kids up to take them with me. My cousin, who was staying at my parents' house, drove us to the hospital and kept Mandy and Allison while I ran into the emergency room. I announced my father's name to the nurse at the front desk, and she told me where he was. I rushed to the bed, eyes on her sneakers as she led the way. Posters on the walls went by in a blur. The fluorescent lights above blinded me as my head spun with all the worst possibilities. The harsh brightness forced me to go faster to my brother and mother, who were standing outside the curtain of my father's bed.

The nurse took leave quietly. The room was so bright, and even though I was warm from my sprint-walk down the corridor, I noticed goosebumps on my arms. I saw no one else other than medical staff in this restricted area. We had been given special access due to my father's dire condition. Nurses walked around in pink scrubs from one partition to another, patients separated by a thin curtain. I searched the room for my father. I caught sight of a green curtain being drawn and saw my father's hand falling off the bed—it seemed to be bouncing. All I could hear were the muffled voices of the people behind that curtain, and I understood that the staff were trying to resuscitate him. My brother explained that my father's heart had stopped. He hadn't taken a breath on his own for almost thirty minutes. I noticed all the tubes on his arms, drugs being pumped into his lifeless body. A loud, singular beep rang, continuously matching the flatline on one of the little monitors.

It was like a horror scene that I couldn't avert my eyes from. I could see a man on top of my father, pounding on his chest. Another young nurse rubbed defibrillators together, placing them on my father's chest and calling "Clear!" as everyone else leaped away from the bed. I could hear the thumping sounds the paddles made on my father's chest, followed by the long continuous beep. My father's body plopped lifeless in the aftershock. She did this repeatedly, so much that I lost any sense of time. It could have been three minutes or an hour. I stood there, paralyzed and watching. My father's arms hung over the sides and flailed up and down each time they tried to resuscitate him. Those hands that had held mine were lifeless. I remembered his hands in mine as we walked together in the Christmas market of Montreux. His hand had touched my forehead and my newborns' as he welcomed his grandchildren. He had held the hand of my first love, a shared promise to take care of me.

The doctor emerged from behind the curtain to pronounce my father's time of death. I screamed. I saw the doctor's sweat-misted face, his eyes red with sympathy and exhaustion.

"No!" I cried. My mother gripped my arm.

"No," I said again, this time more calmly. "It's not time yet. You will keep trying. My father is coming back to me. He can hear me."

The doctor's eyes were moist; what a terrible job he had. "We have done our best. It is customary we call time of death at the thirty-minute mark."

"Daddy! You can hear me! I'm here, and I need you! Please. Please come back, Daddy!" I believed he was still with us, that he could choose not to leave this world and all of us behind.

"You will keep trying," I said to the doctor. I had never been more certain.

He looked hard at me for a good five seconds. "Okay," he said and walked back behind the curtain. He drew it closed and called out medical terms. There were twelve more excruciating minutes of pounding and shouting. "Clear!" There were more numbers and the monotonous beep indicating a lack of a heartbeat. I was plunged into silent, airless horror.

Eeeeeeeeeeeeeeee . . .

"Clear!" the nurse called out as she pressed the paddles onto my father's chest.

Beep. Beep. Beep.

~

My father did come back to us that night. He'd been clinically dead for forty-two minutes, his revival a miracle. No one could believe it. We worried that he wouldn't make it past the night, so family crowded the waiting area. He was discharged after two weeks in the intensive care unit, followed by a week in the regular ward where the doctors monitored his recovery. "He has suffered significant brain damage from oxygen deprivation to the brain. There's no telling how much of it, if any, will come back. I recommend getting in-home help to assist with your father." The doctor also told us that my father was in a fragile state and that they had not anticipated his survival. He called it a miracle.

He was alive, but it wasn't all happy news. His speech was limited to that of a toddler's, and depression descended upon him almost immediately. My mother and little brother were tasked with his care. Once he was home, I felt like it was safe for us to get back to Daniel. We'd been in Malaysia for more than five weeks. I said goodbye to my father, who did not recognize me and refused to kiss me. I remembered his warm lips on my forehead whenever he'd said goodbye in the past. He had given me strong hugs. The love in those gestures had given me courage. Now these were just memories. I looked at him lying in that bed. I memorized every line on his face, the smoothness of his forehead meeting the stubble on his cheek. I didn't know if I'd see him again, given his fragile state.

Once I got home, and with the stress of caring for my father behind me, I was taken over by memories. I remembered him refusing to ask for directions while traveling in London because he couldn't keep up with the accent and fast-speaking Londoners. We never found the place we were looking for. But I remembered my father's belly laugh and his crooked front teeth.

I thought of him incessantly. I knew there was no knowledge, or wisdom, or any fucking psychological bullshit to get through this horrid, undignified state my father was in. There was not a fucking thing that would improve his experience. But in my memories, we existed as we were before. When I fell asleep at night, he was the strongest man I knew, the wisest and funniest. This was despite all we'd been through and the secrets I'd kept from him. I longed to argue with him like I used to, but now all I had were our fights playing in my head like an old movie. I settled on the fact that what happened was part of our journey. I accepted that the father I knew would remain a memory.

Our communication, already challenged by time zone differences, was now further stifled by my father's inability to speak or comprehend much. Most days, he didn't want to talk to me. I didn't know whether it was because he didn't recognize me or didn't have the will to communicate with limited thoughts and words. It was like his journal got wet in the rain, all the words smudged, never to be heard. When we were able to connect, I stared at the screen, smiling. I hoped he would recognize me, that he shared the same memories.

~

Six months after our return to Kentucky, I was grieving and in pain. I realized my grieving was past that of a baseline state and that I had entered a mixed episode—Haddy Maddy and depression walking hand in hand. I had only come up to baseline recently after struggling with Allison, and my father's withdrawal into his own world pushed me back. There were dark times, and they were familiar, like an old friend.

I hadn't eaten all day because I couldn't decide what to cook. I hadn't had a shower in eight days. My anxiety was through the roof. I knew our kids deserved better, but I didn't know what we could do but wait out the episode. I was hardest on myself, crying in guilt to Daniel nightly. I showed appreciation for him whenever I could and tried my best to help around the house. He remained there for me and said that we would get through the episode. He was confident, and I believed him. He carried out all the household responsibilities and supported me as I tried to be more participatory.

These episodes hit me like a sixty-foot rip curl that dragged me a hundred feet deep into the water and left me there to drown. It was a relentless struggle, though no one could see the effort. I tried to distinguish rational thoughts from bipolar thoughts, though this didn't seem useful most of the time because the emotions were excruciating. I wallowed in self-pity, obsessing over what the therapist had said about people with bipolar not being able to raise children. Would I ever be able to do this?

Mandy was a little over three, and Allison was already eighteen months. They were both napping one afternoon. Daniel had just left his office, which meant it would be thirty minutes until he got home. He announced his departure and arrival every day, for my sanity. This particular day, I decided I would sit very quietly and let the kids sleep longer. If I left right away, I could take the sheet I'd enveloped myself in, go to the woodlands across from our house, and hang myself from a tree. It wouldn't be in our house, so the children wouldn't have to see me. Daniel would get home soon enough that they'd never be in danger. By the time he realized what was going on, it would be too late. I'd be gone, but they'd all be better off without me.

It was classic depression. I considered the damage this would have on my girls. The chaos of my emotions was all internal, of course, so I still had to go on doing the things I promised or managing responses to the things I could not. My kids were growing, as were my friendships with moms in the area.

"Hey, how are you doing? Want to get together for wine some time?" The text blinked on my phone. I ignored it. Ghosting people became a skill. I learned to prioritize so I still functioned, but it was fucking agony. It was worse as a mother. Teachers from Mandy's preschool or other moms expected things of me, and "I am depressed" would not have been an appropriate response.

"We need volunteers for the year. Attached is a list of volunteer positions as needed. Please fill out and return to us," read an email from Mandy's preschool. Daniel replied, choosing to feed the chickens at the school for a week. He knew that would be an acceptable task in which I wouldn't need to interact with anyone. I obliged, even though I didn't want to do anything.

People who loved me—Jenny, Sara, my mother-in-law—thought they could help. "If I just support her through this . . ." But it wasn't as simple as someone lifting me out of it. They knew having two toddlers was difficult enough on any mom, but my mental illness made it much worse.

One morning, as she always did when I hadn't called for at least three days, my mother-in-law rang. "Good morning, Amy. How are we doing this morning?" She knew something was wrong but didn't want to pressure me into talking.

"Fine," I said.

"You feeling all right, baby? We can talk if you want to."

"I'm not feeling great, but we can talk." I was desperate for her support, but I didn't know what to say.

"Well, have you seen Jenny lately? Would be nice to spend some time with her." Jenny had come by unannounced the day before, surprising me with lunch. As soon as she saw me, she'd insisted I take a nap. But I didn't want to share this information with my mother-in-law. I knew how much she worried about me, the girls, and Daniel. Instead, I talked about the squirrels we'd seen in our garden and the house projects she was working on.

Finally, she said, "Okay. Call me anytime you need anything, okay? I'm going to get lunch ready." The truth was that I didn't know what I needed other than to clear this fog out of my head so I could be *normal*.

I had learned to go on autopilot. I said things that I wasn't sure were right but were better than nothing. I practiced the fake smile and having to rush away for a fake reason or getting the sudden phone call. I took my kids to their classes—swim, music, dance, and gymnastics—and sat in the car, weeping. I struggled with the madness in my mind and being a mother. In time, I reduced the number of classes they attended outside preschool to manage expectations of myself. I was accepting that I wasn't like all the other moms and that it was okay to have my own boundaries.

I managed what I could, but I didn't talk to anyone very much. I texted close friends, "I'm not doing well. I need space. We'll talk soon." They knew the drill and tried not to worry. I was isolating myself even further. I never knew if they understood because I was unable to communicate with anyone. When I was better, we pussy-footed around the subject, and I brushed it off. There was so much fucking guilt for pushing my best friends away. I didn't want to be that friend that needed everyone all the time, and in my effort to figure it all out, I disappeared.

~

A year passed since my father had been in the emergency room. Allison was two, and Mandy was four. One afternoon, I got anxious and made them bring their paints and easels into my bedroom. They were covered in paint already, and Mandy was confused because they were never allowed to leave the playroom with their art supplies.

I set them up and watched them paint by the window. I lay back down as I watched them. They were carefree and happy. Mandy's hair glistened in the sun that shone through the window as she painted. My sweet Allison squinted from the sun in her big brown eyes.

"These are coping strategies. You do what you have to do to manage," Hilary had told me in our last therapy session. I'd brought the girls with me. They were used to sitting in Hilary's office while I had my hour-long sessions.

"But other moms don't have to do any of this. Their children get to play with other children, go to the park, dance, play soccer." I was never stable long enough to keep up with any of these commitments. I was either anxious or depressed. These were sacrifices my children unknowingly made to accommodate my condition.

"What is a good mom?" Hilary asked.

"A good mom is one who does all the things for her children, all the things children need to be happy," I answered, feeling annoyed that she was forcing me to explain.

"Your children look happy to me," she said, pointing to them. My well-behaved girls sat there, absorbed with games on their iPads. Behind them, I saw pictures on the wall they had made for Hilary the week before. I believed them to be happy. They were well-adjusted children with good manners and jovial demeanors.

I was brought back to the present by Allison's laugh. I looked up, and Mandy was painting Allison's whole face. Mandy chuckled as she painted her sister, and a smile came over my tired face. My children were happy, ergo I was a decent mother.

Allison and I had found each other. She was such an adorable child. Her comedic timing was impeccable. I recognized her efforts to connect with me now, her soft face as she described the injustice experienced in the playroom ruled by her sister. We were deeply and innately connected, and though ours was a bond hard earned, now I could see her more clearly. Perhaps my energy was too intense in her infancy, perhaps she needed to bond in the way she did with her father, or perhaps I needed a break from motherly duties. Perhaps, perhaps, perhaps. It didn't matter. In all that time, I was not the best mother but a solid mother. My children ate and got what they needed. I told them how much I loved them, and I listened to all their stories.

Mandy had fallen over laughing as she painted her own face, and her sister laughed, watching. I grabbed them both, paint and all, and let them paint me. I felt bliss that we were making it as a family. I heard the garage door. Daniel came running up the stairs in excitement, hearing our laughter. He kissed the girls, who loved the mess they were making. He pulled my head on his chest and whispered,

"You're doing it, babe. You're an amazing mother." I allowed his enthusiasm to buoy me. I was coming back; I could feel it.

While it was true that I struggled with everyday life, motherhood had called for me so strongly. Years of therapy had given me the tools to forge a better life despite bipolar. I had learned the navigational system to this beast. This was to be the rest of my life—acceptance of what is and a treatment plan with consistent talk therapy and effective drug therapy. My life would look vastly different than what I saw on the social media of other moms. Planning ahead was critical. I made lists of things to do should I wake up feeling good. My kids got a lot of spontaneous surprises because on my good days, I never took one minute for granted. Sometimes we had "yes" days to compensate for all the shitty ones. All of us had to ride the wave of my ups and downs. It was a high price to pay for my lousy brain situation. But I was committed to staying the course, riding out the hard times, and being present in the good times. I would adapt. I wanted better for my children.

CHAPTER 11

"**M**ercury, Venus, Earth, Mars, Jupiter, Saturn, Uranus, Neptune!" I was awestruck at Mandy's memory and application, her ability to articulate what she learned. I was also smitten by her twenty-month-old baby voice when listing the planets.

She knew that the sun is not a planet but a star made up of hydrogen and helium. She recited astronomy as she played with her cars and blocks, turning to me whenever I asked her something. This was better than the point-and-show she had done with the types of birds in her favorite book, *Jack's Garden*, about four or five months before. I made notes of the birds in my daily reading to her, digesting the names as a necessity because she knew them: yellow warbler, goldfinch, barn swallow, bluebird, mourning dove, catbird, vireo, robin, and brown thrasher. I bought bird feeders and different feeds so we could observe them in real life.

My friends were amazed by how advanced Mandy was and often asked me what books I was reading to her. At the time, I thought her intelligence must have to do with all that reading. But I soon found out what an anomaly she was. When friends came to visit, they seemed to want verification of her intelligence and asked Mandy questions, usually while I was not nearby. At first, I thought they were just curious and marveling at her extraordinary mind. Then I started feeling defensive. *What was it that they were looking for?*

Daniel and I decided that half-day preschool would be good for Mandy. I would get four hours of one-on-one time with the baby, and Mandy would get to socialize with other kids. We also thought it might curb her jealousy of her little sister. Plus, I was struggling with bipolar episodes and felt concerned about Mandy witnessing so much. We sought out a play-based school, and while we thought it was amazing in every way, she spent the first two months crying every time I dropped her off. Her teacher would always follow up with photos of her having fun, so I chalked it up to a little separation anxiety.

But then she started having night terrors. Once that started, she became extremely needy. She stayed awake at night, struggling to initiate sleep, for three weeks in a row. All of this was new behavior. I was assured by our pediatrician that it was normal. Then things got worse. She wouldn't eat the lunches I sent to school, and she wasn't interested in dinner or snacks outside of school. She'd always eaten anything and actually loved bitter gourd, spinach, and fish. There was something in the way the doctors and nurses spoke to me that made me feel condescended to and belittled. At the last appointment, I sat across from the pediatrician, Mandy on my lap, and said, "She's not eating while she's at school, and she's been waking up at night screaming. I'm concerned because she hasn't behaved like this before."

He didn't even look up from his notepad, where he was scribbling away, and said, "That's typical for this age. She's experimenting with foods. Maybe try sending things to school that she likes to eat. Night terrors are also typical for her age group."

He stood up and started to walk out, so I rushed to say, "It's not really typical of her to be this way, though. I'm worried."

He chuckled as his hand reached for the doorknob. "She's perfectly fine, and it's normal to be worried as a first-time mom."

I started to say, "But—"

And he was gone, finishing our appointment from the hallway as he called out, "All right, we'll see Mandy at the next appointment. Have a good day!"

Perhaps I was overly concerned, but I did not feel heard. I shrugged it off as Haddy Maddy putting self-conscious ideas in my head. I held Mandy tighter as the nurse, who remained in the examination room, said to try something for constipation.

Fuck that, I thought. I had a gut feeling it was psychological and that Mandy didn't have the emotional awareness or vocabulary to express it. I tried the constipation stuff anyway, to no avail.

A few days later, Mandy did something that scared me. She was in the playroom, and I was cooking in the kitchen. I popped my head out to check on her, and I saw her stacking magnets very carefully, singing to herself.

"Mandy, baby, you okay?" I just wanted her to know I was nearby.

"Mommy, I'm building a zoo," she said.

Her sweet voice put a smile on my tired face. I got closer to inspect. She smiled at me, then looked at the neatly stacked magnets and started screaming. It was not the baby-whining sort of screaming. She was out of her mind, as if she were possessed, her eyes tight, with a painful grimace. Her face turned red, as if she were holding her breath or choking. I didn't know what was going on, but I stayed calm. I pried her mouth open with my fingers just in case, but there wasn't anything in there, and the screaming didn't stop. I picked her up quickly and inspected her body in case she was hurt. She continued sobbing and screaming. It was so strange and unnerving, as if she were hurt and deathly afraid at the same time. I picked her up and held her. She slowly calmed down, and I asked her, "Are you hurting?"

She said, "Yes."

"In your body or your feelings?"

She gave that some thought. "Both no."

Well, that was confusing, but she seemed like she was snapping out of it. Her shoulders released, and her head slumped on my shoulder.

"Are you feeling better now?"

"Yes."

"Are you feeling safe?"

"Yes."

"Do you need me?"

"No."

"Okay, I love you. Grab a book and hang out with me while I finish cooking dinner, okay?"

The crisis was averted, but the incident was worrisome. A few days later, the same thing happened. Daniel and I talked about how to handle it. I asked some moms I knew, and a few of them suggested maybe something was going on at school.

The next day I visited the school, talked to the director, and tried to understand what was going on with my twenty-month-old. I steeled myself for confrontation, which I dreaded. I sat in the little office between classrooms. There were glass windows in the doors on either side of the office, permitting a view of the children, who were busy with activities. I waited for the director, who was finishing up a conversation with a teacher. My eyes fixated on a little girl pouring colored water into little vials, laughing as the vials overflowed, and a teacher with kind eyes laughing along. All the children looked happy. The environment seemed perfect, like a commercial for wholesome education.

The director stepped in. "Hi. So, what can I do for you today?" She sat across from me.

"Mandy's been having some trouble at home, and I'm worried. I want to know if you've seen anything at school. If you've noticed anything?"

"She's a happy kid," she said. "As you can see, she likes being by herself quite a bit, but that's typical at this age. Nothing out of the norm that I've seen." I looked out the window and caught a glimpse of Mandy sitting by the blocks, just watching the other children.

"How does she do with the teachers? She's afraid of something, and I wonder if she's afraid of the grownups at school? She's never been without me."

I was grasping to understand what was going on with her, but the director, just like the doctor, assured me nothing was wrong. She said almost the same words to placate me. "It's natural to be worried with your first child like this. But nothing out of the ordinary here. She's doing just fine."

I nodded and left.

The whole situation didn't sit right with me, so I wanted to see how she was behaving when I wasn't around. I asked around, and none of the other moms were reporting any issues. Everyone seemed happy with the school. *Was I just the problem?* I was starting to doubt myself, as I was struggling through episodes and my strained relationship with Allison, but I pushed through for Mandy. I wasn't sure if bipolar was clouding my judgment. I showed up at different times to pick Mandy up, when they weren't expecting me. I found my daughter consistently by the book corner, talking to herself. There was no parallel playing, no engagement with anyone. This was not typical for her. My daughter loved playing with other children. She had a best friend, Jared, and they always hugged and played together. I watched the other kids. They were scattered around the room, and they all looked younger than her in their mannerisms. Many were parallel playing, while others were content with their materials. Mandy was the only one who looked unhappy.

With Mandy, I could not surrender as I often did when it came to myself. My past came into full view—all the times I ran away when the going got tough. This was not an option when it came to my child. I started piecing together milestone charts. I was intimidated by the director and the teachers and didn't want to stir shit up. Requesting accommodations for Mandy meant changing things for the teachers. I did not want to be the troublesome mother, and I felt self-conscious about requiring extras for my child. But watching my child suffer forced me to stand up. A comment kept resurfacing from her twelve-month checkup with Dr. Banfor, her pediatrician at the time: "She's extremely bright, this little one. You watch. I've had patients like her. They come in here when they're four, reciting the planets and dinosaurs and all kinds of mind-blowing stuff. I can already see Mandy is in the same club!"

We had moved since then, or I would have sought his advice. I knew Mandy was ahead of her peers. I just had no idea how far ahead. I read a book about parenting gifted children, trying to find qualifiers for her possible giftedness. I talked to our pediatrician and asked his opinion, and he told me that all kids level out at some point and that the school situation was just a case of separation anxiety. When I asked what he thought about giftedness, his answer was condescending. "I wouldn't get ahead of myself here," he said, chuckling.

Frustrated by how he was writing me off, I sought out specialized psychologists in the area and found out that the author of the book I had just read practiced right there in the city. We were excited for the appointment.

I poured my heart out to Dr. Dufftenson. Daniel gave specific examples of my concerns. I was not very good at details, and I was trying to mask my own anxiety. We gave all the information, related or not—that would be the psychologist's job to figure out. Mandy interrupted us to show her writing and drawing. He observed our interactions with Mandy, and her responses. There was an uncomfortable air about this. I was under a microscope too. Mandy showed me a drawing of a stick man with a flower next to it and said, "It's Daddy and a daisy, Mommy!"

I smiled and said, "That's wonderful, baby." I caught a glimpse of the doctor watching us intently with a smile, which I took as approval of my parenting. I felt as if every move I made was being judged. She showed him the alphabet she had written down. She drew more pictures and talked to him.

"This is a car." She liked him.

"Oh yeah? Is that someone or something in it?" the doctor asked.

"Some*one*. That someone is you." She smiled.

I watched the doctor carefully, trusting that we were on the right course to find answers. He explained that with her age group there weren't many reliable measures, but she was ahead of her peers in terms of intelligence. He proposed that it might in fact be her intelligence that was the cause of the anxious behavior she was exhibiting at home. He also suggested that he perform a brief impromptu assessment.

He took Mandy and me to a room where he had charts, pictures, and flash cards and asked Mandy a lot of questions. She seemed comfortable answering. He then asked Daniel, who had been in the waiting room, to join us in his office. His assessment would introduce us to the world of giftedness.

"She seems to be a twenty-month-old processing intellectually close to a three-year-old. Her emotional regulation is not apt to match her comprehension of the world around her." This would be the first time we heard the words "asynchronous development."

"Her intellectual development is sprinting ahead of the rest of her development. Her being in a room with nonverbal or less-verbal children is almost like being in a country where people don't speak your language, and you're trying to communicate, but no one can respond in kind." The guilt set in as I realized I had left her stranded on an island with no concept of rescue. She was not having fun at school. He suggested she spend at least an hour of her time in school with children in the higher age group. She needed mental stimulation as much as she needed play. Dr. Dufftenson suggested we have her tested again at age three. There would be more reliable tests at that age to help us navigate.

In the meantime, he suggested I carry on with enrichment activities I was already doing at home. He recommended we join parenting groups for gifted children and provided us with resources online and in person. For the first time in months, I had something to act on.

～

I had never been one for confrontation. I spoke to the director of Mandy's preschool over the phone and told her the information from the psychologist. She suggested we have a meeting to talk about the assessment in person.

The next morning, I was too distraught by the pending confrontation to enjoy my breakfast. When I tried to eat, the toast was coming up in my throat.

When I got to the school, I was surprised to be met with the school's own assessment: "She's perfectly normal and happy." She assured me that Mandy was no different in her level of language communication than her peers. When I told her what the doctor suggested, she shook her head. She especially didn't want Mandy to be with the older children, not even for one hour a day.

"Can't we just try what the doctor suggested?" I asked.

I was furious. I couldn't believe she had the audacity to counter what the doctor had said or that she thought she could assess Mandy on her own. *By what measures?* I berated myself for crying, for showing weakness, but then had to restrain myself from nearly slapping her when she said, "Aww, do you need a hug?"

We politely removed Mandy from that school the next day. I made up some bullshit excuse because I did not know how to proceed with them. Pulling her out was the best decision. I felt embarrassed about asking for more for my daughter and self-conscious about stating the fact that she was beyond her peers in intellect. Of course, I had my own doubts about everything, but I knew she needed to be supported. I wanted a school that could meet her where she was, that would at least entertain some flexibility around what might help. I wondered if the pediatrician had been right, that this was typical developmentally and she did not need any intervention. On the other hand, Dr. Dufftenson's findings left me anxious to address the needs of my child to alleviate the stress she was clearly having. I did not yet know how to fight for Mandy and thought it was not my place to ask for more.

Supposedly, intelligence is an esteemed privilege. But in this culture, it's believed that it stems from hard work and studious endeavors. It's something laborious and earned. When it exhibited itself in a toddler who was way ahead of her peers, it was brushed off as insignificant. Mandy's intellectual needs were seen as a threat, and I started feeling incredibly isolated as a parent.

Shortly after we pulled her from school, we heeded Dr. Dufftenson's advice and joined a parenting group for gifted children. We found that the other families had similar experiences. Talking about her advanced development felt *normal*. I learned the term "tall poppies," which came from an article I had read. It was about a military general who asked his father what to do with the leaders of a new tribe they had conquered. His father showed him how all the tall poppies in a field were leveled to maintain order and uniformity. The general took his father's advice to heart and eliminated all the tribal leaders—the tall poppies—removing the threat of resistance. Hence the reference of "crushing the tall poppies," which is what the school system often did, even unwittingly so, for the sake of conformity. Gifted children are outliers. The online community we joined was called Raising Poppies, a nod to the idea of children thriving instead of being cut down for the sake of keeping other people comfortable. The group was a wealth of information and supported me so much. I started finding my footing in parenting our poppy.

I also joined online mom groups, where I found advice on how children must first learn how to socialize, free play, and process best in connection with nature. There are more important things to learn than what can be found in academics, and there are no academics for a two-year-old. Rushing the milestones can cause the toddler trauma. The noise surrounding my parenting was deafening. There were formulas, tips, and opinions at every turn. Giftedness is not confirmable until age nine, I was routinely told by other moms in these groups, and that gave me pause. I knew Mandy was gifted, but was I putting too much emphasis on all of this? Familiar guilt surfaced, except that this time it was deeper because it was my child.

Listening to other moms weigh in about anything to do with Mandy became incredibly stressful. I was often defensive, in many cases even fraudulent, playing down the amazing things I learned about my child. I worried that it rubbed other moms the wrong way. I downplayed Mandy's development to avoid the side-eyes of people around me, who would surely take anything I said as bragging. I realized quickly how lonely I would be, parenting a child that was different. I couldn't talk about my child the way the other moms talked about theirs. Loneliness and guilt, my old friends, were now along on the parenting ride. Still, I intended to give Mandy everything she needed.

~

Mandy was two when we placed her in a traditional, regimented school, something that had more challenge and structure. She had classmates who were older than her, and she loved it. She started making friends and actually engaged with them.

I understood Mandy's behaviors—her inability to pull away from activities, her rigid sense of justice—to be atypical, but I was understanding her better. She was physically healthy, and she was happiest when her mind was challenged. I was intent on keeping her with other children instead of homeschooling. I fully bought into the common wisdom that children need to play and be among other children to grow up balanced and healthy. The socialization was going well at her new school, according to reports from her teachers and my observations of her in class.

But then there was a change. A group of students a few months older than Mandy were advancing to the classroom for older kids, and Mandy was staying where she was. The teachers reported that she was self-isolating. I suggested Mandy be moved up as well, but the school was resistant. They wanted to keep her with her age cohort. I couldn't help but think about the poppies.

I was afraid to rattle things, but I was more afraid of my daughter suffering. I stayed focused because what mattered was advocating for Mandy. She was already potty-trained. She was vocal, able to express herself and ask questions. She could read Bob Books and wasn't going to be slowing anyone down academically. Most importantly, her friends were in the older cohort.

The director hesitantly agreed, and a few days later, Mandy joined the older classroom. We sighed in relief. Although resistant, the preschool director was on board with letting us try out the recommendation by the doctor.

Though Mandy seemed perfectly content with the new arrangement, I got a call a couple of weeks into it. When the number from the school appeared on my phone, I panicked.

"Hi. Mandy is not hurt," the director said first. I sighed, feeling the tension. "But I do need you to come and get her. She has been crying profusely the last hour or so, and we can't seem to comfort her."

"Has something happened?"

"No, she's just crying. I was afraid that something like this would happen. I didn't think she was ready for this class."

I resisted saying what I wanted to say, which was that these kids were a mere two months older than Mandy, not so advanced or so old that Mandy couldn't handle it. She had to be crying for some other reason. But I just said, "Okay, I'm on my way."

I got to the school and rushed in, baby carrier on my arm. Thankfully, Allison was calm. I heard shrill screams followed by gasping. I walked into the room. The kids were at different stations, working away. The teachers were going about their business. All this calm was particularly dissonant with the earsplitting screaming that filled the room. Mandy was in the corner, crying loudly. Not yet three, she was violently sobbing by herself, even though there were four adults in the room.

Her body was flailing, her face wet with tears and snot. What was I looking at? I had never seen her like this, not even during the anxiety freak-outs. She was very obviously in pain. No one was offering her comfort. I set the baby carrier down carefully and marched straight toward her.

"Mandy, baby," I said calmly as I reached for her.

The minute my fingers touched her arm, she screamed even louder, "*No, no, no*! I want my snack! I want my snack! I want my snack!"

Her head was moving like a lopsided bobblehead. Her eyes were red and swollen. I did the math quickly in my head—she'd been crying almost two hours. The adults in the room moved toward me. They spoke quickly, reporting all the pertinent information. I was enraged. I turned Mandy toward me and tried to get her attention.

Nothing came out of my mouth because I had to maintain my composure. Nothing good would come out of an impulsive, heated confrontation.

"I didn't finish my work, Mommy. They took away everything, and I didn't get snack. I want my work. I want snack."

Her teacher said sternly, "We were done with coloring, and she was told to put her things away because it's snack time, and she wouldn't. She got upset and wouldn't calm down, so I told her she would get her snack once she calmed down."

This was a fucking preschool, and my two-year-old daughter was left crying for almost two hours *because* she had been crying? I did not say another word, picked up the baby carrier, and stormed out, clutching Mandy tightly. I was horrified that she was left to cry in a corner by herself. Why was my child left in isolation? In the first school, I had suggested a solution but was met with indifference, and I made up an excuse to pull Mandy out. In this second school, I had found my courage and advocated. I'd voiced my daughter's needs, and they punished her in return, putting me in my place. I refused to have my daughter forced into uniformity for the comfort of others, and I was no longer that scared nineteen-year-old. I was now a mother and willing to stand up to anyone.

I kept her home the next few days, and we decided to disenroll her. I was once again in opposition, but this time I felt strength in my conviction to pull her out of school. I was doing right by my child. There would be no more doubts about my choices when it came to my daughters. I had a conversation with the preschool director to pull Mandy out. I had a feeling the incident was to show me yet again that they knew better than I did about child development and what my child needs. This was a pissing contest. They were trying to tell me that I was wrong about her intellectual needs, that I was an arrogant and naive mother who was flexing my entitlement muscles. It was the familiar feeling of punishment, as if I needed to be put in my place.

The outburst had been just like the one at home when she was building a zoo, the one that had scared me to death, only prolonged and with no comfort. I was determined to help her.

～

I was sick to my stomach that I had put my Mandy in that situation. She was already having anxiety, and I wished I had read the preschool director better. I wished that she didn't have to teach me a lesson by hurting my child. I would find someone who understood and an environment that cherished Mandy's growth.

She was about to turn three. We decided to follow through with the formal testing suggested by Dr. Dufftenson. I was informed, prepared, and willing to advocate for my child.

"Her focus is phenomenal! If you're okay with it, I think I can do the full test. It will take another hour or so," the doctor told us after an hour and a half. Daniel and I sat in the waiting room. At the end of the testing, he invited us into his office. Mandy was given some blocks and a squishy brain toy to play with while we talked.

"Okay, I don't want you to be alarmed or afraid of anything," he said.

My mind immediately flooded with possible diagnoses—autism, ADHD, dyslexia? These were all things that had been reported to us by "well-meaning" teachers. I wondered if I had been wrong all along.

He continued. "She is profoundly gifted, and we can handle this with the right strategies. It can be overwhelming, but I want you to be prepared so we can advance her in all areas of development." *Profoundly gifted?* Why would that be alarming?

"Her score is three standard deviations away from the mean and will continue to be in relatively the same ratio to her peers, given optimal environments to nurture her intellect and meet her developmental needs." He gave us a deeper understanding of the way she processed the world, including her hyperfocus. She was hyperfocused at her second school, which was why she couldn't break away from the activity at hand. When she got punished, she could not carry the weight of feeling wronged. Dr. Dufftenson talked about her rigid sense of justice, which was typical of profoundly gifted children like Mandy. He recommended that we explain things when we dealt with her, using age-appropriate language but minimizing sugarcoating, as she had the ability to process the facts.

We were referred to gifted workshops and parenting groups. We would have to learn how to parent Mandy. It would require more than good values and principles we inherited. We needed to understand how to meet her comprehension. Dr. Dufftenson continued with more facts about gifted children. Mandy was engrossed in building with the blocks, talking and giggling to herself in the corner of his office, oblivious to us discussing her future.

Daniel and I learned that giftedness was not widely understood. There was no singular definition of a gifted child. However, there was one way that parents of gifted children learned, and that was an uphill struggle. We would also need a different approach to her education. Dr. Dufftenson suggested homeschooling more than once. He said that I was fully capable, but I wasn't sure I had the confidence to educate her.

I remembered that all the teachers, doctors, nurses, and friends had mentioned how all kids level out at some point, so I brought that up. "She will not be leveling out," he assured me. She had hit the test ceiling, so we didn't know her true potential. All the things I had thought were exceptional and extraordinary about Mandy were truly special. We'd discover over the next months that Mandy needed mental exertion in the way very energetic kids need physical exertion. I started to believe I could be her advocate, maybe even her teacher, but I still wasn't sure. She was only three, but homeschooling had me afraid that I was going to short her on the development that someone more skilled would be able to provide. I had been doing it all along, Dr. Dufftenson said. I understood that, but I also thought about how my bipolar episodes would make for an unstable environment.

～

Feeling vindicated, I looked for schools. At this point she was almost four. The doctor recommended that we still give her opportunities for social development and let her find confidence in being around other kids. We found a new school that advertised individual education that met all children where they were. Things were good in the beginning. She came home happy and was eating and sleeping well. The teachers reported how well-adjusted she was. I felt satisfied that she was in a place that would enable her to grow.

After a few months, Allison, a little over two, joined her in the same Montessori classroom cycle. Whenever I drove by during playtime, I saw Allison sitting on the steps. Crowds and people exhausted my quiet child. Mandy was her best friend. She had been excited about going to school with Mandy, and we were happy to oblige. I watched the children play for a while, but Mandy was nowhere to be seen. It had been about eight months since Mandy joined the preschool. One afternoon, I picked them up. I strapped them into their car seats and asked Allison if everything was okay. She said no, shoveling crackers into her mouth.

"Why? Did something sad happen?" I asked.

"Yes. Mandy was in trouble, and I had to play by myself."

Mandy burst into tears. "I did not want to do cursive writing anymore. I did what you said—she asked me to finish my movable alphabets and I could read the Bob Books. She lied, Mommy. She lied." Guilt hit me. I had told her to ask for what she needs at school, as a way to self-advocate. Dr. Dufftenson had advised us that she would need to learn this because she was the youngest in her class.

As soon as I got home, I called her teacher. It seemed that she had lied to me too, because we had already had a conversation about managing Mandy's expectations. I had asked her to make clear to Mandy about what the expectations were so she would be able to respond and self-regulate. The teacher insisted that she learn how to follow instructions, even if it changes expectations. We recovered and talked about next steps. I had to go in with test results from the psychologist to fortify my defense about her needing something different, explaining how happy we were when we had found this school.

"She is profoundly gifted," I said, as if it meant something. Mandy's teacher nodded. We talked some more. She told us about all the highly intelligent children she had taught, which was the reason her Montessori was so successful. Disappointment washed over me. I didn't think she was listening to me or even capable of it. In her ensuing reports, which were confirmed by my youngest, the more Mandy complied, the more they moved the goalposts. This triggered her rigidity around truth and justice, because they weren't following through on their promises. If it was work she wanted, it was work she would get. When she zoned out, as children do when tasked with something mind-numbing, she was reprimanded and her task extended. If she retaliated, she was removed and placed in isolation in a separate room. Allison spent four of the next ten school days on the steps by herself, waiting on Mandy. Mandy had suffered at the schools she'd attended. They wanted to fit her into a box they could name and reign supreme over. When I defended Mandy, they punished her.

The final straw was when she kicked the teacher. She was told she couldn't do yet another activity she was promised, and she threw a tantrum. The teacher tried to restrain her, and in the scuffle, Mandy kicked her. I was called in, and they were furious about this one display of aggression. If you ask me, this display was delayed in its delivery. They did not know that I knew what had been happening. They listed the many behavioral disorder labels that they believed described Mandy.

"She is not listening to instructions. She is combative, argumentative, and insolent."

"If she is so bright, she should be able to follow simple instructions."

"She's not actually at the level you think she is. She has been asking to read Bob Books, but she needs to do the foundational work first. She cannot read that yet."

I had told Mandy to ask for that because she was bored, and I didn't want to step in just yet. If she was going to move ahead in the future, then she was going to need to stand her ground. I was proud she had heeded my advice and advocated for herself, even though the response she received was less than favorable.

"She's not as advanced as you think," the teacher told me. "I actually have a concern that she may be dyslexic, and we have to keep an eye on this." She was referring to Mandy spelling every word backward on the mat. Dr. Dufftenson explained from his assessment that she was bored, turning her attention to making the letters "fun." I was confident in our psychologist, and I was already planning our next course of action. It was clear to me that they were testing her intellectual boundaries because of my assertion that she was gifted, and now Mandy was paying the price for my demands.

When I got home, Daniel and I discussed what to do. I was not giving power to anyone anymore. It was time to step in. No one we knew had the same experience, but truth be told, Mandy's experience was familiar to me and mirrored my experience growing up in isolation. Parenting based on reference to others was grueling and lonesome. All my angst for my wronged daughter inspired me and put me in touch with my intuition. Mandy was not going to be subject to that isolation. We talked about coping strategies. She was always going to be the odd one out.

We had a heart-to-heart with the teacher, and she ended our journey together. "There isn't much more I can do for her here," she said, which I appreciated because it was the truth—she couldn't help Mandy the way we needed her to. "Public schools will definitely not be able to handle her. It is going to be a big challenge because she's so smart, as you say she is."

I was demoralized by what felt like a slight. I felt attacked. It felt like she was saying that I was the problem and that there wouldn't be a place that could accommodate the requests I was making to meet Mandy's asynchronous development. Statements like these were not considerate of my daughter's whole self. She was digging through quicksand. Every time she learned to rise, she was pulled back by her inability to manage her emotions and behavior, which did not match her intellect. I did not belong in those mom groups, which seemed to garner a special sense of camaraderie for other moms. Like my child, I was an outlier. A strength in me surfaced when it came to my children. I uncovered my voice and my daughter's voice.

∼

When Mandy turned four, we took her for another test with a different psychologist to get a second opinion. The second psychologist confirmed the earlier test results. I wasn't sure what I thought was going to change with a second verification of her profound giftedness, but maybe I wanted additional proof to make a case for extra support.

She then passed an early entrance test for kindergarten at a public school. This school was a dream, and I felt supported in what we needed and wanted for Mandy.

We did not parent alone, either, because we were brought into a village. I breathed a sigh of relief. We'd finally found a school that met Mandy where she was, wasn't threatened by how bright she was, and didn't try to diagnose her because they didn't understand her. This school had a stake in supporting my child with me.

Outside school, we found an endeavor she was passionate about, which was a campaign against single-use plastic. She named it Mandy Luxshmi's Last Straw. She had watched a video on YouTube of a marine biologist removing a straw from a sea turtle's nose and was horrified that straws did that to wild animals. She vowed immediately to give up straws and asked to make a video to show friends, imploring others to say no to single-use plastic straws. Many of our friends watched the video and shared it. An art teacher from the studio where Mandy took classes connected us to a local university. They invited her to talk to their group at the Global Symposium on Waste Plastic after seeing her speak about this in a Facebook video.

My sweet four-year-old stared through the glass walls, her pigtails brushing the plaid dress she had picked out for that day. The red in her dress brought out her rosy cheeks, and the Peter Pan collar was perfect for her studious style. Her eyes were wide, her face serious. She has the prettiest doe eyes, almost like an anime character—large, round, and a gorgeous brown. She read the slides projected on the screen. It had been several months since her last school experience, and Mandy was finding her stride in an environment that cherished her for who she is. She found a place with people who lauded her efforts and offered support within a community of environmentalists. I never could have imagined standing there those few months before as we walked out of yet another school. People were listening intently. Two people looked at Mandy and waved, smiling at her. Mandy was very friendly, and she smiled back. We both looked into the lecture room, where an expert in plastics talked to professors, CEOs, and doctors—important stakeholders in the world of plastics. They had come from all over to attend a global symposium at the University of Kentucky to talk about the future of waste plastics. In just fifteen minutes, they would also be listening to my four-year-old present her plea for the reduction and elimination of single-use plastic waste. The organizers must have imagined that she'd stand up and repeat some of the ideas in her YouTube video, but in fact she'd prepared something much bigger. It was a full-blown talk and PowerPoint presentation, which we helped her to organize at her request. At the tea break, the experts walked out of the room and stopped to talk to Mandy.

The representative from PepsiCo stopped to greet her. "Are you Mandy Luxshmi?"

"Yes, sir, I am. And what should I call you, sir?" she asked confidently.

He smiled. "You can call me Dev."

Mandy smiled, her back straight, and shook his hand. "It's very nice to meet you, Mr. Dev."

Daniel and I beamed with pride. People were curious because the line in the program simply read, "Mandy Luxshmi, Dodson Elementary, Mandy Luxshmi's Last Straw." Many of the attendees commented to us that they were expecting a ten- or eleven-year-old, and we smiled and nodded. "No. She's four." We smiled because we had a newfound confidence in being parents to Mandy. I was beginning to trust myself and the work I was able to do in raising my child.

Mandy walked into the auditorium, where fifty or so people were seated after the break. Her science teacher from her new school was there to support her. We set up, testing the mic.

The coordinator walked us to the podium. Mandy said, "Hello everyone! Can you hear me?" The crowd watched her and smiled. She looked around the room, and her body seemed to shrink. I moved closer to check if she was all right.

"I'm not sure I can do this. I'm scared, Mommy."

"It's okay to be scared. That's absolutely expected at these things. You can back out if you're not up for it, even right this second. Your call. We can duck, and I'll cover you. We'll crawl out of here, and no one will see."

The best way to interact with Mandy when she was scared was to tease her, and it was working. "You're too big! Everyone will see us!" We shared a laugh and a long hug.

"Look, all these people are excited to hear from you. Your words are important, and I promise you, they're words to be heard, because they're yours. Do things that make yourself proud. You know Mommy and Daddy are already proud you're even standing here. You know I've got your back." She glanced over at Daniel, who was setting up our computer to the projector. He smiled and sent her an air hug across the room.

"Okay, I'm doing this. I can do it. Just hold up the cue cards higher, and don't be too slow, okay? It will confuse me."

Her twelve-minute presentation was flawless. She was a natural leader. People were laughing and leaning forward, and the air in the room shifted. Within one minute of her introduction, people pulled out their phones to record. Their fascination moved into more serious consideration of her eloquence.

"Compostable-waste segregation and collection should be readily available, especially where greenwashing exists. Establishments are providing compostable serveware that are only compostable in commercial facilities. These are not readily available in our city. That is an example of plain bad waste management, and we can do better." She furrowed her brow, making the point.

They were listening. Her voice and posture were strong. People were nodding. I held up cue cards with symbols to prompt her thoughts. I held back tears. Fuck yes, that's my girl, my four-year-old badass! I was so proud of her, and Daniel and I were floored yet again. She still amazed us with every new endeavor.

The host wrapped up the talk and thanked her. "I have five minutes for questions if anyone has any," Mandy said, her little voice coming through the speakers. The entire room erupted in laughter. Lots of questions followed. Her poise while answering the questions was impeccable. She thanked everyone for their time and then stepped off the chair they had set up for her to reach the podium. She ran straight to her science teacher, who welcomed her with an embrace. My heart was filled by this interaction, especially given the issues we'd encountered leading up to finding this school for her. All of her previous teachers seemed to find fault with her. At the school she was in now, she was supported.

"I am so, so, so proud of you, my sweet girl," I said.

She possessed an elegance that I didn't think could be taught. Our experience that day boosted the confidence I had in mothering.

At a parent meeting during the first few weeks of kindergarten, we entered a conference room filled with teachers and the principal. They had convened to suggest options for extra classes, substitute classes, and clubs for Mandy and to talk about accelerating her into first grade. They put forward assessments and arguments for her advancement, which was invigorating, especially in light of how her other schools had tried to hold her back. I watched Mandy's teachers acknowledge her talents, and my heart felt huge. I also felt they saw me, too, as Mandy's parent. They spoke with me about what would be best for her. This was what it looked like to no longer be alone. I watched as the heated discussion simmered, and we all agreed on Mandy's acceleration to first grade.

I was invited by a teacher at Mandy's school to showcase Malaysia at a multicultural night in which families from China, Iran, and other countries also presented their cultures. Mandy had only been a student at Dodson Elementary for about three months when we arrived at the school dressed in Malay traditional garb. At the presentation, Malaysia was announced by the emcee, and we entered the stage where we performed a Malay traditional song and dance called *dikir barat*. We sat on the floor, and Mandy led us with a solo. As I sang with my daughter, joined by some of our new friends, my feeling of isolation fell away. I was finally at a school where Mandy's differences and our diversity as a family were celebrated.

Our story about raising Mandy is filled with hardship as well as blessings. She has been in the company of policy makers, activists, researchers, and leaders in our community, all lauding her for her efforts. We've worked to build her sense of self, which is different from that of her peers. Over time, we built a village around my child to support her, to help me guide her into all the wonderful things she can be. Her public appearances, events, and activities motivated her and gave her a sense of belonging to something important. There was great relief in no longer operating alone. We did not belong in any box.

I learned to tune out the noise when it came to Mandy. Our approach to parenting now was to be adventurous and trusting in what we knew about her.

I was not a confident mother in the beginning. My muddled sense of self and where I came from made it difficult. Being confused about raising a child in a culture so different from where I was raised has been tough, and I've always felt eyes on me. Anything I did that was "different" would be scrutinized. The experience increased my feelings of being foreign. Often, my mothering did not come from intuition, but from other people telling me what I should do. Learning how to parent Mandy meant listening to myself.

The biggest gift in parenting Mandy was in what she taught me about not being stuck. If I was willing to fight for her, I could also fight for myself. Most of all, I learned that parenting with bipolar was possible. I was taking responsibilities in stride, and I found my way through the episodes I suffered. I thought back to those moments on the ledge of my apartment in Kuala Lumpur and the subway tracks in Nagoya. I'd pulled back, and it had led me here—to experience the ways in which my children's strength gave me strength. With every realization that I could parent them, I became stronger.

CHAPTER 12

The sun was in my eyes. A cool breeze tickled the corners of my lips. We were on vacation in the Upper Peninsula of Michigan. I had been in this country for seven years, and America still amazed me. COVID-19 had struck a few months earlier, and both girls were home with me. Mandy was in distance learning. This was our time together, avoiding the crowds to stay safe while still enjoying time as a family. My girls, six and four, ran bowlegged, skipping toward the water. They made funny noises, mocking their daddy, who was running from the car. He looked happy. The girls' hair bounced on their little shoulders. My oldest daughter's bangs separated by the wind. Mandy's face was still startlingly cute. She had a deep smile, dimples in her chubby cheeks, and a little line of pearly white teeth. Allison was just beginning to grow into her looks, and it pleased me to no end that she was the spitting image of her father but for her brown eyes. She was now twirling and screaming in excitement: "I'm monster! Big lake monster! I'm gonna eat youuuuuuu!" I watched them both, willing time to slow down, capturing this moment in my mind.

The sound of the waves crashing on the shore was soothing. Daniel's warm hands landed on my hips, followed by a gentle snuggle on that familiar spot on my neck. Oh, how I hated the stubble on his face! His scent and my gratitude for everything he'd given me—this place, our babies—sent waves of sensation into my body. Then he was off and running after the girls, giving me a minute to soak it all in.

The swells from grand Lake Superior rushed toward me with their melodic whoosh and hum. The horizon was astounding. The sky was a dramatic blue, with the warm hues of the sun resting on top. The water extended to the edge of the world, bringing waves to meet the powdery beaches as seagulls patrolled and entertained. Every wave seemed to call to me, "Come rest, for you are home." I was connected to the earth, connected to this country as my chosen home. Over the years, I had fallen in love with this country over and over. I was grateful every day that I'd made the choice to follow Daniel.

I walked toward the icy water. I let it graze my feet, my calves, my thighs. Once I got waist-deep, I lay back and floated, letting go of all the tension. I felt a surge of love, power, and peace. A sense of calm and gratitude came over me. I loved this place—my home, my America.

American pride was one of the first things that fascinated me about Americans, way before I ever got here. In my early days, I played the quiet observer. I worked to assimilate. I'd already stocked up in my memory bank little nuances, phrases, and cultural norms, from TV and from American friends we'd had in Japan and Canada. This was going to be my new home, my children's home, so I set about learning everything.

As I lay in the water, I hummed a country song from the first concert I ever went to, six years earlier. I had grown to love country music. It's what makes me feel most American. The songs were filled with lyrics about Chevy trucks, Budweiser beer, sweet tea, and pecan pie, and the virtues of being strong, kind, and resilient. I had only been in America for about eight months when one of my favorite bands, Zac Brown Band, played at a venue nearby. I had already learned all their songs. I was pregnant with Mandy but wouldn't miss the concert.

When we arrived, I was overwhelmed by the crowd. Everyone had coolers and beers and hands upon shoulders, swaying and singing along as I did. I sang to "Chicken Fried." The lyrics thanked God for life, the stars and stripes, and all who'd given their lives so we could enjoy our freedom. The crowd sang so proudly, with conviction in the words. I saw joyful singing, children dancing, and friends in embrace—I saw freedom. This was American freedom to me, and now I imagined it being bestowed on me too. I was here, and my American daughter would be born here.

I mouthed the words to that song again on the lake in Michigan. I watched my American-born children play in the water and vowed to teach them what those freedoms meant, what I had chosen for them, and why.

~

The children were taking a break on a blanket. They were eating their snacks, giggling at some dad joke that Daniel had made. This was the beautiful family I had built with Daniel. I had approached my initiation into my new country as if I were an interested traveler. Growing up in Malaysia, we were spoiled with TV shows and films from all over the world: Mandarin, Cantonese, Hindi, Tamil, Japanese, Korean, Thai, Singaporean, Australian, British, and American shows. We'd carefully mark up the daily newspaper so we wouldn't miss what we wanted to watch. We had MTV and Channel V. We watched shows that featured American high school students and learned the lingo. Talent shows at school were filled with songs from our favorite American singers or bands, or from movie soundtracks. I felt prepared to make a life here. After all, it wasn't completely alien. Kuala

Lumpur is a big city, Westernized, and I'd arrived feeling fairly cosmopolitan at age thirty. I'd left my home country and lived all over the world.

But arriving in America immediately brought uncertainties and contradictions. There were things I needed to establish to grow roots in this new soil. There was no communal support to guide me in Kentucky. My family were all in Malaysia, and Daniel's was scattered across Texas. His mom, who I was close to, was in Louisiana. I was self-conscious from the beginning, as if I'd started at a new school. I wanted to sort out all the pieces that made up my new home, to absorb all the accents and phrases: "y'all," "way yondah," and "fissin' supper." I'd chuckle as I repeated them, hoping I'd find a way to use them. Perhaps I'd be seen as less of an outsider.

I heard Daniel call out, "Mandy Luxshmi!" She was running to the water without him and stopped in her tracks with a mischievous grin on her face.

That name represented a milestone in my establishing roots in America. It's ironic that growing a family can create more isolation, though maybe this is especially true for mothers. Once I had kids, the isolation hit home. I was just over a year into living in Kentucky. I didn't have any close friends. My parents, who had come to visit and welcome their first grandchild, left convinced I was ready and equipped to care for my baby. When they left, it triggered memories of being abandoned by them. I felt it deep in my stomach, though I wouldn't have said out loud to them how much it still hurt. I was alone in the world, and in many ways that aloneness had been solidified by their choices. This time, it was grating to know that it had been my choice to make a home for myself thousands of miles away from them.

I wanted something different for my children. I wanted them to have connection, to know that I would never leave them. I also had to figure out how to keep my traditions alive in this expanse that was America, which was so quick to engulf the things that mattered to me from my home and culture. There's a singularity to American culture that beckons for us outsiders to fit in. This is especially true when you marry an American and into an American family. The less you sound like a foreigner and the more you fit in, the more comfortable you make other people. I wanted to fit in, wanted to have more in common with Americans. But there were times they dismissed my culture and expressed no interest in my traditions, and I was more accepted when I rejected my roots. Still, I wanted to give my children a sense of their family who loved them from afar.

The first opportunity came, a naming ceremony for my first-born when she turned six months old. Hindu rites and rituals were not designed to be planned by a party of one. The blueprints of the entire affair required a whole village. My family alone—our aunts and uncles and their children—included thirty to forty people. Every single person was pertinent to the ceremony, each a silken thread woven into the rites. It formed the rich textile of our family, our traditions, and the blessings of all our ancestors before us. It was a celebration that every person in my family would be weaving with their assigned task and responsibility. Words would be uttered in careful recitation in a special order commanded by the elders. Our name is a sacred thing, traditionally and carefully chosen in relation to astrology and meaning. Our names are a prayer people make when calling out to us.

In Malaysian-Indian culture, a naming ceremony is usually held when the baby is a newborn, but I didn't have the courage to do it then. I was at a loss as to how I would manage without my whole family present. But it seemed too sacred to skip, as the "Luxshmi" in

Mandy's name held such deep significance. It belonged to my grand-mother who'd raised me. I wanted that name honored with blessings in her memory. I explained the ceremony to the few friends we had as a half-birthday celebration. I simplified the rites so it would be comfortable and quick. I then spent the rest of the time focused on the tea party portion of the afternoon. This would satisfy the parts of our Indian tradition of eating sweets at special—what we call "good"—occasions.

Secretly, I was torn. I resisted my children being too connected to my roots. I felt it important that they find an American identity. I didn't want to cause trouble for them by being the children of an immigrant. They were to be proud Americans. But I would pay a cost for this over time. With no Sanskrit songs of praise, no incense, no rose water, no prayers from the elders, and no silken threads weaving about with preparations for various ceremonies, I became more iso-lated. In denying my children these celebrations, these traditions, I felt even smaller and more alone. I had already felt the displacement of being foreign, and I was even more self-conscious about putting my culture on display. But all my friends in attendance celebrated with curiosity and acceptance of my culture. It made me feel like I could be myself. I could grow roots that extended from my heritage.

With every holiday, the traditions of my upbringing seemed to slip away. Kuala Lumpur felt like a distant memory. That wondrous place seemed so far in the past, only brought forth in conversations with the odd stranger who thought to ask where I was from. I spoke of Malaysia in a "back in the days" way. I told the odd story here or there. I felt a kinship with the old women in Kentucky, who sat on porches in their rocking chairs, inhaling Marlboros between sips of a blue-mountain-decorated can of Coors Light.

~

We took every opportunity we could to see America. Our trip to the Upper Peninsula in Michigan was the twenty-fourth state I'd visited. I had traveled the country with Daniel every chance we got, just as we had traveled the world together before we were married. On our honeymoon, we chose to go on a road trip to the Northeast, covering eleven states. We connected through travels and loved exploring. More than that, I was hungry for America—to experience my new home. I wanted to meet the people, eat the different foods, and ground myself. I wanted in on all that was American.

Despite that wish, I discovered early on that being American holds a deep power that I would never have access to. I'm not talking about flag-flying, gun-toting, we-rule-the-world power. I'm talking about the powerful strength that is the American spirit. As a people, Americans are sincerely and unapologetically loyal to their country and will stand up to defend it. They take their freedoms seriously. Sometimes that can be inspiring, but a lot of times it scares the shit out of me. It took me time to understand Americans' altruistic kindness. It's a very American thing to be part of some altruistic effort. The concepts of society and community are ingrained in America, and I wanted my daughters to experience it all.

I exercised these rights for the first time with my girls at the Women's March in 2018 on the one-year anniversary of Trump's inauguration. We were visiting New York City. We read all the placards against injustices regarding race, sex, policies, immigration, and more. We marched and we chanted. A strong spirit was present that day, and I felt swept up in it. I saw signs that said IMMIGRANTS ARE WELCOME HERE and IMMIGRANT RIGHTS ARE HUMAN RIGHTS, and tears came to my eyes. I felt seen and welcome in that crowd. As an immigrant, I lived in vigilance, afraid of how so many people in this country demonized outsiders. I worried that my day would come.

At the march, I explained to my children what was happening. Mandy smiled and called out "Thank you!" to the woman with the sign that read IMMIGRANTS ARE WELCOME. "My mommy is an immigrant!" she cried. The white lady stopped in her tracks and hugged me, and I thanked her for standing up for me. Holding my daughters' hands, we marched alongside our people. My heart swelled, as this was their future. They were Americans, and this was their birthright. I felt that at least part of America welcomed me. This experience invigorated my desire to become a naturalized citizen, though it would take another two years before that happened.

I had been in America for about six years when I was invited to a football game. The center of the American spirit can be found in the national anthem, which tugs on my heartstrings so much that I cry every time I hear it. We were at a University of Kentucky football game the first time I heard it sung live. It was the first football game I had ever been to. It was so exciting, so prototypically American. There was blue and white everywhere, the University of Kentucky's colors. People stood and sat in waves, cheering and laughing. Everyone was so present, and no one seemed to mind the heat. There were faces painted blue and white, matching the fans' outfits. There was the guy with hot dogs on a tray strapped to his chest, followed by the guy with the cotton candy and popcorn. It was just like I'd seen on TV and in the movies all these years, and now I was actually here. Suddenly, a voice boomed over the speakers, and everyone stood up. Hands flew to hearts, and I placed my palm there too. The national anthem is about strength and pride in victory, and so hopeful. In that moment, I pretended to be American. I was longing to be American. For those few minutes, swept up with the emotion of the crowd, I too was free.

I didn't know if I would ever belong to this land or if it could ever open up its arms entirely. But I knew it had to for my children, and most days, that was enough. Being born here, they had unalienable rights, and possibilities beyond my wildest dreams.

~

During dinner at a Manhattan restaurant the night of the march, I told Daniel that I wanted to apply for citizenship. We had discussed this on many occasions, but I'd always had my doubts. The children were ecstatic. I would be American, like them. Daniel was touched and happy. It hadn't been an easy decision. It's impossible not to be reminded every single day of my outsider status. There are people who ensure that I understand I am not heir to all the promises America holds. My children had been witnesses to my mistreatment. There were many times that I was followed around the store as if I were a shoplifter, treatment that stopped the minute my blond, blue-eyed husband joined me. Sometimes clerks followed me and rearranged products I'd picked up. They did so with much vigor, as if to shake off my brownness. *How dare I touch the products?* I imagined them thinking. Sometimes a clerk would lead me to a different part of the store, where they'd show me cheaper products, implying I couldn't afford whatever I'd been looking at.

These microaggressions and outright hostility cut deep. I'd had to explain to my children how my dark skin and their half-Malaysian, half-American status meant we were different. Even being half of me meant that they would experience life differently from their white peers. I had to instill in them that understanding and the vigilance I felt when I ventured out into the world every day. Still, the children were happy. I played with the pasta on my plate, smiling, knowing that my becoming American would connect us even more deeply.

I would be safer with America as both my chosen and legal home. I would not be deported, like we'd seen happen so many times on the news. We would not be separated, something that terrified Mandy. She had heard about family separation under Trump, even as I tried to protect her from this news.

Daniel took my hand. We had watched the news and read about American immigrants who had been held at airports and denied entry in light of the Muslim ban, even though they held full legal status. I imagined myself not being able to go home to visit my family if Malaysia, a Muslim nation, fell under that ban. The thought of being separated from my husband and children indefinitely was unbearable. Having come into this country legally, through all the required channels, did not provide me with a strong position at all. I let the warmth of Daniel's touch seep into me, reminding me that we were in this together.

Mandy fed Allison pasta. They laughed at how it had dropped before reaching Allison's mouth. I wanted to believe my decision was the right one. My love affair with America might be unrequited or fickle, but my heart held fast. Naturalization was the right thing to do. I shook away my doubts and lifted my own forkful of pasta. I opened my mouth exaggeratingly wide to make the girls laugh. We would be an American family—together, safe, and free.

~

Even though I felt ready to become a citizen, I couldn't shake how doing so might make me complicit in cruelty against people who looked like me. I also believed that the status would give me little protection in the way I was treated because of the color of my skin.

The fact that I love skin products led to one of my more scarring experiences of racism in the States. I like the smells and textures of creams and lotions. They make me feel fancy, and I swear I can see a glow on my face when I find the right concoction.

My eyes looked tired during the struggles with Mandy's schools and her anxiety. While insomnia cannot be concealed, I wanted to try an eye cream I had read about online that claimed to be good for dark circles. The girl reviewing the product in the video I watched was Indian, so sister knew better than anyone about our panda-eye problem.

The girls came with me to the department store. I looked around and found the cream I wanted. I opened the lid of the sample to smell it. I sure did love the scents of creams. I had been standing there no more than thirty seconds. An older woman in a lab coat and a name tag, maybe in her sixties, approached me.

"May I help you with something?" Even though she was smiling at me, her hands moved separate and violently as she ripped the cream out of my hands.

Okay, what was happening right now? I felt a jolt of embarrassment, as if I'd been caught doing something wrong.

"Yes," I managed, pulling up the specific cream I wanted on my phone. I tried to ignore what she'd just done. I avoided looking at the cream she still held in her hand, instead focusing on the smile plastered on her face. I said I would like to try a sample.

"I would, but we ran out of the samples on that one," she said with a neutral tone. It was clear I wasn't going to be able to sample other creams.

"Okay, is there anything else you would recommend?" I was trying, because I always do, to be good, to show through my actions that I was worthy. I didn't want her to think I wasn't a serious buyer, and I was determined to prove I could afford this shit. I wasn't leaving without a purchase.

"No, we don't. We don't have anything for your kind of skin." *My kind of skin?* It was clear what she meant as she raised her eyebrows to indicate there was nothing further to discuss. *I should go now.*

I pretended to look around as I considered my next move. I concentrated on the hook of her nose as she spoke to me. She looked down on me, even though that's not hard to do, as I'm five-foot-two. Wouldn't she get a commission if she sold me something? I tried to will her into seeing me as a paying customer because of my pride and my desire to belong.

I was getting ready to give up when I heard someone from behind me name the same cream I'd just been inquiring about.

"That sample's run out," the saleswoman said, jolly as a fucking fat gnome. "Let me crack open a new one for you." I turned to see a woman who was infinitely paler than me. She had her hair in flawless curls. The powder on her face was so white that she could have been wearing kabuki makeup, yet it matched her nearly translucent complexion.

When I met the saleswoman's eyes again, the word left my lips: "Bitch."

Her eyes got huge; her mouth fell open. I looked away, because as angry as I was, I was also afraid. Ingrained ideas of being an immigrant and my inferiority clouded my head. I looked at her new, worthy customer. She looked "put together" in the *Stepford Wives* sense. Mandy tugged on my hand, and I turned around. My heart was heavy. I would be leaving without a purchase after all. I hung my head in defeat.

On the way home, I wondered if I should have come with Daniel. I thought about other injustices I'd experienced, about the man in Colorado who implied I'd "snagged" myself an American man.

I had brought Mandy to the Olympic Training Center in Colorado

Springs when she was a year old. I wanted to experience this quintes-
sentially American space, where potential and the opportunity to be
the best in the world were celebrated.

We were with a tour group of about eight people. The guide and
I were talking about me being Malaysian, coming to America, and
marrying my American husband.

A man in the group, with whom I'd had no prior exchange,
looked at me and said, "Oh, so you're one of those. Caught yourself
an American man, and came here for the good life, huh?" He looked
smug as he made the harsh accusation.

"Sorry?" I said, unsure of how to respond. My skin was crawling,
and I felt hot. The humiliation was paralyzing.

"I know another Filipino girl just like you. Found a good
American man to get a good life here." He laughed. I left the tour,
unable to hold back my rage.

That time, having a white husband had subjected me to ridicule.
Would he have made that remark if Daniel had been there? Most
times I wished Daniel was with me because he provided a buffer. I
was American by association with him and because we were a family.
Without him, I was a foreigner, and my girls were "other." Without
Daniel, I was without protection, which was worse because my children became targets.

One of the worst of these incidents happened when I was with
the girls at a local barbeque joint. They were four and two, and I was
excited to do this very Kentucky thing with them. We grabbed seats
next to the window. I zoned out for a second, looking at a Ford F-250
truck outside. It was a beast of a truck, which I'd wanted before I had
children. It was a symbol of patriotism and Americanness. I'd fanta-
sized about driving one—country music blaring, mud on the tires,
me shimmying up into the truck.

Then I realized that my children had gone silent. I saw jean-covered legs pressed against the edge of my table. I looked up and saw this behemoth of a man with a sandy mullet. He had a toothpick in the corner of his mouth. His hand rested on his hips as he stared at us. He just stood there staring at us. I didn't know why. But he won—I was piss scared.

I attempted a Southern accent. "Y'all say helloww nahww," I said, but the man ignored me, locking eyes with Mandy.

Before I knew what was happening, he spit his toothpick, along with a ball of saliva, straight into Allison's lap. The loogie landed with a splat, and he kicked our table before he turned around and left. I was shocked, and it took a few minutes to regain my composure.

I did not understand this pure hatred toward us. The interaction was hurtful, but it was just as bad that there wasn't a single ally around. There was no acknowledgment from the other patrons of what we'd experienced. There was us, and there was them. I come from a country that struggles with racism too. Yet I had never been paralyzed with fear for my safety, or for the safety of my children, on account of my skin color.

～

I had discovered over the years that I'd lived in America that there was a deep-seated sickness, cloaked in whiteness, that some would never let go. I felt like I was building sandcastles too close to the water. As soon as I built the beautiful castle, the harsh wave rushed to shore, turning my castle into foam and nothingness. As a foreigner, it took some time to fully grasp the entrenched racism in this country. I thought white people especially would view the privilege of being American as a gift. I didn't realize that entitlement, along with fear of losing their status or superiority, would lead them to demean people or threaten to call the police on people just for existing. I believe that woman at the beauty counter would've done so if I hadn't backed down.

~

On the flip side of these negative experiences are countless kind acts, so my initial concept of America does exist. It is, like many places, full of paradoxes and misconceptions—a place that's difficult to compartmentalize. Its spaces are difficult to define, and its people are varied in their convictions. For this reason, I've always had hope.

When Mandy was almost two and Allison a newborn, wailing as I pushed the grocery cart into the store, I found myself in tears. I had not slept in almost three nights. Mandy was whining about a lollipop or something equally trivial. I was struggling but needed formula and diapers.

I was trying to hush them both when a young man from the floral department came over with a balloon for Mandy. Mandy thanked and hugged him, and I nearly drowned in my own tears of gratitude. We would routinely see the young man after that while shopping. The girls would run and hug him, and he would take them to the floral department to get balloons. Mr. Brandon was part of my children's young lives until he quit a few years later.

As I got more comfortable at Mandy's school, I learned how to embrace my differences and share my culture. I befriended several families there and had many playdates, and this helped bring us closer. A mom from Mandy's school invited me to join a book club. Over wine, the ladies and I had deep conversations about the books. I felt at home and seen as they contemplated my opinions. I listened and learned about America; they listened and learned about my experiences in America. I was learning how to be myself and finding my own version of home.

I've told my children they were born here only because Mommy and Daddy chose to live here. Daddy had lived here because he was born here, and he was born here because his mother lived here, and so on, and it all traced back to his first ancestor immigrating here more than a few hundred years ago. "Home" was a concept I had contemplated incessantly over the years, ever since leaving Malaysia. I would find many ways that homes were made.

When Mandy turned six, she wished to fundraise for a local charity in lieu of gifts. This time it was to provide free food during the pandemic to families having difficulty. Daniel and I organized a 5K for her. For eighteen days leading up to her birthday, she pledged to run a 5K each day. She asked people to donate $25 for each 5K she ran. I was floored when the schedule was filled. The money poured in from the many friends we had made in Lexington. My heart swelled with the love and support they showed my little girl. The connections we had made were true and real, as was their encouragement.

There was also an outpouring of love from people in the city we didn't know, who'd heard about her fundraiser. They also ran 5Ks with her over those eighteen days. There was even a local restaurant that presented her with a gift card and had their staff run 5Ks. Facebook was filling up with videos and pictures of Lexingtonians running for Mandy's fundraiser. They cheered her on, encouraged her spirit, and helped her grow.

On her birthday, we invited people to join us. I wasn't expecting much since we had already met her fundraising goal. We prepared Mandy and also Allison, who had been running quite a few of the 5Ks with her sister. Mandy wore her big blue tutu, a cape with her hand-drawn logo of the charity, and a giant smile. She gulped down the orange juice she asked for in preparation for her run. Allison sat giggling and toying with the funny hats we had prepared for our friends.

I was worried no one would show up. Lo and behold, as I was arranging the party favors and cupcakes outside, car after car arrived. There were so many cars that some had to park on the next street over. Friends emerged wearing masks and filled the front yard and driveway. They were here, families we had come to know and love, to support my daughter. They smiled and waved as we kept our distance, and I wanted to thank them for the gift they were bestowing upon me. It was the greatest blessing of all—love to my child.

Everyone lined up and ran at staggered starts on a marked course through our neighborhood. I watched them power through the 5K—walking, running, or cycling—all to show support. I thanked each person as we said goodbye. I was overwhelmed with gratitude and a deep feeling of belonging. I was welcome, I was home, and there was love where I resided.

~

Being in the water of Lake Superior took my breath away. I was still, present in the experience. I was grateful. Living in America had brought me face-to-face with manic and depressive episodes that plagued me, often triggered by extreme stress. And yet, it was living in America that provided space for my healing, remedy for the illness that had arrived with no invitation. Mental illness holds such a stigma in our world, but in America there is open-mindedness and advocacy. Here, I've had options available for my healing. I've had access to therapists, doctors, and healers, all of whom have been integral to my growth. In America, there's a culture of healing and resolution. In the quest for individual freedom, those who suffer with mental illness and those who have been victims of sexual assault and abuse can insist that their voices be heard. Through the modeling of others, I've been able to create a life I couldn't have imagined. It's a life that is fulfilling, exciting, and—most of all—peaceful. I had grappled with healing before I came to America. I was hushed where I came from and even to a certain degree in Japan. There was little help, due to the stigma that surrounded mental illness. It was hard for me to find Dr. Jacobson, and even he was American. In the States, help was readily available, and I needed only to reach out.

When we got home from Michigan, I spent the next few months contemplating my status—what it meant for me to be an immigrant and what it meant for my children. Mandy and Allison were almost seven and five when I decided to become an American. A few months after I put in my application, I received a letter from the US Citizenship and Immigration Services (USCIS) to complete an interview, which was really a test, and they gave me 128 questions to study. I learned all there was to know about America, from geography to history to civics.

On the morning of the interview, I had Daniel run through the questions with me again and again. I was going to answer every question correctly. I chose my outfit carefully, a soft pink chiffon blouse with gray butterflies—gentle and friendly. I paired it with black slacks and black pumps for a smart and official look. "I am an upstanding citizen of America," the look said. Now, all I had to do was answer the questions correctly without losing my shit, as I was more nervous than I had ever been.

The significance of becoming one with this land was as large as the country itself. I was about to be one with my children, diminishing my fears that we might one day be separated because of my nationality. I wondered if I would absorb those American notions of entitlement myself and fight back against people who called me "other." I would claim my right to be here. "I am an American," I might say.

Daniel approved of my outfit. He kissed my forehead and held me, assuring me I was ready. He had taken the day off from work to drive me to the USCIS office in Louisville, about ninety minutes away. He knew I was anxious, and he wanted to be there for me.

When we arrived, he wasn't allowed into the building due to COVID-19 restrictions. I sat in the waiting area, going over the questions. I watched the people around me who were choosing to become American. A bald man, in a dress shirt and tie and holding two little American flags, approached an old woman. She was in a traditional garb that I could not place. She had a gold chain that made two curves over her forehead and a scarf on her head. I couldn't hear the words exchanged, but I saw him take her two hands as he handed her the little flags. She was beaming, and I saw tears in her eyes. She smiled at me and waved her flag. I managed through tears to say, "Congratulations!" She made it. She was a citizen, as I was hoping to be.

I heard someone call my name. I stood up and walked alongside the man who'd handed the woman her flags. I made small talk to exhibit how assimilated, normal, and pleasant I was—how American I was. He was cordial. I sat across the table from him with a computer screen between us. We completed the first part of the test quickly. He said, "Great! Six out of six. You passed!" A rush left my body. He then asked questions pertaining to personal information. He read me the rights and responsibilities of becoming a US citizen, and I uttered my agreement to every statement, as required. He then had me sign some forms, which I gladly did, until something stopped me in my tracks.

The form said: "Former nationality: Malaysia." My heart sank. Even though I knew this was a prerequisite, it was surreal to see it. I was about to sever ties with the land that birthed and raised me. That beautiful country I came from was about to become "former," a part of my past, like so many parts of me that I'd left behind. I took a deep breath and signed my name, a simple act, but so final. And just like that, it was done.

"Based on the findings of our interview today, I am recommending your application for naturalization be approved," he said. "You will be receiving a letter in the mail determining the date of your oath ceremony." This was going to be my forever home. I was going to be American.

I stood up, crying, and exclaimed, "Thank you, thank you, thank you! You have no idea how much this means to me! Can I hug you? Is that okay? I'm going to hug you!" I stood up and reached across the table where he reluctantly held out his arms.

He laughed. "Congratulations, Ms. Zachry." That was my American name. A life in America lay ahead of me, and this was my home. With all its beauty and dirt, its kindness and brute, America claimed me, and I claimed it back. I was not about to let a few drops of ink taint my entire journey—not the woman at the beauty counter, the man who spat on my daughter, or even the many who told me to go home. I was home. America, for me, had always been a place where dreams come alive. It's now a place where my children have opportunities to become firsts, bests, and awe inspiring, like so many first-generation heroes we celebrate. We are American, and no one can take that away from us.

EPILOGUE

I am back in Sedona, this time with my family on a road trip to the West. I watch Mandy, almost seven, and Allison, now five, skipping and laughing as they hike up Cathedral Rock—the same climb my friends and I had done two years prior.

Here I am again, in the majestic red rocks of Sedona, and it feels like coming home. There's a familiarity here that is heartening. We walk between the red rocks and take in the sights and the breeze. Fresh life teems on rocks millions of years old. I see aspects of myself in this life thriving in the desert. I am still standing, failing to surrender my life. My feet still skim the ground. This was all due to a greater purpose, surely. I chose to grow into the being I am.

The warmth of the sun and Sedona touches me, welcoming me home. The girls scurry along with no hesitation, as if their feet know just where to land. The ease with which they hike this mountain amazes me. These are young women in the making, unperturbed by their world, surefootedly knowing where they are headed—to the top. Their confidence slows me down for a minute. They are already everything I could wish for and then some. I imagine they will face challenges in life head-on. I marvel for a moment at these brave, strong girls Daniel and I are raising.

I can see other buttes in the distance, so beautiful and regal. I want to touch them all, but they seem untouchable, as if thousands of miles away. Yet no matter how far they are, they're not as far away as my family is, truly thousands of miles away. I want to share all this with them, and it saddens me that I'll never be able to.

"This is the life you have chosen," my father once said. With every birthday, wedding, and holiday celebration that passes, I am slowly fading from the family tree. My existence is no longer essential for the harmony of the whole, like the fifth violin in the orchestra that no one would notice if absent. Yet I long for our gatherings, chats over tea with Devi Atthey, and quiet meditations with Uncle Bala. Though they are far away, I know their wisdom and love still guides me, an inseverable link to my roots.

I've lost my father to brain injury. Though he's still alive, he surrendered to a medical condition with no remedy. Our conversations are limited to what he can manage—"I love you" is his response to anything. I try to be grateful for these three words, as they're all I need, but I have remorse for how much is unsaid and forever will be. He will never be able to put words to his thoughts or engage in lively debates and jokes. Memories give me comfort. The fact that I can't and won't go back means that I have lost a tether to home permanently. I ran away when I couldn't face myself anymore. I had wanted it all to end, far away from the love of my family, never realizing how much I would miss them. Now I am here in my new life, a life that is no longer an escape, a life filled with living. It is a life that leaves me wanting for little, a life that is enough for me. I live through the pain of what I used to know, my new life a salve for the wound.

Daniel is waiting for me. He is holding out his hand, helping me up a large rock. We laugh as I huff and puff up that rock, realizing how much older we are than when we hiked Mt. Fuji together eleven years ago. I feel his strong hand in mine, and I am thankful for all that we have together, despite the demons of bipolar. I am here with the love of my life. I see his genuine smile. He has Allison on his shoulders and is running away from Mandy, who is close behind, squealing. With Daniel, I am ready for whatever might come. I am ready to take anything on.

~

The next morning, I sit up in bed to find Mandy with a piece of tissue trying to tickle Daniel's nose as Allison giggles behind her. Daniel sits straight up in bed and grabs Mandy and Allison in one scoop. An eruption of laughter follows that enchants me.

Once we're all dressed, we head out for one last hike. We see a trailhead and decide to try it, not knowing where it will lead. This is not very different from how I live these days. I've let all expectations fall away, a life full of mystery and adventure awaiting me.

We sit on a flat rock as each of us takes in the sights for the last time. Sedona has given me so much. I close my eyes and feel grateful for this life, which I couldn't have dared to imagine.

Mandy picks up a rock and smiles. I had told her about our hostess at the Airbnb where I stayed with Jenny and Sara and how she'd suggested we put our biggest fears and frustrations into a rock and hurl it into the wild.

"Let Sedona take what you cannot handle, and be free of the chains that bog you down," she had said. Mandy was all about hurling rocks, as was Allison. They gleefully look around for rocks until they spot the best ones, scoop them up, and share the treasures they've found. I select a big one, knowing how much I want to leave here in the desert. I hold it tight as I think about all the pain and frustration I want to place into this rock.

My thoughts are suddenly heavy. I think about the violation that brought incomparable pain and suffering and of the perpetual illness that hovers around me like a veil. The pain is large, massive, engulfing me. The rape altered me, and yet every day is an opportunity to get back up and keep walking. I have given up all notions of "why" and am inclined to look toward "what now." I have been the best mother I can be, and I am strong for fighting bipolar while being present for my children. I throw the rock as far as I can, consciously sending with it the limiting constructs of good and bad that have so defined my life. The shame and guilt still live inside of me, but they're more like a bout of food poisoning when they show up—overwhelming, yes, but also able to be purged. Now I know how to fill myself, to rehydrate. I watch as dust blows into the air when my rock collides with the ground in the distance, then settles safely against another rock to remain in its new existence.

As we walk away through the desert, I know that much relies on me. My life isn't perfect, but it is mine to steer. I have a choice. We walk to a nearby swimming hole as we follow the water in the stream. My daughters are ahead of me, speedily walking in the stream over the rocks, and I start to get anxious. Daniel is ahead of the girls, making sure it is safe. I stop and breathe. I am determined to enjoy this moment with my family. I am reminded of all the life choices I made in the past, forgoing things because I couldn't handle my mental state. But this time, something different happens. I am staring straight ahead, and I see my girls joyful and excited by the wilderness. I take my next steps. With every step, the anxiety seems to spill into that stream. I step closer and closer to my children. I realize that I've got this; I can do this. I can do difficult things, and I will keep at it with the mindfulness born of the pain. Mental illness is a part of who I am, but it is not me.

We leave Sedona after our swim and start back to Kentucky, my home, the sweet Bluegrass. We drive across the country, thousands of miles through the beautiful West. As we cross the Kentucky state line, relief fills me, surprising me. But I recognize the feeling—I am home. The life I have built is here, right now. It resides here. Who knows what the future holds? One thing is certain—I am no longer wanting, no longer lost, no longer inadequate. I have had enough. I am enough.

ACKNOWLEDGMENTS

For the birth of this book and the will to have seen it through, my deepest thanks to:

All the remarkable women who came before me, paving the way for my voice. Speaking your truths in words and in songs, in pain and in healing. I stand in your shelter of courage and conviction. Without you, I would still be cloaked in silence.

Laura Kenning, who believed in me when I said I might write a book. Your advice and incredible input on drawing my thoughts into my first words became the heart of this book.

Angie Calderwood, Christina Lord, Carrie Murtha, Jackie McCuddy, your feedback on my very first draft encouraged me to take the big steps. That draft is now a book.

Writing was a whole new world for me, and many times I tried to pull my toes out of the water. Lori Spann, your love and unwavering support kept my feet wet. Thank you for always reminding me to follow my heart. And for your memory of events kept in record books so preciously.

Jenny Mills, you always saw the big picture and drew it up for me with your marvelous vision. Staying the course was hard with my episodes, but you relentlessly persuaded me that I was capable of more than I could see. I would've given up if it wasn't for you pulling me to be me *with a purpose*.

Sara Endicott-Bialczack, your discerning eye and kind critique on my every word erased my self-doubt and fear. Your conviction in my truth is woven in these pages. Our vortex beams strong, always.

Helping me out whenever I was in a jam with edits and queries and standing by me to give me a touch of your brilliance, Jennifer Sciantarelli, you are a gem.

My coach, editor, and mentor who gave my words direction and purpose, Brooke Warner, who taught me to stand by my words. You gave me the courage to be a writer. You gave me so much in our time together. You gave me healing. Your wisdom and kindness gave my voice a chance.

Amanda Oerther, PsyD, I will keep reaching for the ladder, not the shovel thanks to the years you have dedicated to my healing. Your clever words of wisdom in amusing phrases helped me complete this project, coming out only lightly scathed. I will never be able to thank you enough for being the center of my healing, my beacon of light when I lose my way.

My family, who persevered in your love for me. As imperfect and complex as our relationship has been, it is your resilience and fortitude I carry in my veins. My mother, who has sacrificed and dedicated her life to family, and my father, who has given his all for me—I kept the fire in me burning to do you proud.

My daughters, who are proud of my work without reading a word. I pray you will be prouder when the time comes for you to discover these pages. My ride and dies, thank you for riding my highs and lows and making it feel like a buoyant boat on calm seas. I'm forever grateful for your strength, your love, and your pride in me. It is for you that I overcome.

Daniel Zachry, you removed the veil and uncovered my voice to speak my truth, the very seed for this book. For all the hidden moments, the rough moments, the painful moments, it was destiny that brought us together but fierce love that has kept us together. You cared for our children so flawlessly to give me space for writing, for healing. You walked beside me all these years as I battled mental illness and trauma, so patiently and compassionately. I love you forever, then a million times over.

ABOUT THE AUTHOR

© Kelly Spottswood

Amelia Zachry was born and raised in Malaysia. She obtained a bachelor of commerce, majoring in marketing from Curtin University of Technology, Australia. When she met her husband, she moved to live with him in Japan, then Canada. During her time in Canada, she obtained a bachelor's degree in human ecology with a concentration in family studies from the University of Western Ontario. She began writing her debut memoir after finding her voice, bringing to light secrets she had kept: secrets of sexual assault and subsequently bipolar disorder that she suffers from. She is an advocate for mental health and sexual assault awareness, supporting causes to dismantle rape culture and normalize mental health. She maintains a blog where she writes regularly on topics of mental health, sexual assault awareness, immigration, and parenting. When she's not writing, she can be found tending to her many house plants or hiking with her husband and two daughters. Amelia currently resides in Lexington, Kentucky.

SELECTED TITLES FROM SHE WRITES PRESS

She Writes Press is an independent publishing company founded to serve women writers everywhere. Visit us at www.shewritespress.com.

A Leg to Stand On: An Amputee's Walk into Motherhood by Colleen Haggerty. $16.95, 978-1-63152-923-8
Haggerty's candid story of how she overcame the pain of losing a leg at seventeen—and of terminating two pregnancies as a young woman—and went on to become a mother, despite her fears.

At the Narrow Waist of the World: A Memoir by Marlena Maduro Baraf. $16.95, 978-1-63152-588-9
In this lush and vivid coming-of-age memoir about a mother's mental illness and the healing power of a loving Jewish and Hispanic extended family, young Marlena must pull away from her mother, leave her Panama home, and navigate the transition to an American world.

Blooming in Winter: The Story of a Remarkable Twentieth-Century Woman by Pam Valois. $16.95, 978-1-64742-116-8
When Pam Valois met her in the 1970s, Jacomena (Jackie) Maybeck was a model of zestful, hands-on living and aging, still tarring roofs and splitting logs in her seventies—a model for Pam, at the time a young working mother. Here, Pam explores how Jackie's uncommon approach to life encourages us to reflect on our own lives and what it looks like to live exuberantly to the very end.

Breathe: A Memoir of Motherhood, Grief, and Family Conflict by Kelly Kittel. $16.95, 978-1-93831-478-0
A mother's heartbreaking account of losing two sons in the span of nine months—and learning, despite all the obstacles in her way, to find joy in life again.

Finding Venerable Mother: A Daughter's Spiritual Quest to Thailand by Cindy Rasicot. $16.95, 978-1-63152-702-9
In midlife, Cindy travels halfway around the world to Thailand and unexpectedly discovers a Thai Buddhist nun who offers her the unconditional love and acceptance her own mother was never able to provide. This soulful and engaging memoir reminds readers that when we go forward with a truly open heart, faith, forgiveness, and love are all possible.